PS-AXD-260

D0122518

COMPLETING COLLEGE

COMPLETING
College

RETHINKING INSTITUTIONAL ACTION

VINCENT TINTO

The
University of
Chicago Press
*Chicago and
London*

VINCENT TINTO is distinguished professor in the School of Education at Syracuse University. He is the author of *Leaving College: Rethinking the Causes and Cures of Student Attrition* and coauthor of *Where Colleges Are and Who Attends.*

The University of Chicago Press, Chicago 60637
The University of Chicago Press, Ltd., London
© 2012 by The University of Chicago
All rights reserved. Published 2012.
Printed in the United States of America

21 20 19 18 17 16 15 14 13   3 4 5

ISBN-13: 978-0-226-80452-1 (cloth)
ISBN-10: 0-226-80452-6 (cloth)

Library of Congress Cataloging-in-Publication Data

Tinto, Vincent.
    Completing college : rethinking institutional action / Vincent Tinto.
        p. cm.
    Includes bibliographical references and index.
    ISBN-13: 978-0-226-80452-1 (hardcover: alkaline paper)
    ISBN-10: 0-226-80452-6 (hardcover: alkaline paper)   1. College attendance.   2. College dropouts—Prevention.   3. Counseling in higher education.   I. Title.
    LC148.T568 2012
    378.1′6913—dc23
                                                    2011036085

⊗ This paper meets the requirements of ANSI/NISO z39.48-1992 (Permanence of Paper).

CONTENTS

PREFACE

This book represents the closing of a circle that began thirty-six years ago with the publication in 1975 of an article in the *Review of Educational Research*, in which I outlined a theory of student retention. That theory was expanded with the publication in 1983 of the first edition of *Leaving College*, and was modified in the second edition, which followed in 1993. By adapting a largely sociological model to help explain student attrition in higher education, I sought to shed light on the role played by the academic and social environment of an institution in the success of its students. In so doing, I tried to the counter what was until then a tendency to see the lack of student persistence as reflecting the attributes of those who dropped out, or "blaming the victim." Given the racial and class politics in the 1980s, one can see why such blame laying is not only problematic but objectionable. I argued that the pattern of student retention and graduation, as well as its converse, student attrition, was as much a reflection of the academic and social environments of an institution—and therefore of the institutional actions that established those environments—as was the character of the students enrolled in the institution. Since students from low-income or minority backgrounds were less likely to graduate than other students, as they still are today, it followed that at least part of the inequality we observed in educational outcomes, as measured by graduation, can and should be attributed to the actions of the institution.

But knowing what may explain student retention and doing something about it are not the same. Since the publication of the first and second editions of *Leaving College*, I have invested more than a few years in reading about and carrying out research on effective institutional action. I have focused on the building of educational communities that actively engage students in learning. At the same time, I have had the opportunity to speak with many administrators, faculty, and student-affairs professionals in over four hundred institutions—both two- and four-year—across the nation, and to work with TRIO programs through my involvement with the Council for Opportunity in Education and the Pell Institute for the Study of Opportunity in Higher Education. I have come to understand in a way not possible before that when institutions and those who work in them seem unable to enhance the success of their students, it is less for lack of good intentions than for lack of knowledge about the appropriate types of actions, practices, and policies they should adopt. As importantly, I have come to appreciate the centrality of the classroom to student success and the critical role the faculty play in retaining students. But I also learned that the classroom was the domain of institutional action that was given the least attention.

Completing College attempts to bring this learning together in a way that answers the question implicit in my work when first, as a sincere but inexperienced graduate student, I tried to find out what institutions can do to enhance the retention and graduation of students, especially those who have historically not fared well in higher education. This book does not seek to develop a theory of effective institutional action or to propose additional research on student success. Rather it lays out a framework for institutional action and describes the types of actions and policies that institutions can take to enhance student retention and completion. As such, the book is directed not only to those researchers who are interested in translating theory into action, but also and more importantly to institutional administrators, faculty, and staff who are concerned about the experience of their students and have the capacity to take actions that shape that experience.

I attempt to strike a balance between generality of concept and the specificity of application. In proposing a way of thinking about action and describing the sorts of actions and policies that can be applied to all institutions, I also address the needs of particular types of institutions and specific groups of students. Though I provide case studies of various actions taken by different types of institutions to enhance student retention, I have not sought to cover all possible actions and all types of institutions and students. But I hope that the framework for action and the recommendations for action and policy that follow are of sufficient utility that any institution can adapt them to its own context to better promote the retention of all the students it serves.

ACKNOWLEDGMENTS

First and foremost, it is important to acknowledge the many faculty, staff, and administrators with whom I have had the privilege of working during the past two decades. Their wisdom has contributed in countless ways to this work. To those individuals and their institutions I most grateful.

Critical comments and support were provided by a number of individuals. Clifford Adelman, senior associate at the Institute of Higher Education Policy, provided comments on a number of issues, not the least of which concern the ways in which different data sets in higher education can yield different estimates of student retention and completion. Trudy Banta, vice chancellor, Planning and Institutional Improvement, at Indiana University–Indianapolis, helped shaped my thinking on student and institutional assessment. Luis Barrueta, coordinator of Supplemental Instruction at El Camino College, gave invaluable assistance on matters of student academic support. Adolfo Bermeo, senior scholar at the Pell Institute for the Study of Opportunity in Higher Education, and a longtime friend, was instrumental in shaping my thinking about the ways in which the language we use in higher education research serves to harm the very students we seek to help. His passionate support of underserved students from minority backgrounds has long been a source of inspiration. Charles Donaldson, vice chancellor, University of Arkansas, Little Rock, a longtime friend and skilled administrator, provided invaluable insight into issues of the organization and implementation of retention programs. Catherine Engstrom, chair of Higher Education and my colleague at Syracuse University, who was responsible for much of our research on learning communities, helped me to hear the voices of the students we were privileged to have in our study and, in turn, to understand that student voices are essential to reaching the deeper roots of student success. Peter Ewell, vice president, National Center for Higher Education Management Systems, has on various issues been generous with his thoughts and advice. Don Heller, of Pennsylvania State University and a member of the Advisory Board of the Pell Institute for the Study of Opportunity in Higher Education, and Edward St. John, of the University of Michigan, provided valuable input and critical feedback on issues of financial aid. Don Hossler, vice chancellor for enrollment services and professor of leadership and policy studies at Indiana University, gave helpful advice on the impact of enrollment management on student retention. Margaret King, now retired from her position as associate dean for student development at Schenectady County Community College, and past president of the National Academic Advising Association, provided important information, in particular on the different modes by which advising is delivered. Kay McClenney, director of the Community College Survey of Student Engagement at the University of Texas at Austin, has been supportive over the years in a number of ways that go beyond matters pertaining to community colleges. She has long provided a standard by which I judge research and policy in higher education.

Special thanks must be given to two unnamed reviewers, whose honest and forceful reviews of earlier versions of the manuscript proved critical to its development. Their generosity of spirit and time sets a standard of what it means to be a professional colleague.

To my editor, John Tryneski, at the University of Chicago Press, a very special thanks for his patience, understanding, sage advice, and good humor. His support over the past several years in seeing this work through to its conclusion is deeply appreciated. All writers should be so fortunate.

To Margaret Mahan, my copyeditor, I am especially grateful. Her careful editing, thoughtful comments and suggested revisions, and responses to my many questions did much to improve the book.

Finally to Pat, my wife of forty-four years and lifelong partner, and to my daughters Katie and Gabrielle, words cannot convey how much their love, patience, and support over what have sometimes been turbulent waters has meant to me. There are some things in our lives that are more important than books.

INTRODUCTION

1

There is little question that higher education pays. On average, people who go to college and complete a bachelor's degree earn over one million dollars more during their lifetime than do those who do not go to college (Baum and Payea 2004, 2005; Baum and Ma 2007). On a range of outcomes—from personal development, health, and the like—evidence abounds that college graduates fare far better than nongraduates. Furthermore, the gap in earnings, and thus the penalty for not going to college, appears to be increasing (Baum and Payea 2005).[1]

What matters is not simply attending college but completing a degree, especially a four-year degree. Starting but not finishing college yields little earnings benefit in relation to those who do not. The gap in lifetime earnings between these two groups is small, only about $250,000 (Baum and Ma 2007, appendix A, figure 1.2). In other words, the gap in lifetime earnings between those who complete at least a college degree and those who start college but do not graduate is more than $750,000. This is roughly the same as the difference in earnings between those with a bachelor's degree and those with an associate's degree. People with an associate's degree, though earning over their working lifetime about $354,000 more than people who only complete high school, earn approximately $650,000 less than college graduates. This does not mean that going to a two-year college and completing an associate's degree is not valuable in other ways. We know, for instance, that attaining an associate's degree positively influences the attainment of the next generation (Attewell and Lavin 2007a).[2] In terms of a person's working lifetime earnings, however, it pays to complete a four-year college degree, and it does so now more than ever.

The benefits of education accrue to our nation as a

whole. On a range of issues—from voting, health, unemployment, poverty, rates of incarceration, and school readiness of children, to rates of volunteerism—it is evident that the costs to our society of not providing higher education to our citizens are considerable, though the benefits of an education are many (Baum and Payee 2004; Baum and Ma 2007; Carnevale and Rose 2011). The same can be said of the benefits of college education to our standing in the increasingly competitive global marketplace. A college-educated workforce is critical to our nation's ability to remain competitive; but where once we were world leaders in the proportion of our population between the ages of twenty-four and thirty-five holding a college certificate or degree, this is no longer the case. By most estimates we now are rapidly falling behind many other nations in our ability to produce college graduates (National Center for Public Policy and Higher Education 2006; Tierney 2006). Given current demographic trends, there are danger signs aplenty that unless we do a better job in graduating more of our students from college, we will slip even farther behind.

■ Student Retention in Higher Education

It is little wonder, then, that over the past several decades federal and state governments and a range of organizations have invested heavily in programs to increase access to higher education. But as access has more than doubled from nearly 9 million students in 1980 to almost 20 million in 2011, overall college completion rates have increased only slightly, if at all (Bound, Lovenheim, and Turner 2009; Radford, Berkner, Wheeless, and Shepherd 2010; Supiano 2011).[3] Barely more than one-half of all four-year college students in the United States earn their bachelor's degrees within six years from their initial institution (Nagda 2003). Less than one-third of community college students earn an associate's degree or certificate from their initial institution over a six-year period. Some students will take longer than six years to earn their degrees from their initial institution and others will transfer to another institution to do so. The result is that among four-year college entrants nearly 63% will eventually earn their four-year degrees and approximately 40% of community college entrants, if that, will earn a bachelor's degree or an associate's degree or certificate (see table A10).[4]

Not all students graduate from their initial institution at the same rate. Data from a six-year longitudinal study of students who began higher education in 1995 indicate that women earn bachelor's degrees more frequently than men (21.9% versus 19.6%); white students (22.6%) and students from

Asia or the Pacific Island (33.1%) more frequently than African American (14.0%), Hispanic (13.7%), and American Indian / Alaska Native students (8.8%); high-income students more frequently than low-income students (42.0% versus 19.0%); students from college-educated families more frequently than first-generation college students (37.0% versus 12.2%); and students whose high-school grade-point average is greater than 3.25 more frequently than those whose grade-point average is less than 2.25 (29.6% versus 7.5%) (Nagda 2003). Furthermore, only 7.5% of students who are eligible for Pell grants—that is, students who come from low-income backgrounds and are also the first in their generation to attend college—obtain a bachelor's degree within six years from their initial institution, as against 41.1% of those students who are in neither of those categories.[5]

The time taken to earn a degree also varies widely. Of the approximately 55% of those students who complete their bachelor's degree from their initial institution, only about 33% (or 60% of all degree earners) do so within the standard four-year time frame (see Nagda 2003, tables 7.1–7.6). The remaining 22% (or 40% of all degree earners) do so in the following two years. Beyond the fact that some degrees, such as in engineering, require more than four years of full-time study, it is evident that many students take considerably more than four years to earn a four-year degree.

Similarly, rates of attrition vary over time. On average, the percentage of beginning students who leave their initial institution before graduating reflects the well-established finding that institutional attrition is generally highest in the first year and declines thereafter (see table A3). For four-year colleges and universities, whether public or private, 38% of those who leave will do so in their first year, and 29% in their second year.[6] Since much of the attrition in the second year reflects what happened or did not happen in the first year, it is understandable that many institutions allocate a sizable portion of their scarce resources to the first year of college.

There are significant differences among institutions in their rates of student retention. For instance, some private universities graduate over 90% of their beginning students, while some public ones graduate fewer than 30%.[7] That wide variation reflects in part differences both in institutional mission and in the attributes of the students admitted. Institutions that enroll wealthier students, students from college-educated families, and students who have higher high-school grades or entering test scores—in other words, colleges and universities that are more selective—have higher rates of institutional retention and graduation (Astin and Oseguera 2005; Gold and Albert 2006; Horn and Carroll 2006). But even among institutions with similar selectivity, there remains substantial variation in graduation rates (Astin 2005, p. 14). Clearly, there is more to the ability of institutions to graduate its students than is reflected in the students they admit.

However one analyzes the data, one fact remains clear. Institutional rates of four-year and two-year degree completion have not increased substantially since the 1990s (Mortenson 2009b; Radford, Berkner, Wheeless, and Shepherd 2010). Nor have overall rates at which students eventually earn their degrees (Bound, Lovenheim, and Turner 2009).[8] At the same time, though enrollment of low-income students has grown, and the gap in access between them and more affluent students has narrowed, the gap in persistence and completion appears to have increased somewhat over the same period (Horn, Berger and Carroll 2004, table 5-B; Haycock 2006). In 1989–90, for instance, the proportion of low-income students who completed a four-year degree within five years was only 16.7%. In 1995–96 that figure fell to 15.0%. By contrast, the completion rate of four-year degrees for high-income students increased over that period from 38.4% to 41.0%. In other words, high-income students were nearly three times more likely to complete a four-year degree than were low-income students. Since fewer low-income students than high-income students even begin college, the disparity is glaring.

■ **Need for Effective Action**

Despite our nation's success in increasing access to college and reducing the gap in access between high- and low-income students, we have not yet been successful in translating the opportunity access provides into college completion, or what I refer to here as student success. That is the case is not for lack of attention or effort. Indeed, over the past twenty years, if not more, colleges and universities as well as foundations, state governments, and more recently the federal government have invested considerable resources in the development and implementation of a range of retention programs, many directed specifically at low-income and underserved students.[9] Some institutions have been able to improve the rate at which they retain and graduate their students, but many, even those who have sought to do so, have not (Carey 2005b; Carey and Hess 2009).

There are many reasons why this is the case. One has to do with the nature of the research on student attrition, another with the character of most efforts to improve retention. Much of the research on student attrition has not been particularly useful to those in the field who seek to develop and implement programs to improve retention and completion because it assumes, incorrectly, that knowing why students leave is equivalent to knowing why students stay and succeed. The process of persistence is not the mirror image of the process of leaving. Though the two are necessarily related, understanding the reasons for leaving doesn't necessarily translate into helping students to persist (Padilla 1999). Research has also tended to focus on theoretically appealing concepts that do not easily translate into definable courses of action. Take, for instance, the concept of academic and social integration (Tinto 1975, 1993). While it may be useful for theorists to know that what is now referred to as academic and social engagement has a role to play in retention, that insight does not tell practitioners, at least not directly, what they could do to enhance academic and social engagement in their institution.[10] Though a number of researchers have addressed the practical question of "what works" (e.g., Braxton, Hirschy, and McClendon 2004; Engstrom and Tinto 2007; Kuh, Kinzi, Schuh, Whitt, and Associates 2005; Pascarella and Terenzini 1991, 2005; Seidman 2005; and Tinto 1993, 1997; Tinto and Goodsell 1994; Tinto, Goodsell, and Russo 1993; Tinto and Russo 1994), our knowledge of effective action remains fragmented and poorly organized.

The same can be said of institutional action. Despite years of effort, institutions have yet to develop a coherent framework to guide their thinking about which actions matter most and how they should be organized and successfully implemented. Too often, institutions invest in a laundry list of actions, one disconnected from another. The result is an uncoordinated patchwork of actions whose sum impact on student retention is less than it could or should be. Moreover, and just as important, most institutional efforts have been situated at the margins of students' educational life. They have neglected the classroom, the one place on campus, perhaps only place, where the great majority of students meet the faculty and one another and engage in formal learning activities. Lest we forget, so-called traditional students, who enroll full-time in a residential college or university immediately after high school, make up only a quarter of all college students. Most students do not live on campus. A great many work while in college, especially those of low-income backgrounds, and attend part-time. Attending college is only one of many demands on their time and energies. They go to campus, attend class, and quickly leave to attend to other obligations. For them, the experience of college is primarily the experience of the classroom. Their success in college is built upon their success in the classroom.

If institutions are to significantly increase the retention and graduation of their students, especially those from low-income backgrounds, their actions must be centered on the classroom. They must focus on improving success in the classroom, particularly during the first year and lead to changes in the way classes are structured and taught and, in turn, experienced by students, especially those who have not fared well in the past. Furthermore, institutions must align those classrooms, one to another, in ways that provide students coherent pathways of courses that propel them to timely program completion.

The object of this book is to tap the knowledge we have gained from past research on student retention and completion and use it in developing a framework for institutional action that places the classroom at the center. It seeks to provide institutions not only with a systematic way of thinking about what actions they can take to increase retention and graduation, but also with a way of organizing and implementing those actions to enhance their sum impact on student success.

■ A Framework for Institutional Action: The Conditions for Student Success

First, we must recognize that a college or university, once having admitted a student, has an obligation to do what it can to help the student stay and graduate. To improve retention and graduation, the institution must begin by focusing on its own behavior and establishing conditions within its walls that promote those outcomes. This does not preclude efforts beyond the campus to enhance the likelihood of success for its current and future students.[11] Nor does it preclude efforts to recruit students who are themselves more likely to stay and graduate.[12] For most institutions, however, the attributes of new students are largely beyond the immediate institutional control. This is not the case for conditions within colleges and universities in which students are placed. Being already the result of past institutional action, those conditions can be changed. Indeed they must be changed. The long-term improvement in student retention and graduation must begin with efforts to establish those conditions on campus that are known to promote student success. Enhanced student retention and graduation follow.

What, then, does research on student retention tell us about the conditions within colleges and universities that promote retention and graduation? Studies converge on four that are associated with enhanced student retention. These conditions, briefly described below, are expectations, support, assessment and feedback, and involvement (Tinto 2010).

Expectations. Student success is driven, in part, by what students expect of themselves. These self-expectations are shaped, in turn, by a variety of institutional actions, not the least of which have to do with the expectations the institution establishes for student performance and those the faculty establish for their students, especially in the classes they teach. Student success is directly influenced not only by the clarity and consistency of expectations but also by their level. High expectations are a condition for student success, low expectations a harbinger of failure. Simply put, no one rises to low expectations.

Support. It is one thing to hold high expectations; it is another to provide the support students need to achieve them. Without academic, social, and, in some cases, financial support, many students, especially those who enter college academically underprepared, struggle to succeed.[13] At no time is support, especially academic support, more important than during the critical first year of college, when student success is still so much in question and still very responsive to institutional intervention. And in no place is support more needed than in the classroom where success is constructed one course at a time.

Assessment and feedback. Students are more likely to succeed in institutions that assess their performance and provide frequent feedback in ways that enable students, faculty, and staff alike to adjust their behaviors to better promote student success. This is especially true during the first year and in the classrooms of that year, when students are trying to adjust their behaviors to the new academic and social demands of college life.

Involvement. A fourth and perhaps the most important condition for student success is involvement, or what is now commonly referred to as engagement. The more students are academically and socially engaged with faculty, staff, and peers, the more likely they are to succeed in college. Such engagements lead not only to social affiliations and the social and emotional support they provide, but also to greater involvement in educational activities and the learning they produce.

Students are most likely to remain in college when all four conditions exist. Though certain conditions may be more important for some students than others, such as academic support for academically underprepared students, they all matter. The absence of one undermines the efficacy of the others; the absence of feedback, for instance, undermines the ability of the institution to provide support when needed and for students and faculty to adjust their behaviors when called for. Nowhere do these conditions matter more than in the classrooms, and at no time than during the first year of college.

In sum, students are more likely to succeed in settings that establish clear and high expectations for their success, provide academic and social support, frequently assess and provide feedback about their performance, and actively involve them with others on campus, especially in the classroom.

Our focus on the conditions for student retention does not imply that individuals have no say in their own success. Of course individuals matter; their values, commitments, abilities, and prior academic preparation all play a part in their success. Some individuals succeed by sheer willpower, skill, and perseverance, even when conditions would appear to militate against success. Others do not succeed even when placed in settings that are conducive to success. There is only so much an institution can do—and some would argue should do—to promote student success if individuals are themselves not inclined to invest in those activities that lead to success. But none of this relieves a college of its responsibility to establish conditions on campus that are promotive of student success.

We turn, in chapters 2–5, to a discussion of each of the four conditions for student success—expectations, support, assessment and feedback, and involvement—and to the types of actions an institution can take to establish those conditions on campus. In each chapter, case studies of the successful implementation of a particular action are provided. Chapter 6 discusses the kinds of policies an institution should adopt to organize and successfully implement the recommended actions in ways that can be sustained and scaled up over time. Furthermore, it is argued that institutional success in enhancing retention and graduation is not merely the summation of various programs, but a reflection of the systematic nature of those programs and the capacity of an institution to align the actions of its various parts and members to the same goal, namely the success of all students.

The seventh and final chapter issues a call for institutions to take a series of actions to enhance the retention and graduation of their students. Whereas the preceding chapters identify a range of possible actions that institutions could take, this chapter speaks to what institutions should do if they are serious in their pursuit of enhanced student success. Student success does not arise by chance. It requires that institutions commit themselves to intentional, structured, and systematic forms of action that involve faculty, student-affairs staff, and administrators alike. Appendix A provides a detailed analysis of the available data on student retention and student persistence. Appendix B speaks to the issue of accountability and student retention.

EXPECTATIONS

2

Expectations can have a powerful effect on student performance. What students expect of themselves and what they need do to be successful determines in part what they will actually do (Malaney and Shively 1995). As a reflection of institutional action, student expectations are directly and indirectly shaped by a variety of factors, not the least of which are the expectations an institution establishes for its students, as represented, for instance, by the statements and actions of its administrators, faculty, and staff. Those statements and actions that most directly influence student retention have to do with the clarity of expectations and whether they are high or low.[1]

■ Knowing What to Do to Succeed

Student retention and graduation is shaped by the availability of clear and consistent expectations about what is required to be successful in college. Roughly speaking, these expectations fall into three broad areas: success in the institution as a whole, success in a program of study, and success in a course in which the student is enrolled. Expectations of these sorts are typically expressed in concrete ways through orientation activities, program advising, coursework, interactions with course faculty, and individual faculty and staff advising. They are expressed in less concrete ways through informal advising or mentoring, which arises through a variety of formal and informal networks on campus such as student peer groups and student contact with faculty and staff.

Knowing the roadmap to success—the rules, regulations, and requirements for degree completion—is central to students' ability to successfully navigate the path to timely degree completion. To quote Yogi Berra, "You've got to be very careful if you don't know where you're going, because you might not get there." Student expectations as to what is needed to succeed in college are shaped not only by the prior knowledge students possess at entry but also by the academic advice they receive from faculty or staff (Bahr 2008; Elliott and Healy 2001; Frost 1991; Metzner 1989; Ryan and Glenn 2003; Young, Backer, and Rogers 1989). Seidman (1991), for example, found that community college students who received postadmission advising three times during their first semester to discuss issues such as course schedules and academic and social involvement persisted at a rate 20% higher than those who only participated in the college orientation program. Metzner's (1989) study of more than one thousand freshman at a public university found that student satisfaction with the quality of the advice they received was positively related to retention to the second year, in part because it was positively associated with a higher grade-point average during the first year. More recently, Bahr (2008) found that advising improved the attainment of full-time students who enrolled in any of the 107 California semester-based community colleges. The benefits were even greater for students who entered with academic deficiencies. Unfortunately, formal advising by faculty remains a hit-or-miss affair on most campuses; not all students are lucky enough to have an informed adviser (Heverly 1999).

Receiving good advice is essential for the many students who either begin college undecided about their major or change their major during college (Lewallen 1993). The inability to obtain needed advice during the first year or at the point of changing majors can undermine motivation, increase the likelihood of departure, and, for those who continue, lengthen the time to degree completion as students transfer to other degree programs. Though students may earn credits, they may fail to make substantial degree-credit progress. Indeed, some students will continue to the end of the fourth year without completing their degree because they have earned too few degree credits in a major to graduate. In this case, the issue is not just advising undecided students, or what is commonly referred to as developmental advising, but giving specific advice to those students who want to change their major.

A good many students begin higher education without knowing what to expect. First-generation and low-income college students, for instance, typically lack the sorts of shared knowledge, or cultural capital, that more affluent students and those from college-educated families commonly possess about the nature of the college experience and what it takes to succeed.[2] Orientation activities as well as advising and on-campus programs such as Student Support Services can help low-income students and first-generation college students to safely navigate the sometimes turbulent waters of the institution (Engle, Bermeo, and O'Brien 2006).

Knowledge may also be shared through mentoring relationships or, more commonly, informal networks among faculty, staff, and students. New students may gain knowledge from peer groups and from older students from similar backgrounds who are already on campus (Anderson and Ekstrom 1996; Twomey 1991). Attinasi's (1989) research sheds light on the way ethnic peers help new students develop "cognitive maps" of the physical, social, and academic geographies of what might otherwise be a foreign campus.

Nowhere are expectations more important than in the classroom. Success there provides the foundation for student retention and graduation. Classroom expectations are shaped less by advice than by a student's interaction with teachers and, to some degree, with fellow students. The information that faculty members provide in their syllabi, course materials, and conversations with students during the course gives students an idea of what is expected of them academically (e.g., what is required to attain different grades). But teachers' behaviors, especially those pertaining to assessment and grading, often convey more about expectations for success than do faculty statements on formal documents such as syllabi. Here, as elsewhere, consistency matters, and actions speak louder than words.

■ Expectations for Effort

Student retention is also influenced by the expectations the institution establishes for the quality or level of effort required for successful performance (Pace 1980). High expectations are a condition for student success, low expectations a recipe for failure. In their review of the literature on motivation and school performance, Schilling and Schilling (1999, p. 5) conclude "that merely stating an expectation results in enhanced performance, that higher expectations result in higher performance, and that persons with high expectations perform at a higher level than those with low expectations, even though their measured ability is the same." Similarly, a study by Reason, Terenzini, and Domingo (2006) found that students who viewed their institution as more academically challenging were more likely to report greater gains in academic competence during the first year than similar students who saw their institution as less cognitively challenging.

The findings of the National Survey of Student Engagement (NSSE) are even clearer. Student perceptions of the level of effort expected of them by the institution are directly correlated with their level of effort and, in turn, with their success in college (Kuh et al. 2007). Similarly, students in institutions with better-than-expected retention rates perceived their institution has having higher levels of academic challenge (Laird, Chen, and Kuh 2008).

It is regrettable, therefore that students, especially during the critical first year of college, appear to expend too little effort in their studies. Data from the NSSE indicate that first-year students on average spend only about half the time studying that faculty deem necessary for successful learning (Kuh 2003; National Survey of Student Engagement 2006a, p. 19, figure 7). Too frequently we hear of instances where faculty and staff claim to expect one set of behaviors or level of effort by their students, while students seem to expect something entirely different. Not only do students report that they work less than they had expected when they started college, but their expectation of the amount of studying necessary to succeed tends to decline over the course of the first year. This decline occurs regardless of the level of expectations with which students begin or the types of institutions they enter. Even in more selective institutions, whose students enter with higher expectations and exhibit higher levels of effort, students report working two to six hours less per week than they had expected (National Survey of Student Engagement 2006a, p. 20).

Similar findings are reported by Arum and Roska's (2011) study of student learning in the first two years of college. Of the students surveyed, approximately 35% claimed to spend no more than five hours per week studying, and nearly 50% said that in their previous semester they didn't have a single course that required more than twenty pages of writing. Moreover, Arum and Roska found that there has been close to a 50% decline in the number of hours spent studying and preparing for classes over the past several decades.

This relative lack of student effort suggests that faculty, as expressed by their actions, frequently expect too little of their students and fail to construct educational settings that require students to push themselves harder. On average, teachers do not consistently employ pedagogies, give assignments, provide feedback on assignments, and employ assessment tools (e.g., exams or forms of classroom assessment) that lead students to spend more time on task. The settings in which students are placed do not reinforce, indeed may inhibit, what an institution or its teachers claim to expect of students.

Students' expectations are also influenced by their interactions with student peers and the climate they establish for one another (e.g., Astin 1993; Bank, Slavings, and Biddle 1990; Berger and Milem 2000; Bonous-Hammarth 2000; Kaya 2004; and Pascarella and Terenzini 1991, 2005). A recent study by Oseguera and Rhee (2009), for instance, found that the retention climate of an institution, as measured by the aggregate withdrawal intentions of the student body, had an independent effect on the intentions of individual students. In most cases it reinforced what students were encountering in the classroom and administrative offices. That being said, it is still the institution's responsibility to create a climate for individuals and peer groups that promotes clear, consistent, and high expectations. In responding to the needs of individual students, the institution will also improve the expectational climate for other students.

Findings of the recent Survey of Entering Student Engagement (SENSE) nicely summarize the importance of setting clear and high expectations. The survey, administered by the Center for Community College Student Engagement to more than 50,000 new students at 120 community colleges during the fourth and fifth weeks of classes in the fall of 2009, assessed early impressions of institutional practices and student behaviors. It concluded that "when entering students perceive clear, high expectations from college staff and faculty, they are more likely to understand what it takes to be successful and adopt behaviors that lead to achievement" (Center for Community College Student Engagement 2009, p. 6).

Institutions sometimes hold different expectations for different types of students. These expectations may be expressed in labels used to describe certain groups, such as "remedial," or more subtly in the way individuals, whether teachers or students, treat others who are of a different social class, gender, or ethnicity. However expressed, students quickly pick up expectations and are influenced by the degree to which those expectations validate their presence on campus. This is precisely what Rendon (1994) and Barnett (2011) are referring to in their research on validation and the success of community college students, and what Solorzano, Ceja, and Yosso (2000) are referring to in their study of the "microaggressions" that students of color often encounter on a predominantly white campus.

■ Shaping Student Expectations

Institutions act in a variety of ways to shape student expectations. First, they set clear and consistent expectations for student behaviors and the requirements for degree or certificate completion. Second, they help students establish expectations for themselves and provide them with clear roadmaps on what is required for success in their programs of study. Third, working with faculty, they set clear and consistent expectations for what is required for success in the classroom.

Setting Institutional Expectations

Institutional leaders, especially presidents and chancellors, play a major role in shaping the expectational climate of a campus and its students (Carey 2005a, 2005b; Sporn 1996; McLeod and Young 2005). The campus climate creates the expectational context for individual actions, for the way individuals respond to each other and to the multiple and often competing demands upon their time and energies. One example is the way in which faculty balance the competing demands of research and teaching (Wolverton 1998). In an institution that expects superior teaching and provides support for teaching, faculty are more likely to place priority on that part of their job. To the degree that such expectations shape faculty and staff behaviors, they also influence the multiple expectational climates encountered by students.

Stating expectations, of course, is not the same as making them real through institutional behaviors. Expectations for student behavior must be reinforced by matching actions on the part of all members of the institution, especially the faculty. This is certainly the case at Glen Oaks Community College, where admission counselors, faculty, and staff continually remind students of the importance of class attendance. Students are told that if they miss 15% of class time in any semester, instructors have the authority to withdraw them from class. During the first week of class, instructors submit the names of students who miss class to student services staff, who then contact the student. During the third week of class a similar procedure is followed, and this time the student receives a letter from the college, emphasizing the need to attend class regularly.[3]

Most institutions use orientation programs prior to the start of the academic year as a forum in which expectations are stated and information provided about what students need to do in order to succeed (Barefoot 2005;

Mullendore and Banahan 2005; Ward-Roof and Hatch 2003). Though it has never been clear how useful such programs are in setting expectations, anecdotal evidence suggests that they can help family members and others gain a better appreciation of what their child or partner will face in college and, in turn, what they should expect of themselves in relation to the student (Mullendore and Hatch 2000). This understanding is especially useful in the case of first-generation and low-income students, since it may help to reconcile the sometimes conflicting expectations of family and friends with those of the institution.

It can happen, however, that students are overwhelmed with information, so that they have either not read or forgotten much of the material by the time the first semester rolls around. Compounding the problem, students who have yet to begin their first semester often do not know what questions to ask, lacking the experience upon which to base their questions. For that reason, orientation must serve to introduce students to those to whom they can turn when questions arise, and must establish a setting where students will feel comfortable doing so (Ward 2010).[4] In some cases, orientation programs will include current students as guides, possible mentors, or—as in Santiago Canyon College's "Discover SCC: Orientation to College Life"—orientation leaders. In other cases, typically in residential institutions such as Georgetown University and the University of Florida, orientation activities involve outdoor or so-called wilderness programs. Many institutions, such as St. Louis University, extend the orientation program into the first year (Lowe and Cook 2003; Wilcox, Winn, and Fyvie-Gauld 2005). They will do so in a variety of ways, including freshman seminars or first-year experience courses and learning communities. Such activities further the acquisition of information and the development of social affiliations from which students' sense of belonging emerges.

Asnuntuck Community College, among others, uses the popular First Year Experience courses to orient general-studies or liberal arts students to the campus. Instructors in this course invite counselors to work directly with students to ensure that they have a clear understanding of what is expected of them in college and to help them frame expectations for their own educational and career goals. A survey found that students who took the course in their first semester were more likely to remain in college for the next semester than were those who elected to take the course only in their second semester (Center for Community College Student Engagement

2009). Results like these are but one reason why such courses are so widely employed across the nation (see Griffin and Romm 2008).

Enrollment management can also influence student retention by helping to shape the character of the entering class, and indirectly by influencing freshmen's expectations of the setting into which they will enter. These pre-entry expectations serve as an initial lens through which students see and in turn judge the institution. If pre-entry expectations are very different from experience following entry ("this is not what I expected"), students may decide to leave. But if enrollment management helps students form initial expectations that are consistent with experience following entry, its actions can promote retention.

■ Advising: Providing Roadmaps to Success

To succeed, students need a roadmap that guides them through the institution and the field in which they want to earn their degree, the institutional resources available to them in pursuit of that degree, and requirements that have to be completed to earn a degree or certificate in their chosen field of study (Gordon 2007; Gordon and Habley 2000; Gordon, Habley and Grites 2008; King and Kerr 2005). In response to these needs, institutions have established a range of advising programs. These have typically focused on first-year students, in particular those who are undecided about their field of study and those who seek to change it.

Virtually all institutions, whether two- or four-year, have some form of advising for new students, some more structured than others. Many, such as Oakland University, the University of Iowa, and the University of Georgia, rely on intensive early advising. Others, such as the University of Wisconsin–Whitewater, where resources permit, require students to meet with advisers several times during their first year. While most institutions direct their energies to all incoming students, a few, including Sinclair Community College, Louisiana State University, and the University of Cincinnati, provide additional counseling to "at-risk" students. Some, such as Howard Community College, also reach out to high school seniors.

Advising First-Year Students at the
University of Wisconsin–Whitewater

The Academic Advising and Exploration Center at the University of Wisconsin–Whitewater provides proactive and developmental advising to help first-year students make the transition to college and to develop an educational plan to guide their studies at the university. The process begins with a quick "Check-In" at the beginning of the semester, focusing on issues of course registration, and a fifteen-minute "Pre-Advise" meeting to tell students about the many resources available to them on campus. Later in the first semester, each student meets with an adviser for thirty minutes ("Advise") to discuss the registration process and course recommendations for the next semester, along with degree requirements and university probation and progression standards.

As many of 50%, if not more, of all beginning students are undecided or uncertain about their educational and vocational futures (Gaffner and Hazler 2002; Gordon 2007; Lewallen 1993; Kramer, Higley, and Olsen 1994). Since indecision is associated with higher rates of attrition (Lewallen 1993), it is of little surprise that so many institutions (e.g., the University of Illinois, Indiana University, Oregon State University, Pennsylvania State University, and Virginia Commonwealth University) have instituted special advising programs or centers specifically geared to undecided students (Korschgen and Hageseth 1997; Steele 2003). Some institutions (e.g., North Carolina State University) have constructed first-year colleges, providing undecided students with a curricular and advising setting in which decisions about their college future can be made in a careful and informed way (Tagg 2003). Others, such as Monroe Community College in New York, offer students an "undeclared" option, which grants them time and resources to explore possible academic and career choices.[5]

However the programs are constructed, advising undecided students requires professional skills that are not typically found among faculty. Most programs depend on professionally trained advisers who work with undecided students in an advising center. Elsewhere, as in Fox Valley Technical College, they work in partnership with designated faculty from each department or program to facilitate the movement of students into a specific course of study (Frost 1991; Gordon and Habley 2000).

Advising Undecided Students at Pennsylvania State University

Incoming freshman who indicate on their application that they have not yet selected a major are offered enrollment in the university's Division of Undergraduate Studies, whose primary mission is to help beginning students explore majors while making progress toward graduation. Nearly

40% of those offered admission subsequently enroll in the division—a yield rate that is higher than that of most of the colleges at Pennsylvania State University. Currently 20% of the incoming freshman class enroll in the division. Students who begin in other colleges at the university may also enroll in the division if their initial academic plans change and they need advice about their majors.

The division is staffed by some twenty-five professional, mostly full-time advisers, who engage students through online and print materials to explore possible majors and navigate university requirements. Beginning with group meetings with students during the one-day academic orientation program that occurs prior to the first year, advisers track students' progress throughout the year. They e-mail each student about his or her progress and meet individually with most students at least once a semester. As a measure of the division's effectiveness, the six-year graduation rate of its students is similar to that of other students at the university.

Being undecided is not, however, solely a matter of not knowing or being unsure of what academic and career path to follow as one enters college. Many students find that their initial choice of a major was inappropriate (Gordon and Steele 1992; Titley and Titley 1980). Though accurate figures are hard to come by, it is estimated that between a third and a half of all four-year college students change their major at least once while in college (Kramer, Higley, and Olsen 1994; Gordon 2005). They move from decision to indecision. Unfortunately they often do not receive the developmental advising that is provided to students who begin college undecided. Yet such advising as provided at Ohio State University's Alternative Advising Program is as important, if not more important, to their success. It is frequently the case that transcripts of four-year college students who leave in the third or fourth year reveal that although they are earning credits, they are not making progress toward their degree. Failing to get effective advice, they move between majors, without settling on one that fits their interests, and often leave without graduating.

Not surprisingly, career counseling also plays a role in retention and graduation (Luzzo 2000; Nutt 2003). To the degree that career choice and choice of major are connected, effective career counseling helps to steer students toward majors in which they are likely to find value and remain enrolled. It is one of many reasons why some institutions, such as Rowan

University, have combined advising and career services into a single unit, where career counselors and academic advisers are cross-trained to work with students in both areas. Other institutions, such as Quinebaug Valley Community College, refer undecided students to the college's Career Center, where they get help setting and refining their career goals early in their academic career.

Once settled in a program, students need to know about course requirements, scheduling, and other matters related to program and degree completion. Advice in this area, academic rather than career-oriented, is the responsibility of program faculty. Unfortunately, not all faculty are up-to-date on program and degree requirements or student credit histories. This is where degree audit systems, such as the widely used Degree Audit Reporting System (DARS) developed at Miami University of Ohio, are most useful.[6] When run effectively, such systems assist both students and faculty by furnishing accurate and up-to-date information on student degree-credit progress, courses to be completed, scheduling, and course availability. Degree audit systems address some common student complaints concerning faculty academic advising: that some advisers are hard to find, that they are sometimes uninformed about course requirements, and that not infrequently their advice is incorrect. Not all students are lucky enough to have a "great adviser."

One of the virtues of degree audit systems, which can also be a weakness, is that it is sometimes possible for students to get information without having to see an adviser. All registration can be done online, as is the case with the Interactive Degree Audit (IDA) at the University of Texas. Though many institutions only require students to obtain a pin number from their adviser, others that employ a degree-audit system, such as Syracuse University, require students to meet with their advisers and obtain their signatures as a condition for completing registration online. Those meetings give faculty and students an opportunity to talk to each other and allow faculty to do what they do best, namely, to hold conversations with their students about a range of academic matters that are part and parcel of gaining mastery over a field of study.

As already noted, many institutions establish formal advising centers staffed by professional advisers. Understandably, many of these centers focus much of their work on new students for whom advising is needed the most (Commander, Valeri-Gold, and Darnell 2004; Stark 2002). In these centers, advisers may work together with a faculty member whose job it is to provide advice specific to a particular program or department and serve as the adviser to whom students would first go once they enter the program. In this very important respect, first-year advising centers coordinate and align the actions of professional advisers and faculty advisers to ensure, within reason, that the advice students receive is accurate and consistent over time.

A number of institutions, such the Fox Valley Technical College, the University of California–Davis, and the University of New Hampshire, also use trained peer advisers as part of their first-year advising programs. Peer mentors may serve particular members of the entering class (e.g., students of a particular race/ethnicity or program) or take part in first-year seminars. Though peer advisers can never take the place of professional advisers and trained faculty, they can provide a valuable type of informal advising; for example, they can direct students to the person who can fix a particular problem, or let them know of the best places to study (Koring and Campbell 2004). Peer advisers also can serve, as we will see when we turn to assessment and feedback, as the ears and eyes of an "early warning" system, alerting institutions of student difficulties (e.g., social or personal problems) in time to intervene before those difficulties undermine progress and lead to withdrawal. It is important for peer advisers to have faculty and staff they can call on for assistance. In no instance should peer advisers feel obliged to provide advice on issues they are inadequately prepared to deal with. For this reason, effective peer advising systems invest in training programs for peer mentors and provide them structured support. The same applies to all advising programs. Their effectiveness depends on an institution's willingness to invest in a range of support services for faculty and staff, not the least of which is the provision of training programs. In the final analysis, the success of any program, advising or otherwise, depends on the skills of those responsible for implementing it (Nutt et al. 2003; Folsom 2007).

The question remains as to the organizational model institutions should use to build their advising programs (Pardee 2000; King 2003). Among the seven models of advising described by King and Kerr (2005), the one these authors recommend for two-year colleges is a centralized advising office that attends to all students who enter the institution (a total intake model). A corps of trained advisers, which may include faculty and peers, advise all first-year students and continue advising those who are undecided or change majors. For four-year colleges, especially larger ones, King and Kerr recommend a dual model, with trained advisers and knowledgeable full-time faculty working together. The former advise undecided students and all first-year students regarding academic policies, registration, and so forth, while faculty members advise students who have selected a major, informing them of the specific requirements of their field of study.[7]

Regardless of the model an institution adopts, there are rarely enough advisers to talk with every student. For that reason some institutions supplement individual advising with the kind that reaches groups of students. Foothill College, for instance, embeds advising in courses such as the Freshman Seminar. Though group advising cannot answer each student's questions, it often leads to higher utilization of individual advising services. As we will discuss in chapter 3, this principle of embedding services in classrooms is being used to help both first-year and academically underprepared students.

An increasing number of institutions invest either in online advising or—as do Arizona State University, University of Louisville, and Valencia Community College—in a combination of online and professional advising. Valencia Community College maintains an advising center as well as an online developmental advising program called Life Map, which guides students through the various steps leading from indecision to a concrete course of action and ultimately to graduation.[8] A number of institutions such as Capella University and Rio Salado College, both on-line institutions, and Saddleback College and Irving Valley College of the South Orange Community College District, have employed predictive analytics to advise students (see Norris et al. 2008). Similar to the way Amazon and Netflix uses a person's recent purchases to recommend similar items, information on students' preferences, schedule, and current courses is utilized to suggest other courses that would enable the student to make progress to program completion. As we will discuss in chapters 4 and 5, similar methods are being employed both as early warning systems and as tools for institutional decision-making.

■ **Setting Expectations for Success in Classrooms**

Student expectations, specifically those that most directly shape learning, are primarily framed by the expectations teachers establish in their classrooms as to the amount of effort required of their students (Kirk 2005). It is worth repeating that no one rises to low expectations; student success is enhanced when expectations for effort are high and clearly enunciated. Yet data from the National Survey of Student Engagement (NSSE) reveal that student expectations as to the effort required in college not only begin lower than that of the faculty but decline over the course of the first year.

Here is where faculty behaviors are critical. Teachers must not only set high expectations but must constantly reinforce them. Therefore, while expressing high expectations both in their written course syllabi and by oral communication with students in class, teachers must reinforce those expectations by their own behaviors. Such behaviors range from grading standards, feedback on assignments and examinations, and the modeling of exemplary effort, to the use of pedagogic methods that require, by their very nature, high levels of effort.

■ Expectations and Student Success: A Comment

Establishing an environment that provides students with a clear road-map and high expectations for their success requires collaborative efforts of all members of the institution, especially the faculty. They must understand that their actions speak as loudly as their words. Once such an environment is achieved, its effect on student success can be powerful. Colleges with environments of this kind not only will help its existing students to succeed but will attract many others who seek such environments.

SUPPORT

3 Just as expectations matter for student success, so does support. Without academic, social, and in some cases financial support, many students struggle to meet institutional expectations and succeed in college (Community College Survey of Student Engagement 2008; Ward, Trautvetter, and Braskamp 2005; Zhao and Kuh 2004; Belcheir 2001; Filkins and Doyle 2002; Upcraft, Gardner, and Barefoot 2005). Numerous studies have documented the relationship between first-year students' perceptions of institutional support and a range of social and personal development outcomes (Belcheir 2001; Laird, Chen and Kuh 2008; Polewchak 2002; Zhao and Kuh 2004). Filkins and Doyle's (2002) study of low-income and first-generation first year students at six urban colleges, for example, found that students' evaluation of institutional support was positively associated with self-reported gains in social and personal development. More recently, a study by Reason, Terenzini, and Domingo (2006) of 6,687 first-year full-time and part-time students in thirty four-year campuses nationwide found that students' perceptions of the degree to which the institution was supportive of their academic, personal, and social needs were the most powerful predictor, among a wide range of variables, of increased academic competence during the first year.

That high expectations and support go hand in hand with student success is not a new notion. Sanford (1966) and Erickson (1968) both argued that learning environments should provide a balance of challenge (or what we now call expectations) and support. Too much challenge and/or too little concurrent support could prompt maladaptive coping strategies such as ignoring the challenge or escaping it by leaving college (as cited by Hamrick,

Evans, and Schuh 2002). As Baxter Magolda (1999a, p. 23) puts it, "support for students' current way of making meaning is central to promoting complex meaning-making."

■ Academic Support

Nothing is more important to student retention than academic support, especially during the critical first year of college, when student retention is still very responsive to institutional intervention. Unfortunately, more than a few students begin college academically underprepared. The U.S. Department of Education reported that at least 28% of all beginning college students in 2000 enrolled in at least one basic-skills or "remedial" course in reading, writing, or mathematics (National Center for Education Statistics 2004, p. 17). Not surprisingly, the percentage of students enrolled in basic-skills courses was higher in two-year colleges (42% in public two-year versus 20% in public four-year) (National Center for Education Statistics 2004, table 4). But even these percentages may not reflect the number of students who need remediation, since not all students directed to those courses actually take them (Attewell, Lavin, Domina, and Levey 2006).

For many students the availability of academic support—in the form of basic-skills, developmental, or remedial courses; tutoring; study groups; supplemental instruction; and summer bridge programs—is critical to their ability to succeed in college (Barefoot 1993; Blanc, DeBuhr, and Martin 1983; Blanc and Martin 1994; Commander, Stratton, Callahan, and Smith 1996; Congos, Langsam, and Schoeps 1997; Peterfreund, Rath, Xenos, and Bayliss 2008; Ryan and Glenn 2003; Upcraft, Gardner, and Barefoot 2005). In no subject is academic support more important than in reading. As demonstrated by Adelman (2004), students whose reading skills require remediation are less likely to graduate from college than are students with other "remedial" needs, such as mathematics.[1]

According to a study of students in the City University of New York, merely being placed in remedial courses did little to increase students' ultimate success, but completing those courses improved their chances, relative to comparably skilled nonremedial students (Lavin, Alba, and Silberstein 1981). In other words, what matters is seeing a course through to completion. Similar conclusions were reached in a study by Bettinger and Long (2004a, 2005) of approximately eight thousand first-time freshman enrolled in nonselective, public four-year colleges in the state of Ohio, and a study by Attewell, Lavin, Domina, and Levey (2006) of two-year college students, members of the National Educational Longitudinal Study who had graduated from high school in 1992.

Not just the underprepared require academic support. Attewell, Lavin, Domina, and Levey's (2006) analysis of high-school graduates in 1992, for example, revealed that a good number of students with relatively strong academic skills take remedial courses in colleges. For these students too, support in the form of freshman seminars or study-skills courses contributes to their success in the first year (Barefoot 1993; Davis 1992). A statewide study by the Florida Department of Education, for instance, followed 36,123 full-time community college students, who first enrolled in fall 1999, for more than five years (Windham 2006). Of those students, 10,716 (42%) took a Study Life Skills course designed to give them the skills needed to succeed in college. Students who completed that course achieved their associate's degree or certificate at a rate of 58%, as compared to 41% for those who did not take it. The course proved to be "beneficial to all students regardless of their preparation for college" (Windham 2006, p. 7).

Academic support is especially effective when aligned with the immediate task of learning within a classroom (Perin 2011). Such alignment allows support to be contextualized to learning in specific courses. This is but one reason why actions such as supplemental instruction, basic-skills learning communities, and the embedding of basic skills within academic courses have proved particularly helpful to students (Kenney and Kallison 1994; Engstrom and Tinto 2008). Though most institutions have learning centers, the kind of generic support typically offered in those learning centers too often leaves students ill equipped to apply that support to the specific demands of the classroom.

At no time is academic support more important than in the first year—indeed, in the first semester and first weeks of that semester. Early success—whether in the beginning classes of a course or in the first courses of a program of study—increases the likelihood of future success. Conversely, early failure substantially undermines future success. Consequently, academic support activities such as those noted above are most commonly applied to key first-semester courses and, where appropriate, as early as possible.

■ **Self-Efficacy and Student Success**

One way of understanding the impact of early classroom successes on subsequent success is through Bandura's (1986) social cognitive theory.

Social cognitive theory argues that individuals' interpretation of their performance alters their sense of self-efficacy and, in turn, their future performance. These self-evaluations are based in "beliefs in one's capabilities to organize and execute the courses of action required to manage prospective situations" (Bandura 1995, p. 2). These beliefs influence the choices people make and the courses of action they pursue in the future (Pajares 1996). Feelings of competence encourage individuals to engage in complex tasks and influence the amount of effort they will expend on those tasks and how long they will persevere when confronting obstacles. This is particularly true for those who have struggled in the past to succeed in school and college (Zajacova, Lynch, and Espenshade 2005; Vuong, Brown-Welty, and Tracz 2010).

To the degree that support programs focusing on the first semester help students succeed in that semester, they enhance students' sense of self-efficacy, reduce stress, and in turn increase the likelihood of subsequent success (Chemers, Hu, and Garcia 2001; Coffman 2002; Fencl and Scheel 2005; Grant-Vallone, Reid, Umali, and Pohler 2003; Lent, Brown, and Lark 1984; Multon, Brown, and Lent 1991; Ostrow, Dark, and Berhman 1986). For those students who enter college academically underprepared or who have struggled academically in the past, success depends as much on their coming to see themselves as being able to succeed as it does the acquisition of basic skills (Hall and Ponton 2005). This is also true for many minority and first-generation college students, especially those from low-income backgrounds (Hall and Ponton 2005; Solberg and Villarreal 1997; Torres 2004; Filkins and Doyle 2002). In part, it is what Rendon (1994) and Barnett (2011) means by the importance of validation for success of underserved students, and what Torres (2006) means when she speaks of the importance of affirmation for student success.

■ Social Support

Student retention is also shaped, directly and indirectly, by social forces internal and external to the campus, especially those that influence students' sense of belonging and membership in the social communities of the institution. This is especially important during the first year of college, when students have to make a series of adjustments to existing social relationships (including their family and friends), while forming new relationships with people on campus: faculty, staff, and students alike (Gloria, Kurpius, Hamilton, and Wilson 1999; Gloria and Kurpuis 2001; Somera and Ellis 1996; Skahill 2002). Social membership, or, in Schlossberg's language, mattering (Schlossberg 1989), yields a number of benefits that promote retention (e.g., Astin 1984; Lotkowski, Robbins, and Noeth 2004; Pascarella and Terenzini 1991, 2005; Thomas 2000; Tinto 1993). First, it leads to a range of social support that eases the transition to college and reduces academic stress levels (Rayle and Chung 2007; Sand, Kurpuis, and Rayle 2004; Torres and Solberg 2001). Second, it enables students to more easily access informal knowledge from their peers, helping them navigate the often foreign terrain of the institution (Attinasi 1989; Torres 2004). Third, it promotes a sense of self-worth, which in turn influences academic performance (Rendon 1994; Barnett 2011). Finally, it enhances students' attachment or commitment to the institution and their willingness to remain enrolled (Karp, Hughes, and O'Gara 2010), which is especially important for underrepresented students, who sometimes find themselves out of place in a largely majority-serving institution (Hausmann, Ye, Schofield, and Woods 2007, 2009; Torres and Solberg 2001). By contrast, the absence of social membership often leads to problems of adjustment and subsequent withdrawal (Cabrera, Nora, Terenzini, Pascarella, and Hagedorn 1999; Gohn, Swartz, and Donnelly 2000; Jackson, Soderlind, and Weiss 2000). Fleming's (1984) study documents how a sense of marginalization and the absence of social support for students of color on a predominantly white campus can drain the emotional energies they need to endure what they perceive as a hostile climate.

Not all social adjustments come easily. For many students, social support in the form of counseling, mentoring, and faculty and peer advising can spell the difference between staying and leaving (Bahr 2008; Lidy and Kahn 2006; Morales 2009; Salinitri 2005; Sorrentino 2007). Crisp's (2010) study of mentoring in community colleges, for example, found that students who were mentored became better integrated both socially and academically, and more committed to earning their degree.

Mentoring is especially important for low-income, first-generation college students (Crisp and Cruz 2009; Torres 2004) as well as for academically underprepared entrants (Salinitri 2005). It also helps many students of color on predominantly white campuses, who sometimes find the environment unsupportive and inhospitable (Fleming 1984; Hurtado and Carter 1997; Johnson et al. 2007). For these students, mentoring programs and ethnic study centers and organizations can contribute to success by providing social and emotional support for individual students, as well as a safe haven for groups of students who might otherwise find themselves out of place in a setting where they are a distinct minority (e.g., Attinasi 1989; Fleming 1984; Guiffrida 2003; Torres 2004). For new students, these centers can also serve as secure, knowable ports of entry, enabling them to develop cognitive maps of the academic and social geography of the campus (Attinasi 1989; London 1989; Terenzini et al. 1994; Torres 2004). They also provide a place where students can "let their hair down" and restore their emotional energy (Fleming 1984).

Social support can also come from interaction with faculty and staff and from student peers both inside and outside the classroom (Diel-Amen 2011; Giddan 1988; Johnson et al. 2007; Swenson, Nordstrom, and Hiester 2008; Thomas 2000). Student groups or communities that provide social support, especially during the critical first year of college, may take the form of residential settings, extracurricular activities, and in some cases in shared learning programs like learning communities.

■ Financial Support

Though the research evidence is somewhat mixed, greater amounts of financial aid appear to be associated with higher rates of student retention (Gansermer-Topf and Schuh 2005, 2008), especially for those from low-income backgrounds (Heller 2003; Pascarella and Terenzini 2005; Paulsen and St. John 2002; St. John 1991, 2000). This seems particularly true of grants as opposed to loans (Bettinger 2004; Dowd and Coury 2006; Dynarski 2002, 2003; Gross, Hossler and Ziskin 2007; Hossler et al. 2009).[2]

Differing amounts of aid, loans, and grants influence a student's choice of public versus private college; a four-year versus a two-year college; whether a student attends full-time or part-time; and whether he or she maintains a job while in college (St. John 1990; Heller 1996, Advisory Committee on Student Financial Assistance 2010).[3] Especially for low-income students, a lower level of aid is associated with attendance at two-year institutions and, in turn, with lower levels of retention and eventual completion (Bettinger 2004). This remains the case even after controlling for differences in academic preparation (Bound, Lovenheim, and Turner 2009). Attending college only part-time and holding a job have the net consequence of lowering levels of academic engagement, increasing the amount of time it takes to complete a program of study and the likelihood of retention (St. John 2004). A study of completion among students who began two- or four-year colleges in 2003–4 indicates that nearly 70% of those who always attended part-time left without a degree within three years of enrolling. Among full-time students, by contrast, only 17% of those in a four-year college and 40% of those in a two-year college left within three years (Berkner et al. 2007).[4]

It is therefore regrettable not only that the purchasing power of Pell grants have, until recently, declined over the past thirty years (Fischer 2007; Farrell 2007), but also that institutional aid has shifted from need-based to merit-based aid and away from low-income students to students from more affluent backgrounds (St. John 2001). During the 2003–4 academic year, for example, it is estimated that of the roughly $10.2 billion in financial aid provided by institutions in the United States to full-time students, approximately 54% was distributed in the form of merit-based aid, of which nearly 60% went to students whose families earned $60,176 per year or more and only about 20% to students whose families earned $33,346 or less. But even in the distribution of need-based aid, only about 21% went to the latter families (Heller 2008).[5] Ironically, while there is a positive relationship between aid or net price and graduation for low- and moderate-income students, that relationship does not appear to exist for students from families in the top half of the income distribution (Bowen, Chingos, and McPherson 2009, p. 231).

Varying amounts of aid may also influence student retention by determining the amount of time students have to be socially and academically engaged in college (Herzog 2005; Lichtenstein 2005; St. John 2004). Cabrera, Nora and Castaneda's (1992) analysis of the combined effects of student engagement and student financial aid indicated that though engagement variables have stronger direct impacts on retention, financial aid has an indirect effect via its impact on levels of student engagement. This may help explain why many work-study programs appear to enhance student retention (Astin 1975, DesJardins, Ahlberg, and McCall 2002; Hossler et al. 2009; St. John, Hu, and Tuttle 2000; St. John, Hu, and Weber 2001). In such programs, students are able to gain financial support while being engaged with others on campus.

The direct effect of financial support on retention is most apparent when students, especially low-income students, experience financial difficulties while in college (McGrath and Braunstein 1997; Gross, Hossler, and Ziskin 2007). Though one typically thinks of such difficulties as involving family emergencies, some low-income students find themselves unable to purchase needed books and supplies until their grants are cleared by the institution's financial aid office. In this case, short-term institutional financial support is vital to students if they are to keep pace with the demands of classroom work.

A cautionary note about the impact of financial support is warranted. Like any other form of investment, a student's response to the cost of investing in higher education is necessarily conditioned by the perceived value of that investment. Though there are obvious limits to a person's ability to respond to cost, especially among low-income students, the perception of value may lead some students to persist even when costs dictate part-time attendance, holding down a job while attending college, or both. By contrast, others may choose to leave college, even with little financial pressure, when they perceive the value of college as marginal. While colleges may have limited ability to influence the net cost of college attendance, they can influence the value of attendance by enhancing the quality of the education they offer.

■ Academic Support Programs

Academic support programs abound. They take on a variety of forms, including summer bridge programs, freshman or first-year seminars, learning and tutoring centers, basic-skills or developmental-education courses, accelerated courses, study-skill courses, supplemental instruction, academic-assistance learning communities, and embedded academic assistance.

Summer Bridge Programs

Summer bridge programs are designed to facilitate the transition from high school to college and to place incoming students on an equal footing with other students (Fenske, Geranios, Keller, and Moore 1997; Kezar 2000; Pascarella and Terenzini 2005). They occur in community colleges, such as Highland Community College, Capital Community College, Lone Star College–North Harris, and Santa Fe Community College; in university colleges, such as the one at Indiana University–Purdue University at Indianapolis; and in public and private colleges and universities, such as Holy Cross College (Indiana), Morgan State University, Bowie State University, California Polytechnic University, Eastern Kentucky University, San Francisco State University, and Syracuse University. Although these programs have come to serve a wide variety of students—international and non-English-speaking, underrepresented, disabled, and those in specific fields such as the STEM disciplines (science, technology, engineering, and mathematics)—and provide a range of academic and social services, their primary focus has been and continues to be academic support for underprepared students (Kezar 2000; Walpole et al. 2008). Students are brought to campus before the start of the first semester for an intensive academic and social support program, including advising and counseling, that runs anywhere from one to four weeks. They are typically required to live on campus, where they participate in various enrichment activities and take a range of college courses to help bridge the gap between high school and college coursework. By gaining an academic as well as a social head start on their first year of college, these students typically need less support during that year. Summer bridge programs thus enhance rates of retention (Critical Issues Bibliography 2001; Buck 1985; Evans 1999; Gancarz, Lowry, McIntyre, and Moss 1998; Gold 1992; Garcia 1991; Walpole et al. 2008). The long-term impact of summer bridge programs is even greater when they are connected to support programs that follow immediately at the beginning of the fall semester. This requires that faculty and staff of the two programs collaborate, so that the activities of the summer program are coherently linked to those that follow.[6]

Summer Bridge at the University of California–San Diego

Between 120 and 150 freshmen participate annually in a four-week OASIS Summer Bridge program, which is designed to enhance students' academic, social, and leadership skills. Students enroll in two credit-bearing courses—Contemporary Issues I: The University in Society, and Education Studies 20: Introduction to Principles of Learning, whose credits can be applied to the total credits required for graduation. Throughout the program, students work with undergraduates who serve as academic transition counselors, and with tutors who help orient students to the university and provide both academic and social support. All Summer Bridge students, including those who will be commuters in the fall, live together in a residence hall during the program. Their common experience in both academic courses and residential life enables them to form important friendships, which ease their transition. The students also receive extensive, personalized information about campus resources.

An important feature of the program is its connection to other programs that follow in the fall quarter. Summer Bridge students transition into the

OASIS Learning Communities and Academic Transition Program, which provide each student with an individualized package of tutoring, mentoring, counseling, and networking. Students are assigned a peer mentor known as an academic transition counselor (ATC), who meets with them and follows their progress throughout the entire freshman year. In addition, students participate as a group in weekly learning-community seminars, focusing on college success throughout the first year. These provide students with a consistent small group of peers with whom they can collaborate for study groups and other activities throughout the year. Data indicate that Summer Bridge participants, whether educationally disadvantaged or not, persist and achieve at rates as high as or higher than nonparticipants. Freshman who participated in the program in 2001 had a freshman-to-sophomore-year retention rate of 96%, as against the 92% rate of nonparticipants, and fewer experienced academic difficulty—defined as having a GPA below 2.0. For freshmen who participated in the program in 1995, 81% graduated within five years, as compared to 78% of nonparticipating freshmen. It should be noted that unlike some other summer bridge programs, the one at the University of California–San Diego, views itself as providing opportunity to students who might not otherwise be able to attend a selective institution of higher education and therefore has prioritized service to the most at-risk students.

The First-Year Seminar

The popular first-year seminar, once a form of extended orientation, now occurs in a wide variety of forms (Upcraft, Gardner, and Barefoot 2005; Hunter and Linder 2005).[7] Some of these seminars serve, as they did when they began, to provide information about academic requirements and an introduction to the intellectual life of the institution. Others take the form of college success courses, focusing on study skills, time management, and other skills designed to improve academic performance. Some seminars may combine orientation and academic skills with a range of academic and social activities designed to build involvement in the life of the campus. Others are strictly academic courses. Some are offered to all students, while others are targeted to specific groups, such as academically underprepared students. Some are voluntary, while others are required of all students, such as those at Community College of Baltimore County. Though often taught as stand-alone courses, an increasing number of first-year seminars are linked to other courses in the form of a learning community—of which we will speak later—such as those at Appalachian State University and Baruch College (Friedman and Alexander 2007; Henscheid 2004, Swing 2004).

College Success Courses at Chaffey College

Chaffey College established a two-semester program for students on probation entitled Enhanced Opening Doors. Students are required to take two college-success courses taught by a counselor. These courses provide basic information on study skills and the requirements of the college. Students are also required to visit the college's success centers, where they receive individualized assistance in reading, writing, and mathematics. A recent study by the Manpower Demonstration Research Corporation (MDRC) found that the Enhanced Opening Door program increased the average number of credits each student earned, the number of students who earned a grade-point average of 2.0 or higher, and the proportion who moved off probationary status (Scrivener, Sommo, and Collado 2009).

College Success Courses at Community College of Baltimore County

All new students at Community College of Baltimore County are required to take a one-credit course for 1.5 contact hours entitled Transitioning to College. It is delivered in four college divisions (known there as academies): Liberal Arts, STEM, Health Professions, and Business / Social Sciences. Though its primary focus is developing an academic plan, it also helps student locate and utilize a range of support services on campus, such as advising, financial aid, disability services, and tutoring and writing centers. In addition, the course presents effective strategies for managing a variety of individual "time-money-life" issues. Full- and part-time faculty who teach the course receive a full week of training and are credited 1.5 hours toward their teaching load. The various course sections are similar in student composition, except for five sections for African American students and those sections that are part of learning communities. While fourteen sections of the course are offered entirely online, some of the classes in each section take place in a computer lab, thereby promoting students' technology skills.

Regardless of form and focus, evidence of the effectiveness of freshman seminars, when properly implemented, is widespread (Barefoot 1993; Davis 1992; Goodman and Pascarella 2006; Pascarella and Terenzini 2005; Scrivener, Sommo, and Collado 2009; Tobolowsky, Cox and Wagner 2005). Zeidenberg, Jenkins, and Calcagno (2007) followed for almost six years community college students, both remedial and nonremedial, in the state of Florida, of whom some took a college success course, and others did not. For both remedial and nonremedial students, taking the course was associated with higher rates of certificate or degree completion even after student attributes were controlled.

Effective implementation is no easy task. Much depends, among other things, on the nature and training of staff, the number of contact hours, and the alignment of the seminar's content and activities to the other courses in which students are enrolled (Hunter and Linder 2005; Hunter 2006). For example, it has been shown that the impact of the seminar on student retention increases if the contact hours are increased (from the typical one hour to two or three hours), if it is co-taught by an undergraduate student leader, and if it is paired or linked with another course or courses in a learning community (Swing 2003, 2004). But even with proper implementation, first-year seminars face a number of continuing challenges, not the least of which is that of academic credit. Many institutions are reluctant to grant more than one credit if that is for a course that they may see as non-academic even when evidence suggests otherwise. Perhaps for this reason, an increasing number of first-year seminar programs are being integrated into curricular learning communities, about which we will speak further (Friedman and Alexander 2007; Henscheid 2004; Swing 2004). In this case, the content and activities of the first-year seminar will vary according to the needs of the students enrolled in the learning community in which the seminar is part.

Like summer bridge programs, first-year freshman seminars employ a range of activities to build social connections among students and consequent social support (Smith, MacGregor, Matthews, and Gabelnick 2004; Tinto, Goodsell, and Russo 1993; Tinto and Goodsell 1994). This is particularly apparent in living-learning communities—such as those at the University of Arizona, the University of South Carolina, the University of Maryland, and Western Kentucky University—in which students live together while also taking two or more courses together (Kanoy and Bruhn 1996; Pike 1999).[8] In some cases, faculty are involved in residential settings (Golde and Pribbenow 2000). In other cases, peer mentors are attached to those programs—as they are at Appalachian State University,

Creighton University, Millersville University, and the University of Hawaii at Manoa—as a way of better aligning their work with those of the faculty and staff directing the seminars or learning communities (Wilkie and Jones 1994). In either case, living-learning communities and other forms of student support that are embedded within or connected to academic programs provide an effective way of bridging the gap between a student's social and academic engagements.

Supplemental Instruction

Supplemental instruction is primarily an academic support strategy that provides support in the form of study groups connected to a specific course (Blanc, DeBuhr, and Martin 1983; Blanc and Martin 1994; Commander, Stratton, Callahan, and Smith 1996; Congos, Langsam, and Schoeps 1997; Hodges, Dochen, and Joy 2001; Hurley, Jacobs, and Gilbert 2006; McGuire 2006; Muhr and Martin 2006; Peterfreund, Rath, Xenos, and Bayliss 2008; Stone and Jacobs 2006; Zaritsky and Toce 2006). The academic support they receive in a supplemental study group enables the students to immediately apply that support to the tasks required by the course to which the group is connected.

For many or most students, as already pointed out, success is constructed one course at a time. Since no courses are more important than those in the first semester, in particular those that are considered foundational or gateway to other courses, those are the ones to which supplemental instruction is most often applied, as they are at Texas A&M University and the University of South Carolina. Unless students are successful in those courses, they are unlikely to be successful in the courses that follow (Ogden, Thompson, Russell, and Simons 2003). Supplemental instruction is also employed for courses that have relatively high failure rates; El Camino College and Manchester Community College use this strategy. In both cases, supplemental instruction tends to improve the average performance of students by reducing the number of students who either fail or achieve barely passing grades (e.g., Congos 2003; Congos and Schoeps 2003; Hodges, Dochen, and Joy 2001; Wolfe 1998; Wright, Wright, and Lamb 2002). The strategy owes part of its success to the increased time students spend studying with other students in their groups (Maxwell 1998). Like the freshman seminar, supplemental instruction is being employed by a wide range of two- and four-year institutions in the United States as well as overseas.[9]

Nonetheless, not all students who need supplemental instruction take advantage of the study groups or do so consistently. Some attend only when an exam approaches. Beyond making attendance mandatory (Hodges, Dochen, and Joy 2001), colleges encourage attendance in a variety of ways: scheduling supplemental instruction immediately before or after the class to which it is attached, employing video or web-based alternatives (Martin and Blanc 2001; Wang 2005), and ensuring that there is a clear relationship between the activities of the supplemental instructional units and the materials covered in each class throughout the semester.

Supplemental Instruction at El Camino College

Supplemental Instruction (SI) at El Camino College, California, began in 2002 under the direction of Luis Barrueta, with funding from a Title V grant for the development of first-year programs. SI supports many disciplines but focuses on mathematics courses, specifically Pre-Algebra, Beginning Algebra, and Intermediate Algebra. Initially established with four sections as part of a small, controlled test of its feasibility, it has grown to serve as many as thirty-five sections in one semester. It was able to do so by starting small and using evidence from its assessments, not only to improve over time but also to gain support for its continuance, following the end of the Title V grant, both from the college and from the deans of the departments where SI is employed. The program works hard to recruit able leaders and to carefully align the SI sessions to the courses to which they are attached. Evidence of the program's effectiveness from summer 2002 to spring 2009 is clear: 77.4% of the students who attend the Pre-Algebra SI sessions are successful (that is, they earn grades of A, B, or C) versus 59.5% who do not attend the sessions; 73.4% of students attending the Beginning Algebra SI sessions are successful, versus 41.9% who do not attend; and 75.5% who attend the Intermediate Algebra SI sessions are successful, versus 42.8% who do not attend.[10]

Supplemental Instruction at Richard J. Daley College

Richard J. Daley College's supplemental instruction program, "Comprehensive Academic Support and Help to Return on Investment" (CASH-to-ROI), requires students in remedial math, English, and reading comprehension who choose to participate to meet eight times over the course of the semester in smaller groups of seven to ten, with each group assigned a part-time staff member as a "tutor-facilitator" to lead discussions. Using material that takes the form of a multichapter science-fiction adventure story, students respond to assignments and discussion questions that require them to integrate and apply all three subject areas to solve problems that are described in the story. Fifteen percent of a student's grade is determined by attendance in the CASH-to-ROI study groups. Between 80% and 90% of students participating in the program have received passing grades in remedial math, English, and reading comprehension courses, a rate that is twice as high as the pass rate of students who did not participate.[11]

Learning Communities

Although I will discuss learning communities at greater length in chapter 5, I should point out here that an increasing number of institutions have adapted learning communities to the task of providing academic support. They do so by including a course in study skills or, as noted above, a freshman seminar, as one of the linked courses (Friedman and Alexander 2007; Maxwell 1998; Tinto 1999). Such learning communities have proved most effective when the instructors of the courses that constitute a particular community coordinate the activities of their courses with those of other instructors (Engstrom and Tinto 2007, 2008). As with supplemental instruction, the coherent linking of support activities among courses in the learning community enables students to quickly apply what they learn in the support course to the academic demands of the other courses. The result is improved performance. Friedman and Alexander's (2007) study, for example, assessed the performance of 1,294 first-year students in three categories: those enrolled in thirty-seven different learning communities for which Freshman Seminar served as the anchor course, those enrolled in a nonlinked seminar; and those who did not enroll in a seminar at all. Students enrolled in a linked section of Freshman Seminar earned the highest grades in the learning community course, followed by the other two groups, in that order.

Because many students enter college academically underprepared, a number of institutions have adapted learning communities to the needs of basic-skills students. Such institutions include DeAnza College, Hillsborough Community College, Kingsborough Community College, LaGuardia Community College, Metropolitan Community College, Seattle Central Community College, California State University East Bay, Temple University, and the University of Texas–El Paso. These institutions have combined one or more basic-skills course with a content course. In this case, the structure of the learning community provides a vehicle for the alignment of basic-skills instruction with instruction in the relevant content course (Malnarich et al. 2003; Tinto 1999).

At Kingsborough Community College, for example, students in the developmental education learning communities took, as a group, a remedial English course, an academic course in health or psychology, and a one-credit orientation course. On a wide range of factors, students had more success than similar students in a control group not enrolled in the learning community. On average, they took more courses, passed more classes, earned more credits, and were more likely to be enrolled in the college in the following year. Furthermore, they had statistically higher rates of passing the English tests necessary to qualify for college-level work and degrees at the City University of New York (Scrivener et al. 2008; Bloom and Sommo 2005).

A national study of the basic-skills learning communities by Engstrom and Tinto (2007, 2008) reveals the way basic-skills students make sense of their experience in a learning community. With a grant from the Lumina Foundation for Education and additional support from the William and Flora Hewlett Foundation, the researchers studied basic-skills learning communities in thirteen two-year and six four-year colleges in California, Florida, Massachusetts, Maryland, New Jersey, New York, North Carolina, Pennsylvania, Tennessee, Texas, and Washington.[12] They used a variant of the Community College Survey of Student Engagement (CCSSE) to survey academically underprepared students in basic-skills learning communities, comparing them with similar students in classrooms not part of a learning community, to define patterns in their academic and social engagement, their perceptions, and their academic plans. To determine their subsequent persistence, students were followed over several years. Case studies were carried out for three two-year and two four-year institutions, and longitudinal interviews were conducted over three years with students in the basic-skills learning communities.[13] It was found that academically underprepared students in learning communities were significantly more engaged in a variety of activities, including classroom work and activities involving their faculty and classmates in and outside of class, than were similar students on their campuses. They also perceived themselves as having received a good deal more encouragement, support, and intellectual gain than did similar students not enrolled in those programs.

One student described how linking a basic-skills course to a content course improved performance in the latter: "The relationship in classes between accounting and ESL [English as a second language] is helping a lot because the accounting professor is teaching us to answer questions in complete sentences . . . to write better. And we are more motivated to learn vocabulary because it is accounting vocabulary, something we want to learn about. I am learning accounting better by learning the accounting language."

Another student spoke about the impact of her experience on her self-respect as learner: "So you are constantly having to think, re-think, and even re-re-think what's going on in light of all the feedback you're getting from all these different points of view . . . ; you realize you know something, like you're not dumb."

A third said that his experience shaped his confidence and in turn his academic performance: "Being the same classes, it's comforting. You are scared and maybe somebody speaks much better than you and writes better, so you feel more comfortable seeing the same faces every day, and you communicate more and more often, little by little. . . . I got the confidence from seeing the same faces. . . . I'm not afraid of saying anything now, but I was. . . . The more confident I feel, the better I do . . . . I think I have gotten smarter since I have been here. I can feel it."

Not surprisingly, students in the learning-community programs were more apt to persist to the following academic year. The average difference in persistence between learning-community and comparison-group students in the four-year colleges was nearly 10%; in the two-year colleges it was slightly more than 5% (though on some campuses it was as high as 15%).

A number of factors contributed to that persistence. First, the learning communities were intentionally designed to promote interconnections among the courses they comprised. The same principle of alignment applies, as noted earlier, to supplemental instruction. But in this case, support is connected to one course. In basic-skills learning communities, support can be connected to several courses. Second, the learning communities were designed to provide students with additional student support services, enabling them to access support in ways unavailable to those not in learning communities. Third, faculty and staff set high expectations for their students and emphasized the building of a supportive climate within the community for students seeking to acquire skills they had not possessed prior to beginning college.

A number of programs for basic-skills students include counseling and other support services, such as those at Cerritos College and Skagit Valley

College. They do so because there is ample evidence that academically un- derprepared students, in particular those of low-income and underserved backgrounds, often require social as well as academic support to succeed in college. The Hulu'ena program at Hawai'i Community College, for exam- ple, places academically underprepared Native Hawaiian students in three courses during the first semester: a developmental education course appro- priate to their particular needs, a college success course in which a range of support activities are embedded, and a course in Hawaiian culture. Advis- ing, counseling, and case management are mandatory, and expectations for student success are high.

ESL Learning Communities at Kingsborough Community College
Learning communities at Kingsborough began in 1995 with the Inten- sive ESL Program. It served about ten cohorts of up to twenty-five first- semester ESL students, who took five linked courses: ESL, Speech, two Student Development courses, and a General Education course such as Psychology, History, or Sociology. Now, via the Opening Doors Program, over thirty learning communities are offered each semester, serving more than twelve hundred incoming freshmen annually. In this program, three courses—English, Student Development, and General Education—are linked. Students in all learning communities, ESL or otherwise, are of- fered extensive support to help them become part of the Kingsborough community, make a smooth transition into college life, and succeed aca- demically. Students in the Intensive ESL Program and those in Opening Doors who are in the lowest developmental English courses have sched- uled time in the Reading and Writing Center, working with tutors who also sit in on classes once a week. Students in the Second Semester Pro- gram are offered supplemental instruction via small group or one-on-one support by Kingsborough faculty.

A longitudinal study of 385 ESL students who began their studies in the Intensive ESL program indicated that students in the program not only achieved higher pass rates and better grades in the regular ESL course than a similar number who had not taken the intensive one, but also per- formed better in subsequent ESL and developmental English courses. In addition, the content-linked ESL students had better long-term academic success rates than non-content-linked ESL students in measures such as English proficiency-test pass rates, graduation and retention rates, and overall GPA (Song 2006).

**Developmental Education Learning Communities
at Metropolitan Community College**
The Academic Improvement for Success Program (known as AIM) at
Metropolitan, begun in 1998–99, enrolls students as a cohort in learning
communities comprising two or more courses in reading, writing, math,
and personal or career development during a quarter. Like Cerritos College and Skagit Valley College, Metropolitan integrates student services
personnel into the program. Career counselors meet with students and
make class presentations. Many of the faculty, specifically those in math
and English, are members of their respective departments, yet all are required to participate in annual training sessions and meet together over
the course of the year to share their experiences and consider possible
changes. Though they are not paid extra to teach in the program, they are
given a stipend at the outset of their participation for the additional time
required to plan their activities. Central to the success of the program is
not only its recruitment of full- and part-time faculty who are willing to
be flexible and work collaboratively with others and its staff development
programs, but also the support provided by dean-level administrators in
both educational and student services. Indeed, the college has provided
a separate budget line to support the initiative. Modified over the years,
by incorporating strategies such as problem-based learning, for instance,
the program has significantly improved student performance and retention. Of students in AIM, 81% continue to the next quarter, and 61% remain throughout the academic year, versus 68% and 52% respectively for
students in the regular developmental courses. AIM students graduate at
approximately the same rate as do students generally (Raftery 2005).

Embedded Academic Support
Another strategy, now being widely used in the technical and community
colleges in the state of Washington, such as Highline Community College,
Lower Columbia Community College, and Tacoma Community College, is
to embed basic skills in technical and vocational courses serving basic-skills
adult students. Students in the Integrated Basic Education and Skills Training program (I-BEST), receive support from basic-skills instructors, while
earning credit toward a certificate or degree. The program requires collaboration between basic-skills and course instructors such that both must be
present in the classroom for at least 50% of the total instructional time. The
resulting alignment of support to content enables students to acquire basic

skills within the context of a course and to apply those skills as they seek to learn the course's content. It is the same sort of alignment that occurs in supplemental instruction and in basic-skills learning communities.

A study by Jenkins, Zeidenberg, and Kienzl (2009) of thirty-one thousand students included nearly all of the approximately nine hundred who enrolled in I-BEST courses. Even after controlling for differences in background characters, these researchers found that students participating in I-BEST, including those who enrolled in at least one non-I-BEST workforce course, achieved better educational outcomes than did other basic-skills students. I-BEST students were more likely than others to continue into credit-bearing coursework, earn credits that count toward a college credential, earn occupational certificates, and make point gains on basic-skills tests.

I-BEST at Highline Community College

The I-BEST program at Highline involves the collaboration between the technical/vocational and ESL instructors, who work together on curricula that integrates basic-skills competencies with those of the technical/vocational program. In order for the program to qualify for 1.75 FTE toward an AAS (associate of arts and sciences), the state requires a 50% overlap in instructional time—that is, content and basic-skills instructors must both be present in the classroom for at least half of the total time of instruction but teach solo the rest of the time. I-BEST classes include five hours a week of noncredit adult basic education and ESL instruction.

Central to the program is the way in which basic-skills are contextualized to the learning needs of students and the skills and knowledge they need to acquire in a particular field of work. The paired instructors spend a considerable time co-planning the course and assessing student competency-based learning outcomes. Impetus and continued support for the program comes largely from teachers whose experience in I-BEST reinforces their belief that it is more effective than traditional basic-skills instruction.[14]

Basic-Skills Courses

The most common form of academic support for those judged to be academically underprepared is the ubiquitous basic-skills course. Though a long-standing feature of higher education, the effectiveness of basic-skills courses has come into question. As documented by Bailey, Jeong, and Cho (2009a, 2009b), not many students who begin at the lowest level of developmental education complete the full sequence of courses. These authors' study of progression rates through developmental courses among the Achieving the Dream colleges, typically involving three levels of coursework below a degree-credit bearing course to which that coursework provides entry, indicates that only 31% of students referred to math remediation and 44% referred to reading remediation completed the full sequence to which they were referred within three years. Furthermore, only a little more than 50% of each of those groups went on to pass a credit-bearing course. Such research underscores efforts such as those by the Carnegie Foundation for the Advancement of Teaching (Strengthening Pre-College Education in Community College) and the Lumina Foundation for Education to improve existing practice (see Zachry 2008).

To this end, an increasing number of colleges are taking several actions. First, they are better aligning the courses within their developmental course sequence so that requirements for success in one course are more clearly related to success in the subsequent courses of the sequence (Bailey, Jeong, and Cho 2009a, 2009b; Roksa, Jenkins, Jaggars, Zeidenberg, and Cho 2009) and the degree-credit bearing courses to which they provide entry (Grubb and Cox 2005).[15] Second, colleges have begun to address the pedagogical skills of faculty who teach basic-skills courses and have adopted a range of pedagogies beyond those typically employed in those courses. The Strengthening Pre-Collegiate Education in Community Colleges (SPECC) project, a partnership of the Carnegie Foundation for the Advancement of Teaching and the William and Flora Hewlett Foundation, brought together faculty from eleven California community colleges who teach pre-collegiate mathematics and English language courses.[16] These teachers, both together and separately on each of their campuses, explored different approaches to classroom practice, academic support, and faculty development. Their work was guided by the principle that teaching, and hence student success, is enhanced by on-going collaborative inquiry and evidence about teaching and learning. One of the outcomes of the project was the adoption by several participating colleges of cooperative learning in the instruction of basic skills. Other colleges, such as Richland College in Texas and Patrick Henry Community College in Virginia, acting on their own, did likewise.[17]

Several states, including California, Connecticut, Indiana, Kentucky, Massachusetts, and Washington, have already initiated or are planning statewide efforts to improve the teaching of basic-skills courses, especially in the colleges where the need is most pressing. In California, for instance, where it is estimated that nearly 75% of community college students require some form of basic-skills instruction, the state has allotted funds to what is known as the Basic Skills Initiative.[18] Currently those funds are distributed to community colleges with the requirement that they be invested in programs to promote improved basis skills instruction. A series of other initiatives to further basic-skills instruction are under way, such as the Basic Skills Resource Network and the Strategic Literacy Initiative, pointing up the growing recognition of the importance of faculty development to the success of academically underprepared students in the courses they teach.[19]

Some colleges have looked into course redesign and have questioned the skills that are currently being taught in most basic-skills courses (Conley 2005). Too often, judgments about needed skills are based solely on high-school standards, with little regard to what we may already know about the skills that differentiate successful from unsuccessful performance in the programs of study to which developmental courses provide entry. It is one thing to see developmental courses as helping students gain entry to the transfer course sequence in a community college; it is another to view them as providing entry to technical/vocational courses whose purpose is to prepare students for specific fields of work. Instructors should know not only the skills students need to acquire in the developmental and certificate or degree credit courses but also the best way of teaching those skills. Here is where the I-BEST initiative in the state of Washington is so promising, because it embeds basic skills in technical/vocational courses and asks students to apply those skills in the context in which they will be used.

Other colleges have sought to address students' slow progress through developmental education by accelerating instruction for students whose skills are stronger than other academically underprepared students. Mountain Empire Community College, for example, in revising its mathematics sequence, has utilized what it calls Peer-Led Team Learning to provide additional support for students in developmental mathematics courses. Mountain Empire, like Montgomery College in Maryland, has implemented a program that provides a quick review of math concepts for students who already have a solid background in the course material: these Fast Track Math courses condense a full semester of developmental Arithmetic and Algebra I into one- and two-credit review classes, respectively (see Zachry 2008).

Other institutions—Austin Community College, Chaffey College, Community College of Denver, Dean College, Howard Community College, Ivy

Tech Community College of Indiana, Middle Tennessee State University, Montgomery County Community College, Pasadena Community College (Math Jam), Prince George's Community College, and the University of Southern Maine, among others—have also employed accelerated learning programs. They vary in their approaches. Some use a form of supplemental instruction, like Mountain Empire; others, summer bridge programs, like Pasadena Community College Math Jam; others, modified forms of a supplemental instruction/learning community, like Community College of Baltimore County; and still others, like Austin Community College (Capital IDEA), an embedded basic-skills instruction much like the I-BEST program in the State of Washington. What they share is their desire to eliminate the need for a stand-alone developmental course when students are only one level below college-level work.

Peer-Led Team Learning at Mountain Empire Community College

The Peer-Led Team Learning (PLTL) program at Mountain Empire, a form of supplemental instruction, focuses on developmental mathematics, specifically Algebra I. It is based on small, highly interactive groups that are facilitated by students who in the past were successful in that course and are trained as peer tutors. The PLTL sessions, named the Power Hour, are built into the class schedule one day a week, just before the regular Friday class. That hour is always open to students. Though attendance at the Power Hour is voluntary, students are given incentives to attend, such as extra credit points. The PLTL Power Hours sessions were begun in the spring semester 2007 and have continued in both spring and fall. For each semester, two Algebra I classes have been chosen to have PLTL Power Hour sessions. Three peer leaders are assigned to each class, and the class is divided into small groups, which meet at different locations throughout the campus. The peer leaders attend one hour of class on Monday and Wednesday, and meet once a week with the faculty instructor. Because the college already has a successful TRIO tutoring program, the PLTL leaders work under the direction of the tutor coordinator of the TRIO program.[20]

Attendance at PLTL sessions is correlated with improved success in developmental math (Algebra I). Students who participate in the PLTL sessions perform better on quizzes, tests, and the exit exam. The students have very positive comments about the time spent. They report that they learn from working with the other students and that the sessions help them understand the material better. Some have requested that the PLTL sessions be extended into Algebra II.

Accelerated Learning at Community College of Baltimore County
The accelerated learning program at Community College of Baltimore County, begun in 2007, is intended for students who test one level below college-level English. Rather than being placed in a stand-alone developmental writing course, eight basic-skills students are registered in the college-level English course with twelve other non-basic-skills students. At the same time, they are registered in a developmental English course or seminar linked to the college-level course, which is taught by the same instructor. By participating in what amounts to a learning community composed of two courses, students are able to earn college credit while attending to their basic-skills needs. As compared to the 27% pass rate in college-level English that characterized the prior use of a stand-alone developmental writing course, students in the accelerated program passed the college-level English course at a rate of 63%.[21]

Guilford Technical Community College takes a different approach by focusing on students with the lowest levels of academic skills and those who frequently fail one or more basic-skills courses. Their Transitions program combines components of adult basic education with developmental education in ways that allow students to make quicker progress through the developmental course sequence. It does so, in part, by providing more intensive instruction and employing student COMPASS scores, rather than grades, to determine progress. It also facilitates the acquisition of skills through the use of learning communities, as do many other colleges (e.g., Cerritos College, DeAnza College, LaGuardia Community College, and Seattle Central Community College).

Another recent and quite different approach to basic-skills courses, specifically those in mathematics, is to replace those courses with a yearlong sequence of statistics. The Statistics Pathway (Statway), directed by the Carnegie Foundation for the Advancement of Teaching and Learning in collaboration with the Charles A. Dana Center at The University of Texas at Austin, is designed as a one-year pathway that culminates in college-level statistics.[22] It concentrates on statistical content with requisite arithmetic and algebraic concepts taught and applied in the context of statistics. Statway is structured to serve students planning to continue their studies in the humanities or the social sciences, for whom statistics is likely to be more useful in their careers than the mathematics taught in the basic-skills sequence. The concept is now being tested in nineteen community colleges in five states (California, Washington, Florida, Texas, and Connecticut).

Social Support Programs

Social support programs range from advising, mentoring, residential life, and campus recreation programs to counseling, health services, career services, religious services, and services for particular groups of students including underrepresented students, adults, those from abroad, and those with disabilities. Like academic support, social support is often most needed during the first year of college when students are making a variety of social transitions and adjustments. Freshman seminars, advising, and residential programs abound. So do a range of counseling and health services, such as those at Collin County Community College, Cornell University, George Mason University, St. Mary's University, and Western Kentucky University, which are designed to help new students deal with the stress that sometimes accompanies the transition to college, especially when it involves living away from home (e.g., Sharkin 2004; Lee et al. 2009). Wilson, Mason, and Ewing (1997) examined the relationship between counseling and retention as a function of the amount of counseling received. Those who received counseling were more likely to be retained than those who requested but did not receive it. Turner and Berry (2000), having tracked a cohort of students over six years, found similar differences in retention.

But while need for student counseling on health-related or psychological issues has increased, students, especially those in their first year, are often reluctant to seek out those services because they are embarrassed or do not acknowledge their need for help. For this reason, effective programs, such as that at Kentucky Western University, tend to be carefully interwoven with academic advising, career guidance, and other services and activities that are part of the student experience (Kadar 2001; Sharkin 2004). As with the academic support programs discussed above, embedding a service with others increases its use and effectiveness.

Social support can also be provided through mentoring programs that attach student peers, faculty, or administrators to specific groups of new students (Campbell and Campbell 1997; Jacobi 1991; Shotton, Oosahwe, and Cintron 2007; Institute of Higher Education Policy 2011). Peer mentors, such as those at Appalachian State University, Creighton University,

Estrella Mountain Community College, the University of Georgia, and the University of Vermont, can help familiarize new students with the strange new world of campus life in ways that faculty and staff cannot. Peer mentoring programs are also found in residential settings, as in Bowling Green State University, Frostburg State University, and the University of West Georgia, where upperclassmen act as "buddies" to new students. Where students work as residential hall staff, they typically receive training and have access to professional staff who can be called upon for assistance. Student peer advisers/mentors will often learn of student difficulties before anyone else and can alert appropriate professional staff so that action can be taken before those difficulties cause students to leave.

Peer Mentoring at Buffalo State College
The purpose of the Peer Mentor Program at Buffalo State's University College is to provide a student-to-student connection for first-year students in the classroom. A peer mentors wear many hats: he or she may serve as a role model of a successful student, a coach for academic skills, a tutor for course content, and a resource for campus information. The duties of the peer mentor include holding three mandatory sessions with students throughout the semester; hosting a "Getting to Know You" session, whose goal is to understand new students' academic and social situation; organizing a "Pre-Advisement" session to help students understand first-year requirements; and providing information on campus social and academic resources. In addition, a peer mentor holds tutoring sessions to help students who have demonstrated problems in class, have received mid-semester grades below a "C," or have requested additional help. Where appropriate, a peer mentor will meet with course faculty to better understand schedule, material, and goals.[23]

Social support is particularly important to low-income students, first-generation college students, and minority students on predominantly white campuses (Levin and Levin 1991; Gloria, Kurpius, Hamilton, and M. Wilson 1999; Merriam, Thomas, and Zeph 1987; Pagan and Edwards-Wilson 2002; Thayer 2000; Santos and Riegadas 2004; Shotton, Oosahwe, and Cintron 2007; Morales 2009). Mentoring programs, ethnic studies programs, student clubs and centers, and state and federally funded programs like Student Support Services (SSS) all provide students with a supportive community of peers. Mentoring programs for minority students, such as those at North Carolina State University and Pomona College, serve as important ports of entry to an unfamiliar institution (Attinasi 1989; Shotton, Oosahwe, and Cintron 2007). The same can be said of programs, such as those at Santa Barbara City College and the University of Miami, that serve the needs of international students for whom the transition to college involves both a new institution and a new country. The SSS program, part of TRIO, also provides academic and social support to its students. Limited to those institutions that are able to obtain funding, SSS serves students who are from low-income backgrounds, are first-generation college students, or have disabilities evidencing academic need. Two-thirds of the participants in any SSS project must be either disabled or first-generation college students from low-income families. One-third of the disabled participants must also be low-income.[24] SSS is largely a funding mechanism that enables colleges to package a variety of services for their students. As a result, though the overall results of the programs are positive, their impact varies from institution to institution (Chaney, Muraskin, Cahalan, and Rak 1997). In many institutions, such as Indiana University–Purdue University Indianapolis, the SSS program adds an extra layer of support and guidance as well as membership in a community of students who are on a similar journey. Many states, such as California, New Jersey, and New York, fund similar programs. For instance, New York State's Higher Education Opportunity Program (HEOP) is a partnership between the state of New York and its independent institutions, which provides economically and educationally disadvantaged residents the possibility of a college education. The State University of New York's Educational Opportunity Program (EOP) provides similar assistance to low-income, full-time students enrolled in the state university system.

Regardless of its form, student support programming is increasingly being seen as part and parcel of college education, involving intellectual, social, and emotional development. For such programming to work well, however, academic and student affairs professionals must collaborate in ways that allow students to integrate their academic and social experiences in a coherent manner (see American Association for Higher Education 1998).

A final note: the challenge of academic and social support programs is less in their creation than in their utilization, especially among first-year students. Experience tells us that intervention matters.[25] Rather than wait for students to avail themselves of services, effective institutions generally monitor student performance and quickly reach out to them when indicators warrant action. This is the same principle of effective early warning systems that will be discussed in chapter 4.

Financial Support Programs

Both two- and four-year institutions have established financial support programs to help students pay for college. Many, such as the College of the Ozarks, the College of Western Idaho, Columbia College, Mercy College, and Merced College, employ work-study programs as part of their aid packages, often with funds from the Federal Work-Study Program and state work-study programs.[26] Such programs, when properly constructed, promote student retention by involving students with faculty, staff, and fellow students in ways that further their success (Astin 1975; Adelman 1999; Beeson and Wessel 2002; Heller 2003). This seems to be particularly true when work-study placements are directly related to a student's field of study or interest (Broughton and Otto 1999).

An increasing number of institutions are combining financial aid for low-income students, typically involving work-study, with other institutional services. The University of North Carolina's Covenant program, for example, not only provides financial aid and work-study but also academic and personal support services to help Covenant Scholars complete their undergraduate degree programs. Since its establishment, the four-year retention rate of Covenant Scholars has increased to 66.3%, a rate 9.5% higher than similar students entering at the same time.[27] Syracuse University runs a comparable program for Native American students.

Overreliance on work-study, however, may hinder retention when time spent in work takes away from the time required to meet the academic demands of college. For this reason, a number of well-resourced institutions, typically the elite private colleges and universities, have moved to provide grants, in some cases with work-study, to cover the full cost of attendance for those admitted students whose family incomes would not cover the cost of their attendance. Stanford University, for instance, no longer requires families earning less than $60,000 a year to contribute to the cost of education.[28] Unfortunately, most institutions do not have the financial resources to follow suit. Some, such as Hamilton College, have opted instead to end merit-based aid in favor of putting more resources into need-based aid.

In a different approach, low-income students at two colleges in the New Orleans area, Delgado Community College and the Louisiana Technical College–West Jefferson, were offered a $1,000 scholarship for each of two semesters ($2,000 total) if they met two conditions: to remain enrolled at least half-time and to maintain at least a 2.0 (or C) average. Program counselors monitored students' performance, and paid students who met these conditions in three increments: $250 upon enrollment, $250 at midterm, and $500 at the completion of the semester. The scholarships were paid on top of Pell grants and other financial aid for which students qualified. Scholarship recipients were not only 5.3% more likely to register; they were 6.4% more likely to register full-time, although only half-time enrollment was required to maintain the scholarship. Enrollees in the program were more likely than nonenrollees to register for college, to persist once they entered, and to earn more credits and higher grade-point averages through four semesters (Richburg-Hayes et al. 2009). The program proved so successful that more than four thousand students will receive scholarships at two- and four-year institutions in four states: Borough of Manhattan and Hostos Community Colleges in New York City; Lorain County, Owens, and Sinclair Community Colleges in Ohio; the University of New Mexico; and all state colleges in California.[29] The University of New Mexico's program that provides low-income freshmen with financial support if they enrolled full time, maintained a "C" average, and receive enhanced academic advising yields similar benefits (Miller, Binder, Harris, and Krause 2011).

A number of institutions and several states have financial aid programs that require students to meet certain requirements before they begin college. In Indiana's Twenty-First Century Scholars Program, income-eligible sixth-, seventh-, and eighth-graders who enroll in the program and meet a number of requirements while in high school (e.g., maintain a cumulative grade-point average of 2.0 on a 4.0 scale) are guaranteed the cost of four years of undergraduate tuition at any participating college or university in the state.[30] Oklahoma, Washington and Wisconsin have similar programs, as do a number of institutions elsewhere (see Blanco 2005). Syracuse University, for example, has established the Haudenosaunee Promise Program, which provides similar financial guarantees and support to members of the eligible Haudenosaunee territories.[31]

Haudenosaunee Promise Program at Syracuse University

The Haudenosaunee Promise Program provides a range of financial as well as academic and social support for qualified members of Haudenosaunee nations (Mohawk, Oneida, Onondaga, Cayuga, Seneca, and Tuscarora). Eligible students have to be admitted to the university as a first-year or transfer student, maintain satisfactory full-time academic status, and have resided in one the nations a minimum of four years prior to admission. All program students are provided with financial assistance equal to the cost of tuition, housing, and meals (on-campus) and mandatory fees for each year of full-time undergraduate study. Recently the program joined the university's Project Advance, which offers qualified Haudenosaunee high-school students financial assistance to enroll in Syracuse University courses while still completing high school.[32]

All these actions presume that students are at least somewhat aware of their financial aid options. Unfortunately this is not the case. In the 1999–2000 academic year, for instance, it is estimated that approximately 850,000 students who were likely to be eligible for a Pell grant did not file a Free Application for Federal Student Aid (FAFSA) (King 2004). Though some may not have applied because of the complexity of the application, others were unaware of the availability of aid or failed to apply by the established deadline. For this reason, an increasing number of institutions, such as the State University of New York Cortland, the University of California–Los Angeles, and the University of Houston, are investing in financial aid advising programs, which, together with existing web-based services (e.g., FinAid, NASFA-Student Aid), seek to provide students with the information they need concerning alternative financial aid strategies. A number of organizations, such as the Advisory Committee on Student Financial Assistance, the College Board, and the Lumina Foundation for Education, have issued reports calling for simplification of the process of applying for financial aid, and College Goal Sunday has drawn more than a hundred thousand college-bound students since its inception.[33]

However constructed, financial support aims not just to make access to college possible, but to allow students "to participate fully in the educational experiences and benefits" that access is intended to provide (Pascarella et al. 2004, p. 281), and thus to promote their success.

■ Support and Student Success: A Comment

Support matters, especially that which addresses the academic needs of students. To make it matter, however, requires that institutions go beyond making it available to those who wish or have time to access it. Institutions must to carefully align support to the learning needs of students in the classroom and must adopt policies that facilitate student success in the classroom.

ASSESSMENT AND FEEDBACK

4

An environment rich in assessment of students' performance and in feedback of information about student performance to students, faculty, and staff is another important condition for student success. Students are more likely to succeed in settings that enable all parties—students, faculty, and staff—to adjust their behaviors to better promote student success. In such settings, students become more involved in learning activities, and more effective in self-assessment to improve their learning strategies and study habits.[1] Feedback is particularly helpful when it creates a slight cognitive dissonance between what a person thinks of his or her performance and what a person discovers from feedback, because such dissonance can cause profound changes in behavior (Carroll 1988). This is especially true in the classrooms and during the first year, when students are seeking to adjust their behaviors to the academic and social demands of college life (Angelo and Cross 1993; Huba and Freed 2000).

To be effective, assessments must be frequent, early, and formative as well as summative in character. Frequent assignment-based mini-exams and periodic pauses for assessment and feedback within the class improve motivation (Becker and Devine 2007) as well as attention and comprehension (Bligh 2000). This is particularly true of classroom assessment techniques, such as the one-minute paper, described by Angelo and Cross (1993) and Cross and Steadman (1996), because they allow students to adjust their study behaviors, and faculty their teaching, as the course progresses (Kwan 2010). As documented by Stetson (1993), faculty who employed those techniques during a four-year trial reported that students improved their grades, final examination scores, and class projects. The impact of such assessments on student outcomes appears to vary little, with respect both to instructors and to students' ability level (Chizmar and Ostrosky 1998). This is also true of those forms of classroom assessment that employ classroom response systems (Bruff 2009, 2010; Hodges 2010; Kaleta and Joosten 2007; Patry 2009; Roschelle, Penuel and Abrahamson 2004) and those that involve the use of learning portfolios (Barton and Collins 1997; White 2005; Zubizarreta 2009).

The most common forms of student assessment employed by colleges are those that assess student learning skills at entry, monitor student progress during college, gauge student performance within the classroom, and provide early warning system of student difficulties.

■ Assessment at Entry

Entry-assessment materials come in many forms. Some are produced by firms such as the College Board (Accuplacer) and the American College Testing Program (ASSET and COMPASS), others are designed by individual institutions to suit their particular needs. Certain institutions, such as Coastline Community College, use multiple assessments to assess different skills, such as reading and mathematics. Almost all are designed to assess readiness for college-level work and are used to determine appropriate course placement and identify students who may require remediation or additional academic support. Some institutions, such as those in the California State University system's Early Assessment Program (EAP), the Florida community college system, and, in Texas, the El Paso Area College Readiness Initiative, have employed readiness-for-college assessments as early as the junior year of high school in order to alert students that unless they improve their skills they may be required to enroll in basic-skills courses at the outset of their college careers.[2] Such assessments provide an opportunity for additional preparation in the twelfth grade, and professional development activities for high school English and mathematics teachers. Long Beach City College, the Long Beach Unified School District, and California State University–Long Beach, have joined together to provide such services.[3] By doing so, colleges and universities hope to reduce the burden they face in addressing the academic needs of entering students.[4] A recent study of the impact of the program found that students at one California State University campus who had taken the EAP—regardless of their scores—were 4%–6% less likely to require remediation than those who had not (Howell, Kurlaender, and Grodsky 2010). In Florida, Senate Bill 1908 offers eleventh-grade high-school students who express an interest in post-secondary education an opportunity to take courses such as mathematics in their senior year, thereby avoiding the possible need to do so in college.

Regardless of its form, the effectiveness of an entry assessment depends not only on accuracy but also on how it is used to place a student in courses suited to his or her abilities.[5] Typically such placements are based on cutoff scores, so that students who score below a certain level are placed in, or advised to enroll in, courses such as basic skills.[6] Experience tells us, however, that the use of cutoff scores can result in incorrect placements, especially for those who test just above or just below the cutoff score. Some who score above the cutoff may still need additional academic preparation in the form of a basic-skills course, while some who score just below would do better to attend a learning center rather than follow a full course. Incorrect placement not only results in students finding themselves out of place in a class, but also in classrooms in which students manifest such a wide range of knowledge and skills that instructors cannot effectively teach all members of the class. Such situations can influence the success not only of those who are incorrectly placed, but also the other students in the class. For this reason, faculty sometimes carry out their own assessments at the start of a course or very soon after, and recommend, if appropriate, new placements for some of their students.[7]

Some entry assessments (e.g., CIRP Freshman Survey), typically those for four-year residential institutions, also assess a range of social issues such as residential placement that may impact student experience. Still others, such the College Student Inventory (CSI), seek to assess dropout proneness and to predict the likelihood that students will struggle during their first year of college.[8] Typically, these assessments are based on a range of student data, including attitudinal measures, that together have been shown to be associated with the likelihood of attrition. The aim of such assessments is to encourage faculty and staff to reach out to the students so identified and to provide counseling, support, and other services to head off potential difficulties.

Though such assessments can be valuable, they must be used with care. Predictions of the likelihood of attrition are based on a series of aggregate relationships between attributes and attrition that may or may not be reflective of any particular institution or individual. Further, they unavoidably ignore the well-documented fact that retention depends more heavily on what students experience after entering college than on what happened before.

Of course, a student's personality and the environment interact. Student responses to an environment are part and parcel of the process of retention. But by focusing on the attributes of students alone, a college risks neglecting the way changes in the college environment can increase retention for all students, not just those whose assessment scores suggests the need for additional services.

New forms of assessment are being designed that focus less on the kind of knowledge and skills defined by high school curriculum. Instead, they draw on what we know about the character of student success in college, and those skills and behaviors associated with college success, such as contextual skills, cognitive strategies, and academic behaviors (e.g., Conley 2005, 2007). Assessing a student's readiness for college by no means predicts the likelihood of graduation from college. One possible form of assessment, based on five key cognitive skills, appears promising (Conley, Lombardi, Seburn and McCaughy 2009). Another, developed at the Law School of the University of California–Berkeley, is designed to predict "successful lawyering" (Shultz and Zedeck 2008).[9] A related movement that seeks to better align the high-school curriculum to the demands of college underlies the American Diploma Project (ADP).[10] A partnership of four national organizations and five state agencies, ADP is a collaborative effort involving over thirty states to reorganize the high-school curriculum to ensure that graduating students have the knowledge and skills necessary for success in college. The project seeks to streamline assessment systems so that the tests students take in high school also serve to gauge student readiness for college.

■ Classroom Assessment

Assessment and feedback is also utilized within classrooms to create "feedback loops." These provide faculty and students alike with continuing information needed to improve both faculty teaching and student learning (Brookhart 1999; Huba and Freed 2000; Yao and Grady 2005). Techniques such as the "one-minute" paper described by Angelo and Cross (1993) are being successfully used by a wide range of institutions such as the College of DuPage, Honolulu Community College, Lansing Community College, Southern Illinois University at Edwardsville, Indiana University, Michigan State University, and Vanderbilt University.

A number of institutions—including Ohio State University, Vanderbilt University, the University of Minnesota, the University of Texas at Austin,

Mount St. Mary's College, York College of the City University of New York, Hillsborough Community College, Johnson County Community College, Mesa Community College, Palm Beach Community College, and the University of Wisconsin campuses at Milwaukee, Eau Claire, Oshkosh, and Whitewater—are now using immediate feedback techniques, referred to as student response systems, that employ system software and personal response units or clickers (Beatty 2004; Duncan 2005; Kaleta and Joosten 2007; Martyn 2007). These enable students to respond to a question asked by the class instructor and thereby allow the instructor to ascertain in real time the degree of student comprehension during class. By this means the instructor can clear up any confusion before the end of class or design activities for the next class. Though such systems can be quite effective in improving student classroom learning (Kennedy and Cutts 2005; Patry 2009; Poirier and Feldman 2007), they have a steep learning curve and can take up a good deal of classroom time (Kaleta and Joosten 2007). Nevertheless they add another tool that can be used to assess student performance in the classroom.

Many institutions use learning portfolios to assess student performance (Barton and Collins 1997; Zubizarreta 2009). Beyond the feedback they provide, consistent use of student portfolios also promotes the development of critical reflection that is in turn related to further learning and development (Cambridge 2010).[11] To facilitate their use, institutions such as Alverno College, Elon College, Evergreen State College, Kalamazoo College, LaGuardia Community College, Miami University of Ohio, and Montana State University have employed web-based portfolios that enable students and in some cases faculty to collect and reflect upon their experiences and accomplishments across their college years.[12] In some instances, as in the School of Education at Syracuse University, graduating students use their portfolios as part of an electronic résumé when applying for work or postgraduate opportunities.[13]

■ Early-Warning Systems

Classroom assessment can also be employed as part of an early warning system to alert faculty and support staff alike to students who are struggling in class. Such systems are used at Bossier Parish Community College, Florida Southern College, Navarro College, Northern Virginia Community College, Northwestern State University, Pennsylvania State University, Purdue University, Tallahassee Community College, Virginia Commonwealth University, and the University of South Carolina. When shared with student support staff, classroom assessments allow both staff and faculty to intervene in timely fashion.[14]

To be effective, early warning systems must be employed as close as possible to the beginning of the semester. Early classroom difficulties, if left unattended, can snowball over time and undermine student learning. The longer intervention is delayed, the more difficult it is to reverse the momentum toward withdrawal that is established by a student's earlier difficulties. Early warning is especially important in courses considered foundational to student academic skills because failure in those courses tends to undermine success in the courses that follow.[15]

Early Warning at Allegheny College

In 2004, Allegheny College implemented an early warning system (Academic Performance Report), which was adopted by virtually all faculty members, that has helped reduce the number of student withdrawals or failures, in particular during the first year. When faculty become concerned about a student in one of their courses, they use a web form that interfaces with the college's student information system (SIS) to alert staff in the college's Learning Commons (Academic Support Center). A member of the Learning Commons staff monitors the reports and determines the best person to contact the student (perhaps someone from the Learning Commons staff or the Dean of Students office, a residential life professional, or a member of the athletic coaching staff assigned to academic support). Reports range from missing class, to inadequate performance, to a general concern for a student. The assigned staff member may e-mail, meet with, or phone the student. He or she often follows up with the faculty member to determine the best course of action. In any case, the staff person does not wait for the student to initiate contact.

After a first report on a student, alerts for that student are automatically copied to the staff member assigned to assist the student; responses can thus be coordinated and students can develop a relationship with one person. All alerts and notes on follow-up are tracked in the college's SIS, so that if the student contacts any of the college's support services, the assigned staff member will be able to assess the student's situation, know what has already been done, and make recommendations that are

consistent with the messages the student is already receiving from institutional representatives.

In the first weeks of the semester, faculty receive an e-mail from the
dean of the college reminding them of the early alert system and the importance of using it In addition, the Learning Commons generates a report each semester identifying students who received a D or F in a course
but did not receive an early alert warning before the end of the semester.

Some institutions, such as Purdue University, Rio Salado College, and Saddleback College, have automated early warning systems. Like an increasing number of institutions, they have sought to employ predictive analysis and technology in ways to develop and facilitate programs for student
success. Rio Salado College, an online institution under Maricopa Community College, employs data-mining and predictive analysis to identify
at-risk students by combining demographic and personal information and
past behaviors with real-time class behaviors and performance. Embedding
this analysis within the classroom has resulted in a predictive accuracy of
over 70%. More importantly, it has led to the development and testing of a
range of interventions to improve online classroom success. Others, such
as Cleveland Community College, Estrella Mountain Community College,
and Paul Smith College, have employed commercial software, which, once
a faculty member has indicated a problem on a predefined list of student
behaviors, automatically sends alerts to support staff, who then connect
with the student.

Purdue University Signals for Student Success

The Signals program at Purdue combines predictive modeling with data-
mining from Blackboard Vista, the university's course management system, to identify students who are at risk of failing or doing poorly in a
course. Its student-success algorithm uses a range of measures, from
entry data to course performance data, to assign each student to one of
three risk groups: green (not at risk), yellow (may be at risk), and red (at
risk). E-mails, composed by the instructor, can then be sent, as appropriate, to students in each risk group, indicating what students need to do to
improve their performance. The Signals program urges students to use
available resources on campus. The strength of Signals is that in using
real-time data, it provides real-time feedback as early at the second week
of class, and it can do so frequently over the course of the semester.

■ Assessment and Course Redesign

Technology is being employed not simply to modify but to transform individual courses. Working with Carol Twigg's National Center for Academic Transformation, institutions such as Brigham Young University, Drexel University, Florida Gulf Coast University, Iowa State University, Portland State University, Tallahassee Community College, and the University of New Mexico have transformed many of their large enrollment courses in ways that have led to increases in student course success.[16] For instance, the drop-failure-withdrawal (DFW) rate for redesigned courses at the University of New Mexico declined from 42% to 25%, and the rate at Florida Gulf Coast University from 45% to 11%. But those declines did not come from simply adding technology to existing course structures, but transforming the course in ways that emphasize student involvement and active learning (Twigg 2005). Other institutions, such as the University of Texas at Austin, are taking similar steps to improve student success in large, lower-division gateway courses.[17]

Course Transformation through Technology
at the University of New Mexico

The University of New Mexico's redesigned General Psychology, its largest and most popular undergraduate course, enrolls 2,250 students annually. The primary goal of the redesign was to improve the course's high DFW rate (42%); among the DFW students, 30% failed the course, and a disproportionate number were minority students. High failure rates in core curriculum courses such as General Psychology are known to have a strong negative impact on the university's low overall retention and graduation rates. The course redesign reduced the number of lectures each week from three to two and incorporated a weekly 50-minute studio session led by undergraduate teaching assistants, strong students from previous sections of General Psychology, or upper-division honors students. In-class activities were supplemented by interactive Web- or CD-ROM-based activities and quizzes, offered on a 24/7 schedule. Students were able to interact online with other students and review concepts based on individual need. Commercially available software was used that contained interactive activities, simulations, and movies. Each week, students took repeatable quizzes requiring a C level of mastery. An active intervention strategy ensured that students were making progress. Graduate teaching assistants monitored quiz performance, counseling students with weak performance.

The failure rate was reduced from 30% to 12%, and the DFW rate fell from 42% to 18%. The number of students who received a C or higher rose from 60% to 76.5%, and there were more A and B grades than recorded in previous semesters. At the same time, the course was arguably more difficult, requiring students to completely cover a high-level introductory text. Three factors were seen to be particularly important in improving student learning: first, the use of online mastery quizzes, which tested both factual and conceptual knowledge, structured students' learning, and kept students on task; second, requiring students who scored 75% or less on the first exam to attend a weekly 50-minute studio for the remainder of the semester for additional tutoring from undergraduate teaching assistants; and third, requiring all sections to use the same materials and perform the same amount of work, thereby providing a more consistent learning experience for all students.[18]

■ Institutional Assessment of Student Experience

Assessing student classroom experiences institution-wide can also lead to improvements in student retention. One way to do so is to employ detailed data on student classroom performance along with data on student experience, as provided, for instance, by the National Survey of Student Engagement (NSSE) and the Community College Survey of Student Engagement (CCSSE). Though similar in the sorts of data they provide, they differ in how they obtain data. To develop a representative portrait of student experience, the NSSE relies on a random sampling of the student population and specific yearly cohorts (e.g., first-year students), whereas the CCSSE relies on a random sampling of classrooms in which all students are sampled. Institutions can, of course, develop their own surveys, tailored to the specifics of their student body and institutional functions; or, with additional investment, they can use the NSSE and CCSSE surveys but with additional questions. Regardless of their form, the data they provide can lead to institutional improvements in student success (CSSE 2006; NSSE 2006b; Yao and Grady 2005).

More than a few institutions have employed such surveys to improve student performance in class. The Lone Star College System in Texas, for instance, instituted a Classroom Research Initiative involving ten faculty members of each of the system's campuses; these teachers explored how the use of their CCSSE data would enable them to design new classroom activities to promote greater student engagement. The program, which includes professional development for the entire faculty, focuses its efforts on helping individual teachers develop action plans for classroom improvement. Each faculty member designs a data-based classroom strategy, implements it, evaluates it, and shares results with colleagues and administrators (Community College Survey of Student Engagement 2010).[19]

■ **Assessment, Feedback, and Enhancing**
  Student Retention: A Comment

While entry assessment, end-of-first-year assessment, and other forms of course, program, and institutional assessment be can be useful and, in varying ways, indirectly affect student retention, the most effective form of assessment is that which monitors actual student performance in the classroom. To the degree that such assessments are shared with students, faculty, and staff and used to trigger action, as in early warning systems, they address the issue of student success within most directly by focusing on student performance in the classroom. As a result, they recognize that all students may struggle at one time or another, not just those who are thought to be at risk. Furthermore, the use of these assessments raises the question of how classrooms and other places of learning can be changed to increase the likelihood that students will succeed in class and, in turn, complete college.

INVOLVEMENT

5

The fourth condition for student retention, perhaps the most important, is involvement, or what is now commonly referred as engagement (Astin 1984; Kuh, Schuh, Whitt, and Associates 1991; Kuh et al. 2005; Tinto 1975, 1993).[1] The more students are academically and socially engaged with other people on campus, especially with faculty and student peers, the more likely (other things being equal) they will stay and graduate from college (Astin 1984, 1993; Borglum and Kubala 2000; Braxton and McClendon 2001; Carini, Kuh, and Klein 2006; Kuh et al. 2005; Pascarella 1980; Pascarella and Chapman 1983; Terenzini, Lorang, and Pascarella 1981; Tinto 1975, 1987, 1993). During the critical first year, involvement serves as a foundation upon which subsequent student and faculty affiliations are built and academic and social memberships established (Tinto 1993; Upcraft, Gardner, and Associates 1989).[2] This appears to be true for all students, majority and minority alike, and applies even after controlling for background attributes (Greene 2005; Kuh et al. 2007).

Fischer's 2007 study of engagement employed data from approximately four thousand students, who participated in the National Longitudinal Survey of Freshmen. The survey studied the way different forms of engagement in the first year of college were related to student satisfaction, academic achievement, and remaining in college for a second year. Among all the students, regardless of ethnicity and race, those having a larger number of formal academic connections with faculty, as well as a larger number of formal and informal social connections with faculty, staff, and peers, were found to enjoy greater satisfaction and higher retention. Conversely, the absence of such ties proved to be a predictor of leaving. The effects of involvement on retention extend beyond the first year (Graunke and Woolsey 2005). Coghlan, Fowler, and Messel's (2010) study of the retention of sophomores to the third year of college found that students who returned for the third year had been more involved during their first and second year, especially with their peers, than those who left.

Academic and social involvement influences retention in a variety of ways. The impact of academic involvement arises primarily from classroom involvement and student-faculty contact (e.g., Astin 1984, 1993; Friedlander 1980; Ory and Braskamp 1988; Parker and Schmidt 1982; Pascarella and Terenzini 1991). Greater engagement in learning activities in the classroom, especially those that are seen as meaningful and validating, leads to greater time and effort students put into their studies, which, in turn, heightens academic performance and retention (Barnett 2011; Engstrom and Tinto 2007; Kuh, Carini, and Klein 2004). Similarly, students who report greater contact with faculty, both inside and outside the classroom, do better on a range of educational outcomes (e.g., Endo and Harpel 1982; Pascarella and Terenzini 1980; Reason, Terenzini, and Domingo 2006; Terenzini and Pascarella 1980). Not the least of these is the sense of validation that comes from positive interactions with faculty (Barnett 2011). Even among those who persist to graduation, students who report higher levels of contact with faculty and peers in class demonstrate higher levels of learning gain and student development (Astin 1993; Endo and Harpel 1982; Pascarella and Terenzini 1980; Wilson, Wood, and Gaff 1974).

Social involvement and the emotional support that accrues from involvement also affect retention (Gloria, Kurpius, Hamilton, and Wilson 1999; Gloria and Kurpuis 2001; Mallinckrodt 1988). By contrast, the absence of social involvement and the social isolation and loneliness that follow often lead to withdrawal (Fleming 1984; Nicpon et al. 2006; Rotenberg and Morrison 1993). So it is not surprising that students living in residence halls on campus are found to have higher retention rates than those who live off campus (Pike 1999; Pike, Schroeder, and Berry 1997).

Academic and social involvement, though conceptually distinct, overlap and influence each other. Academic involvement in class through the use of cooperative group work, for instance, has been shown to promote social involvement that extends beyond the class (Tinto 1997). Similarly, social involvement in academically oriented social organizations and clubs can promote academic involvement. Some forms of social involvement, however, such as those that may occur among fraternities and sororities, may weaken academic commitments or detract from the time needed to attend to the academic demands of college (Pike 2000).[3]

The relationship between engagement and learning outcomes varies among institutions. Carini, Kuh, and Klein's (2006) study of students at fourteen four-year colleges and universities found that student engagement was more positively associated with student performance among some institutions than others. In other words, the impact of engagement on student performance in any institution reflects in part the institutional setting in which involvement occurs, not the least of which is the cultural context that gives meaning to student interactions with people on campus.

Involvement appears to matter more for some students than for others. A recent analysis of NSSE data of student performance suggests that the impact of engagement on first-year grades and retention to the second year may be greater for students of lower ability and students of color than for white students (Cruce, Wolniak, Seifert, and Pascarella 2006; Kuh et al. 2008). For academically underprepared students, in particular, engagement appears to help offset the otherwise negative effects of lower academic skills.[4]

■ Involvement, Meaning, and the Sense of Belonging

Involvements, academic or social, do not occur in a vacuum. They take place within specific social and cultural settings and among individuals whose values give them meaning. It is not simply the degree of involvement that affects retention, but the way involvement leads to forms of social and academic membership and the resulting "sense of belonging" (Schlossberg 1989; Tucker 1999; Harris 2006; Hoffman, Richmond, Morrow, and Salomone 2003). Decisions to stay or leave are shaped, in part, by the meaning students attach to their involvement, the sense that their involvement is valued and that the community with which they interact is supportive of their presence on campus.[5] This is precisely what Hurtado (1994) and Hurtado and Carter (1997) argue in their analysis of "hostile climates" for minority students.[6] The supportive climate of a campus fosters student retention by establishing the broader context within which involvements occur and are interpreted (Hausmann, Ye, Schofield, and Woods 2009).

A sense of belonging is a generalized sense of membership that stems from students' perception of their involvement in a variety of settings and the support they experience from those around them (Hoffman, Richmond, Morrow, and Salomone 2003). As most institutions, except perhaps for small private colleges, consist of a variety of communities—faculty, staff, and students—whose values and norms may differ, students may feel a sense of belonging with one community but not with others or with the institution generally. When exploring student involvement, one must ask with whom, in what settings, and about what issues involvement occurs and how, in turn, the student interprets those involvements. Retention requires that a student see him- or herself as belonging to at least one significant community and find meaning in the involvements that occur within that community. When speaking, for instance, of the retention of students of color on primarily white campuses, researchers have stressed the importance of a "critical mass" of like persons on campus in order for such communities to form (Rendon, Jalomo, and Nora 2000; Grier-Reed, Madyun, and Buckley 2008).

Involvement or, better yet, the quality of involvement also depends on the degree to which individuals see their involvement as relevant. Individuals are more likely to become involved in those forms of activity that are perceived to be relevant or at least meaningfully related to their interests broadly understood. For institutions, then, the question is not whether students want to be involved—students go to college precisely to be involved—but to which forms of involvement they will direct their energies and how those involvements will shape their success in college.

■ Promoting Involvement for Student Success

As a practical matter, colleges must determine how they can involve their students in ways that promote retention and how to do so in settings such as urban two and four-year institutions that serve large numbers of students who hold jobs, attend part-time, and have substantial obligations beyond the campus (e.g., work, family). For these students the more traditional practices that institutions have used to engage their students, such as extracurricular activities, residential programming, and clubs (as described by Kinzie 2005; Kuh 2003; and Kuh, Schuh, Whitt, and Associates 1991), yield relatively little relative benefit, if only because few students have the luxury of being able to spend time on campus beyond the classroom. This is not to say that out-of-class involvements are needless. For many students and for many institutions, especially residential ones, out-of-class involvement can play an important role in student development, learning, and retention (Attinasi 1989; Belgarde and Lore 2003; Kuh 1994; Kuh, Schuh, Whitt, and Associates 1991; Kuh et al. 2005). Nor is it to say that all two- and four-year colleges should not invest in student government, clubs, sports and other out-of-class activities. For many students, however, especially those in community colleges, if involvement does not occur in the class-room, it is unlikely to occur at all (Donaldson, Graham, Martindill, and Bradley 2000, Tinto 1997). Furthermore, if involvement in the classroom is interpreted as uninvolving, unsupportive, or uncaring, it is unlikely that students will want to expend the effort needed to succeed (Allen and Madden 2006; Barnett 2011; Giaquinto 2009–10; Hoffman, Richmond, Morrow, and Salomone 2003).

Student classroom experiences also influence student-faculty contact outside the classroom. The faculty's teaching styles, classroom behaviors, and evaluation practices, for example, serve as indicators to students not only of the availability of faculty for out-of-class contact but also its desirability (Wilson, Wood, and Gaff 1974). Some teachers and certain pedagogical practices seem to foster that engagement, while others do not. Furthermore, not all students are equally influenced by faculty behaviors within the classroom (Allen and Madden 2006). Out-of-classroom involvements, in the academic realm at least, come to matter in large measure as a result of what occurs within the classroom.

An increasing number of institutions are beginning to focus on the classroom and the spaces adjoining it as sites for involving their students (Braxton and McClendon 2001; Heiberger and Harper 2008; Tinto 1997). Three strategies warrant mention: the use of pedagogies of engagement, the construction of learning communities, and the use of service learning.

■ **Pedagogies of Engagement**

Unlike the traditional lecture, where students are typically passive, especially in the many large first-year classrooms that dot the postsecondary landscape, pedagogies of engagement require students to be actively engaged in learning with other students in the classroom (Barkley 2010; Barkley, Cross, and Major 2005). The most commonly employed of these pedagogies are cooperative or collaborative learning, and problem- or project-based learning.[7] Both have been shown to positively impact student success because they lead not only to greater academic engagement but also to social relationships with other students (Pascarella and Terenzini 2005).

Cooperative or collaborative learning, though somewhat different as the former is more structured than the latter (see Bruffee 1995) requires students to become actively involved in learning groups with other students so that the work of the group cannot be accomplished without each member doing his or her part.[8] Problem-based learning, like cooperative learning, requires students to work together during class, but it does so by focusing the curriculum on applying knowledge and skills acquired during the course to solving a problem or set of problems that form the foundation of the course (Amador, Miles, and Peters 2006; Wilkerson and Gijselaers 1996).[9] Project-based learning is similar, but it also requires students to publicly present the results of their work (Blumenfeld et al. 1991; Ravitz 2009; Strobel and Barneveld 2008). In both cases, learning is enhanced because students have to apply what they are learning to solve a problem being addressed (Ebert-May, Brewer, and Alfred 1997). Though often used in smaller classrooms, both methods have been successfully employed in large classes in a number of large universities (Ebert-May, Brewer, and Alfred 1997; Smith 2000; Cooper and Robinson 2000; MacGregor 2000).

Research on the effectiveness of cooperative/collaborative learning and problem/project-based learning in improving student learning is widespread (Blumberg 2000; Johnson, Johnson, and Smith 1998b).[10] Of particular note is that pedagogies of engagement enhance students' processing skills, relative to lecture classes, while not substantially diminishing content acquisition (Ebert-May, Brewer, and Alfred 1997). Cooperative activities also enhance retention by promoting social as well as academic involvement (Braxton, Milem, and Sullivan 2000; Braxton, Jones, Hirschy, and Hartley 2008; Pascarella, Seifert, and Whitt 2008).

It should be noted that the impact of pedagogy on student success appears to be mediated, in part, by the effect different pedagogies have on students' sense of their own capacities as learners. Fencl and Scheel (2005), for instance, found that teaching strategies, especially those that emphasize collaborative learning, enhance students' sense of self-efficacy while also increasing their learning of course content (p. 23).[11] Enhanced self-efficacy promotes, in turn, behaviors that further the likelihood of success.

Many programs are already using these or similar pedagogies. Schools of business, for example, typically use team learning and case-study methods (Michaelsen and Pelton-Sweet 2008; Sweet and Pelton-Sweet 2008; Mulcare and Ruget 2010). So do schools of nursing. The University of Delaware has long been an advocate for problem-based learning. Their Institute for Transforming Undergraduate Education promotes reform of undergraduate education through faculty development and course design.[12] Institute fellows receive hands-on experience in employing active learning strategies, particularly problem-based learning, and effective use of technology in their courses.

Cooperative Learning at Northern Essex Community College

The faculty development program at Northern Essex Community College operates with the belief that investing in the college faculty provides a key to student success. Some of the programs and projects encouraging co-operative learning have included the Carnegie Foundation's Scholarship of Teaching and Learning, yearlong projects on Critically Reflective Teaching, a summer institute on Cooperative Learning led by Barbara Millis, interdisciplinary Learning Communities, annual Teaching and Learning Conferences, and Staff and Faculty Inquiry Groups (SFIGs).

The college's most recent commitment to cooperative learning involves the re-creation and expansion of its College Success Skills program, which had been primarily focused on late-registering adult students. Beginning in the fall of 2010, the course has been transformed into a cooperative teaching and learning experience involving hundreds of students and faculty from a wide variety of disciplines. The faculty are provided with special professional development to teach the course, including a two-day summer institute with Barbara Millis, followed by a two-day retreat, which reinforces cooperative learning strategies, research, course design, and focus group instruction based on the Millis model.[13]

Problem-Based Learning at the University of Delaware

The Institute for Transforming Undergraduate Education at the University of Delaware has played a central role in the implementation of Problem-Based Learning (PBL) at the university and elsewhere across the United States. To date, over four hundred members of the University of Delaware faculty have participated in PBL workshops, where they create active learning strategies that require students to work cooperatively, to apply critical thinking and problem-solving skills, and to utilize technology to enhance their learning. After creating PBL cases, participating faculty are encouraged to share them online in the university's Problem-Based Learning Clearinghouse.

Although PBL originated with the sciences, the clearinghouse contains problems designed to address the arts, social sciences, and the humanities as well. All undergraduates at the university are required to take three credits of a Discovery Learning Experience (DLE), a course that involves experiential learning and out-of-class instructional experiences. The DLEs are often structured as PBLs to ensure that students make connections between their discipline and the real world. Further exploration of DLE listings indicates a plethora of PBL courses available in all seven colleges of the university for students to engage in a collaborative experience.[14]

■ Learning Communities

Learning communities are another increasingly popular strategy. Their effectiveness in promoting student involvement, learning, and retention in both two- and four-year settings has been well established (Engstrom and Tinto 2007; Taylor, Moore, MacGregor, and Lindblad 2003; Tinto 1999; Zhao and Kuh 2004).[15] In their most basic form, learning communities constitute a kind of co-registration or block scheduling. The same group of students registers for two or more courses, forming a sort of study team. In a few cases, they may follow the curriculum together over an entire semester, all studying the same material. Sometimes a learning community will link students by tying two courses together—for example, a course in writing with a course in history or current social problems. In some large universities, students may attend lectures with two or three hundred students who may not be in a learning community but stay together in a smaller discussion section led by a graduate student or upperclassman. In other cases, students in a learning community may take all their courses together in one block of time, meeting two or three times a week for four to six hours each time.

Though co-registration facilitates the development of socially supportive peer groups (Tinto and Goodsell 1994), it is not sufficient to ensure enhanced student learning and retention. Learning communities require a central theme or problem that links the courses in which the students co-register. The aim is to construct an interdisciplinary or multidisciplinary learning environment in which students are able to connect what they are learning in one course to what they are learning in another. Co-registration is simply the structure upon which learning communities are built. It provides the faculty in the separate courses the opportunity to coherently link the content of their courses with that of courses taught by colleagues.

More and more learning communities are also utilizing pedagogies of engagement. Students not only pursue a common body of knowledge but also share the experience of gaining that knowledge together. They form communities within and between classes that reinforce the impact of their shared learning experience. A study by Lichtenstein (2005) of students enrolled in several learning communities on a university campus found higher grades and retention among students in those communities that provided a stronger sense of community and clearer linkage between faculty, subject matter, and course organization. In other words, the impact of a learning community depends very much upon how it is implemented.

When developed for the needs of new students, learning communities frequently include a first-year seminar as one of the linked courses (Baker and Pomerantz 2001). In some cases, students will live together in a residence hall in what is commonly referred to as a living-learning community (Pike 1999; Pike, Schroeder, and Berry 1997). The experience of living and learning together, when properly implemented, promotes a social cohesiveness that furthers retention while helping to bridge the academic-social divide that typifies many students' lives (Kaya 2004). When applied to the needs of academically underprepared students, learning communities often connect a study-skills course or one or more developmental-level courses such as writing to a credit-bearing course such as history, so that the skills being acquired in the developmental course can be directly applied to the content course (Tinto 1999; Malnarich et al. 2003; Smith, MacGregor, Matthews, and Gabelnick 2004; Engstrom 2008). Whether for new or academically underprepared students, learning communities support the daily learning needs of students, thereby facilitating success in courses to which support is connected (Engstrom and Tinto 2007, 2008). In this and other ways, learning communities provide a structure that enables a college to align its various actions on behalf of student learning and retention. This alignment is most likely to occur when faculty and in some cases faculty and staff form collaborative partnerships to promote the success of their students.

When fully implemented, learning communities have enhanced student retention by increasing both academic and social engagement (Pike, Kuh, and McCormick 2008; Rocconi 2010). Comments from students surveyed in a multi-institutional study of learning communities typify student experiences in learning communities (Tinto, Goodsell, and Russo 1993; Tinto and Goodsell 1994; Tinto and Russo 1994). Reflecting on the way a learning community in an urban community college encouraged her to continue in college, one student observed: "In the cluster we knew each other, we were friends, we discussed everything from all the classes. We knew things very, very well because we discussed it all so much. We had discussions about everything . . . it was like a raft running the rapids of my life." For her and for many of the classmates, the shared activities of the learning community gave rise to the development of supportive peer groups, whose support was essential to being able to continue in college. It is a type of support that busy faculty and staff cannot easily provide.

Participation in the learning community also shaped engagement in ways that extended beyond the classroom. Another student, also in an urban community college, noted: "You know, the more I talk to other people about our class stuff, the homework, the tests, the more I'm actually learning . . . and the more I learn not only about other people, but also about the subject, because my brain is getting more, because I'm getting more involved with the other students in the class. I'm getting more involved with the class even after class." The shared activities of the learning community, constructed in part through the use of collaborative pedagogy, promoted engagement in learning not only within class, but beyond it as well.

A study undertaken at Kingsborough Community College in New York City sought to ascertain whether the impact of a learning community depended largely on the characteristics of the students who volunteered to participate in the learning community, the so-called volunteer effect (Scrivener 2007; Scrivener et al. 2008). Students who volunteered for the learning community were randomly assigned to one of two groups; one group was enrolled in the learning community, the other was not. It was determined that students who participated in the learning community did better on a range of measures than did students who did not participate. In other words, the impact of the learning community did not reflect the attributes of the students but the characteristics of their experiences within the learning community.

It must be noted, however, that learning communities, at least on community college campuses, will typically reach a relatively small proportion of students, if only because of the more varied forms of enrollment that mark student participation. By contrast, a number of private four-year colleges use learning communities for all their first-year students (e.g., Wagner College). That being said, effective learning communities range from programs in four-year institutions such as the University of Southern Maine, California State University–East Bay, Johnson C. Smith University, St. Lawrence University, and the University of Texas San Antonio, to programs in two-year colleges such as DeAnza College in California, Kingsborough Community College and LaGuardia Community College in New York, Seattle Central Community College, and Skagit Valley College.

In addition, several organizations—most notably the Learning Communities Resource Center of the Washington Center for Improving the Quality of Undergraduate Education at Evergreen State College—provide support for the development and assessment of learning communities.

Learning Communities at DeAnza College

DeAnza College's interdisciplinary learning community program, LinC, links two or more classes together with a common theme or question, content, and assignments. For example, Don't Believe Everything You Think is linked to Reading and Writing / Language Arts; and Mind Control: Persuasion and Propaganda is linked both to Psychology with Fundamentals and to Oral Communication. Over the course of an academic year, LinC offers between twenty-five and thirty different learning communities, serving a range of students including those in the college's transfer program, ESL students, and those requiring basic-skills courses. Each offers from seven to sixteen quarter-units, constituting either a portion or the whole of an academic load for a student. All learning communities are collaboratively designed by faculty, and many are team-taught. A counselor is assigned to each learning community team to provide study-skills support, academic advising, and personal counseling. LinC is directed by a faculty coordinator and a seven-member advisory group consisting of faculty, counselors, and the director of staff development.

Faculty interesting in participating in the program must submit a written proposal that includes integrated course content and assignments along with plans for including student services interventions and designated formative and summative assessment instruments. An important feature of DeAnza's learning-community work is its extensive, ongoing faculty development program, undertaken in collaboration with the Office of Staff and Organizational Development. Expectations and guidelines for designing, implementing, and assessing learning-community curriculum are explicit; faculty who want to teach in a learning community are supported by workshops and in-service professional development. Faculty are also introduced to the LinC program's use of Small Group Instructional Feedback (SGIF), routinely administered by staff in the fourth and tenth week of the quarter, so that students can collectively reflect on what is and is not working in their learning community. An analysis of student feedback is used to identify areas where faculty, collectively, need more training. The college provides budgetary support for conference travel, release time, workshops, and a retreat off campus every quarter for faculty and staff in the LinC program and anyone else who is interested.

Ongoing assessment is viewed as a critical means for sustaining, improving, and expanding LinC. With the support of the college and the district's institutional researchers, multiple assessment measures are used, including the Student Profile, success and persistence rates, Small Group Instructional Feedback, reflective student essays, a student survey, student focus groups and a faculty survey. Retention (defined as completing a course) in the LinC program is 85% or higher, compared to the college-wide average of 60%. Student success (defined as passing a course with a grade of C or better) in LinC is 90% or better. In the general education classes that are linked to, or clustered with, pre-collegiate classes, success rates are between 10% and 25% higher than those in general-education classes not in a learning community.[16]

■ Service Learning

Service learning is another way of engaging students by requiring them to get involved with service activities beyond the campus (Bringle 1996). Unlike voluntarism, the service students provide must be linked in an educative way to a course in which they are enrolled (Vogelgesang and Astin 2000). For instance, service in a homeless shelter might be linked to a course in urban sociology. The educative character of that linkage is reinforced through the use of reflective journals or essays, in which students are asked not only to reflect on their experience but also to describe how their service experience relates to their course work (Eyler 2002; Hatcher, Bringle, and Muthiah 2004; Simons and Cleary 2006). The impact of service learning can be both immediate and long-term (Astin, Vogelgesang, Ikeda, and Yee 2000; Eyler, Giles, Stenson, and Gray 2001; Steinke and Buresh 2002). Jones and Abes (2004) found that even two to four years after taking a service-learning course, participants continued to describe the importance of that experience to their evolving sense of self and self-authority.

However constructed, effective service learning requires the collaborative efforts of faculty and student-affairs professionals to establish and monitor the service activities deemed appropriate for the relevant course (Bringle and Hatcher 1996; Heffernan 2001). In this respect, service learning, like learning communities, provides yet another tool to better align the actions of various members of the institution on behalf of student success.

Service-learning programs are found in a range of two- and four-year in-stitutions. Among the former are Brevard Community College, Brookdale Community College, Chandler-Gilbert Community College, Colin County Community College, Evergreen Valley College, Kapi'olani Community College, Kirkland Community College, Miami-Dade Community College, Monroe Community College, Portland Community College, and Raritan Valley Community College; and among the latter are Alverno College, An-tioch College, Berea College, Boston College, Brown University, Indiana University-Purdue University Indianapolis, Portland State University, and Wayne State University.[17]

Service Learning at Raritan Valley Community College

Service Learning at Raritan Valley, at first a relatively small program, was initiated in 1993 by faculty and staff who believed in the power of service learning not only to improve society but also to transform student lives in ways that go beyond the curriculum. Now, over seventy faculty mem-bers from all academic departments connect the learning objectives of their courses, as well as reflection exercises, to community service. With the assistance of service-learning staff, who coordinate placements in community sites, more than eight hundred students in more than eighty courses provide at least seventeen thousand hours of service to some two hundred community organizations. The staff not only help individual faculty members to integrate service learning into their courses; they also provide class-based presentations and organize campus workshops on service learning.

Service learning is an all-encompassing theme at Raritan Valley Com-munity College with students serving at many different kinds of organiza-tions—schools, social- service and governmental agencies, and nonprofit bodies. Many students work in pre-school through secondary educational systems, after-school programs, nursing homes, adult day-care centers, assisted living facilities, animal shelters, museums, courthouses, proba-tion departments, youth correctional facilities, consumer affairs offices, churches, youth programs, and homeless shelters. In helping disadvan-taged populations, the service-learning students served as tutors for at-risk middle and high school students and assist with ESL classes. They plan and deliver workshops on career and college planning at homeless shelters and collaborate with staff at mental health and developmental agencies to improve learning for students with disabilities.[18]

■ Promoting Involvement and Faculty Development

Since pedagogies of engagement have been shown to improve student success within the classroom and, in turn, to increase student retention and completion, one might expect wide use of such methods. According to two recent surveys of faculty, however, they are used less than one would hope. Among nearly 3,600 faculty in 39 community colleges across the nation who were surveyed in the fall of 2004, approximately 42% reported having spent 50% or more of their class time lecturing and leading discussions, whereas less than 10% of class time was given to small-group activities and student presentations (Community College Survey of Student Engagement 2005). In a similar survey of over 19,000 faculty in 109 four-year institutions, 48% reported spending 50% or more time class time lecturing or leading discussions, while 54% reported using less than 10% of class time on small-group activities; almost 75% of the entire sample spent less than 20% of class time on small group activities (Laird, Buckeley, and Schwarz 2005). But even these figures may overstate the degree to which faculty are employing pedagogies such as cooperative or problem-based learning, for small group activities and structured cooperative activities are not identical. What many teachers call small-group activities are little more than loosely organized conversation groups. These lack the structure that underlies effective cooperative group work, which requires each participant to take part in the learning activities of the group. Clearly, there is still much to do to promote the effective use of pedagogies of engagement for student success.

One of the ironies of higher education is that most college faculty, unlike the faculty in elementary and secondary school, have had no formal training to teach. This does not mean that there are not many talented and well-prepared faculty members who bring to the task of educating students a broad repertoire of teaching and assessment skills. Most college teachers, however, enter the profession untrained for the task of educating students. Given the centrality of the classroom for student success and the role of pedagogy and assessment in the construction of effective classrooms, it follows that faculty development must be a key feature of any institutional plan of action designed to enhance student retention.

Institutions are, of course, not blind to the importance of faculty development. Virtually all institutions invest in some form of it. The most common form occurs in centers for teaching and learning.[19] Found in both two- and four-year institutions, these centers serve a variety of staff development functions, not the least of which is the enhancement of teaching skills among faculty. They do so most commonly through meetings, seminars, on-campus conferences, mentoring programs, individual consultation, and targeted grants. A number of institutions have formed faculty academies, which call for faculty to work in teams over a period of time to learn new teaching and assessment skills (Cox 2001; Fayne and Ortquist-Ahrens 2006). They do so because it is becoming increasingly clear that effective faculty development requires on-going collaborative engagement and inquiry that is typically not achieved through stand alone activities to which different faculty attend.

Taking a cue from the effectiveness of learning communities for students, a number of institutions such as Miami University of Ohio, Chaffey College, and Johnson C. Smith University have promoted similar communities for faculty (Cox 2001; Cox and Richlin 2004; Shulman, Cox, and Richlin 2004).[20] Typically, faculty from different disciplines work together over a semester or a year in active conversations about teaching and learning.[21] At Chaffey College, for example, full-time as well as adjunct faculty are encouraged to participate in a two-week summer institute, during which they learn not only about pedagogy and assessment but also about student backgrounds and how issues of income and ethnicity shape student learning. Participants are required to develop new strategies to improve and assess student learning in their classes during the following year. During that year, they continue to meet to discuss their experiences in implementing those strategies and the results of their assessments. Their experiences are then shared with the faculty broadly in the form of a handbook on "what works."

Most faculty learning communities are cohort based or topic based. Among the former, those at the University of Texas at El Paso and Chandler-Gilbert Community College involve new faculty in the same way that student learning communities usually focus on first-year students (Fayne and Ortquist-Ahrens 2006). In the case of Chandler-Gilbert Community College, new faculty are encouraged, and offered incentives, to participate twice a month in a yearlong staff-development program; it consists of a variety of activities in the college's Network for Excellence program and New Faculty Orientation Series. In addition, new faculty are required to take a twenty-one-hour course on active learning strategies, which provides hands-on classroom experience. The college also requires faculty to submit annual self-assessment of their practice. For new faculty, such assessment is normally tied to their participation in the Network for Excellence. These teachers are then encouraged to continue in the network's second- and third-year learning communities. In this way, the college provides an intentional structure that promotes ongoing collaboration and inquiry about effective practice.

Some institutions—including Chaffey College, Foothill Community College, Leeward Community College, Richland College, South Texas College, Mountain View College, North Lake College, Stonehill College, Tallahassee Community College, Valencia Community College, and to some degree Chandler-Gilbert—make participation in faculty development activities, whether in the form of a learning community or otherwise, mandatory for new faculty (Fayne and Ortquist-Ahrens 2006; Kreaden 2001). At Mountain View College, for instance, new faculty are assigned a faculty mentor, whereas at Leeward Community College, North Lake College, and Stonehill College new faculty are organized into teaching squares over the course of the first year, which provide faculty with an opportunity to visit each other's classes over the course of a semester and discuss what they have learned from their observations. Some programs, such as those at Valencia Community College and Richland College, also provide incentives for adjunct faculty to participate (see Valley 2004a, 2004b).[22]

New Faculty Development at Richland College
Richmond is one of seven separately accredited community colleges in the Dallas County Community College District. Its new-faculty development program grew out of its involvement (in 2000) in the district's program for all new faculty within its borders. That program, entitled Visions of Excellence, called for all new faculty to attend one of two weekend retreats as well as one session each month throughout the year, not only to be oriented to the district but also to be introduced to issues of pedagogy, assessment, learning styles, and the like. Though the "requirement" to attend varies among the seven district colleges, attendance has been universally very high.

Beginning in 2002, Richland College developed its own mandatory program for new faculty, above and beyond that required by the district. Richland now requires all new faculty to participate in a three-year initiative. Throughout their first year, they meet for three hours every second Friday of the month, to be oriented to the college and to participate in a series of modules that expose them to a range of pedagogical and assessment issues. Master Teachers share their teaching methods with the participants. During their second year, faculty have to complete a fifteen-hour module on cooperative learning strategies, during which they have an opportunity to practice the skills they acquire. The college's focus on cooperative learning reflects their assessment of research evidence that classroom-level engagement in learning is a key to student success. During the third and final year of the program, faculty are required to select one of three options: two focus on the development of shared faculty conversation communities and the development of a values-informed culture at Richland College, and the third focuses on student engagement and what faculty can do to more fully engage their students in learning.

Evidence of the effectiveness of the program is reflected in feedback from faculty participants and from CCSSE data. As regards the former, new faculty complete Visions of Excellence surveys, evaluate the cooperative learning workshops, and provide feedback to the program as members of an advisory committee, which helps the college improve the program over time. Feedback has been overwhelmingly positive. Over the years since its inception, about forty new full-time faculty—and, though not required, four hundred part-time faculty—have gone through the program.

Good pedagogic practices are especially important to those who teach the critical first-year courses (Erickson, Peters, and Strommer 2006). Syracuse University, for example, established Gateway Fellowship, a program within its Center for Support of Teaching and Learning. It includes faculty who teach the large freshman introductory courses that dot the first-year landscape. Since the first year is critical to students' success, it is best to invest resources, if limited, in that year and in the faculty who teach the introductory classes.

Another aspect of faculty development is the growing movement to prepare doctoral students for a teaching career. Syracuse University and the University of Southern California have joined many other universities in what is known as the Preparing Future Faculty program.[23] Begun in 1993 as a partnership between the Council of Graduate Schools and the Association of American Colleges and Universities, and supported by the Pew Charitable Trusts, the National Science Foundation, and the Atlantic Philanthropies, the program has been implemented in more than forty-five doctoral degree–granting institutions and nearly three hundred two- and four-year colleges (DeNeef 2002).

What, then, is the impact of faculty development programs on students? Given the widespread investment in faculty and staff development programs, surprisingly few studies connect faculty development to student outcomes. The few that do, however, suggest that such programs affect student success in a number of ways (Braxton, Bray, and Berger 2000; McShannon 2002; Bothell and Henderson 2004). By influencing the pedagogic and assessment practices of faculty, they impact student behaviors within the classroom and in turn student learning. They also appear to increase student satisfaction with their classroom experience. Other evidence, if only anecdotal, indicates that faculty development programs yield benefits beyond student learning and student satisfaction. Not the least of these is greater engagement with other faculty on campus. This is especially apparent in cohort or learning community models that require participants to engage in ongoing collaboration over an extended period of time. That engagement impacts faculty learning. In the same way that students learn better together, so do faculty.

■ Involvement for Student Success: A Comment

One of the findings of our research on learning communities was that students in these communities spend more time than those in a comparison group on a range of activities related to student involvement and learning (Engstrom and Tinto 2007). Yet in response to a survey question about hours spent studying, they indicated that they spent somewhat fewer hours studying than did students in the other group. When queried about their answers to that question, however, they told us that they thought the question referred to hours spent alone at a desk, working on their assignments. They did not see working together in groups on their assignments, within and outside the classroom, as "studying." As one student said, "it was too much fun." Students, especially traditional-aged students, enjoy being involved with their peers. The challenge facing higher education is to take advantage of that understandable inclination by actively involving students in meaningful learning activities within the classroom. A study by Arum and Roska (2011) suggests that we have not yet done so on a scale that would impact student learning in higher education generally.

ADMINISTRATIVE ACTION

6

Substantial improvement in a college's ability to promote student success does not arise by chance. It is the result of a series of intentional, structured, and proactive actions that are consistently applied over the long term (Carey 2005b). The actions described in the preceding chapter do not, of themselves, ensure significant long-term gains in institutional rates of student success. While the leadership of an institution should speak forcefully about the importance of student success (American Association of State Colleges and Universities 2005; Carey 2005b; McLeod and Young 2005), it must also establish a series of policies that support and guide those actions and those who are responsible for implementing them. Without strong support, programs tend to stagnate or fold. The success of an institution reflects the ability of its various programs to improve, endure, and scale up over time in ways that are systematic and aligned to the achievement of the same goal: enhanced student retention and graduation.

In this chapter, we speak of institutional policy in a broad sense. Specific attributes of administrative policy are necessarily a reflection of the particular context within which those actions are taken and the unique values that inspire them. We therefore discuss only those that are generic in the sense that they would apply to most institutions, two- and four-year, and are essential for institutional improvement. Although rates of student retention and graduation, especially in public institutions, are influenced by the actions of state, federal, and in some cases nongovernmental organizations (e.g., private foundations), our focus is on the actions that institutions need to take on their own to improve those rates.

■ Investing in Assessment

First and foremost, improved rates of retention and graduation depend on the investment of institutional resources in those areas of institutional functioning that most directly impact student retention, in particular those pertaining to instructional and academic support (Ryan 2004). Whether budget lines are allocated to pilot programs, to new programs, to greater academic and social support, or to actions that indirectly impact those activities, such investments matter.

Effective investing begins with institutional assessments to pinpoint those aspects of institutional functioning that require improvement.[1] With respect to student retention, an institution needs to assess student experience and its effects on retention. One way to do so is to employ detailed data on student progression through the institution, stratified by student attributes, with data on student experience as provided by the National Survey of Student Engagement and the Community College Survey of Student Engagement, described earlier. Institutions can, of course, modify those surveys or develop their own, tailored to the specifics of their student body and institutional functions.

The use of surveys, whether institutional or purchased from external organizations, should not be a one-time affair. They should part of an ongoing process of assessment, to determine whether actions the college has taken have improved student experience and in turn student retention. This is in part the reasoning underlying the Lumina Foundation for Education's Achieving the Dream initiative, which had participating community colleges begin the process of institutional improvement by first collecting and analyzing data on student performance.[2]

Though useful, surveys are only a first step. They should be followed by a more focused assessment of areas identified as requiring attention—particular courses, first-year experiences, and so forth—and a search for actions that have proved effective in similar institutions in addressing those areas. Many such actions have been described in the preceding chapters.

Another approach to assessment, which relies on readily available data, is the analysis of student transcripts (Banta, Lund, Black, and Oblander 1995; Banta, Jones, and Black 2009; Hagedorn 2005). Analyzing patterns of student progress through the curriculum—for instance, noting when different patterns of course-taking are associated with high or low completion rates—can reveal blockage points in the curriculum (e.g., courses in which performance affects performance in related or subsequent courses or those with high failure or withdrawal rates). When applied to students who leave late as opposed to early in their academic careers, transcript analysis can identify students whose course-taking behavior results in credit progress but insufficient degree credit progress for graduation (Douglas College 2002; Obetz 1998). Since these students tend to change their majors one or more times, a college may institute specific advising or counseling for these students. As applied by Adelman (1999a, 1999b, 2004, 2006), transcript analysis can reveal patterns and intensity of course-taking that shape subsequent performance; it can also, as employed by Chen and Carroll (2005), show how first-generation college students study. In program assessment, it may reveal that the courses making up a program are poorly aligned or articulated (Grinnell College 2008; Reichard 2001).

In a transcript analysis of student course-taking patterns at West Chester University of Pennsylvania, it was found that students in professional programs tended not only to graduate more frequently than did those majoring in liberal arts, but also to take courses in a more orderly fashion (Zhai, Ronco, Feng, and Feiner 2001). Another study of the course-taking patterns of students in an urban community college found that students who were classified as course-shoppers earned lower grade-point averages than other students (Hagedorn at al. 2007).

Another way in which transcripts are being applied to institutional assessment is through the analysis of momentum point attainment (Adelman 1999, 2006; Leinbach and Jenkins 2008). Key points in the curriculum are identified, referred to as momentum points or milestones, whose timely attainment is associated with student progress to degree completion (Ewell 2009). Identifying momentum points enables the institution to break down the longitudinal process of student achievement into a series of concrete, intermediate steps, thereby allowing it to focus on the way different institutional actions should be timed and sequenced to move students to and beyond these points. For many institutions, momentum points may include the successful completion of developmental coursework, the timely declaration of a major, and the earning within particular time periods of a set number of credit hours.

The Washington State Board for Community and Technical Colleges is now employing momentum point analysis of more than eighty-seven thousand first-time community and technical college students who entered the Washington system in the 2001–2 academic year as part of their Student Achievement Initiative. Student attainment benchmarks can thus be established and will be used to assess the progress of each community and technical college in increasing student achievement (Prince, Seppanen, Stephens, and Stewart 2010; Pettit and Prince 2010). At Tacoma Community College, analysis of transcripts has identified six distinct momentum points: passing a basic-skills course, passing a pre-college writing or mathematics course, earning the first fifteen college-level credits, earning the first thirty college-level credits, passing a required mathematics course for a technical or associate degree, and being awarded a degree or a completion-of-apprenticeship certificate. The college's efforts to increase student achievement of each of these momentum points has resulted in gains across each point, ranging from a 7% increase in degree/certificate completion to a 47% increase in basic-skills attainment.[3] Other states such as Indiana and Ohio also plan to use momentum point analysis.[4]

■ Investing in Program Development

A college needs to invest in programs in ways that enable them to develop over time. It should not only support program startup but should also provide incentives and rewards to promote program continuation over time. Too many programs begin but fail to endure. They fade away because the people who initiated them either tire of the effort or leave the institution and are not replaced. A program may also die because of the departure of an administrator whose support was critical to its birth. A program's ability to endure requires a commitment on the part of the institution to provide incentives and rewards over the long term. Without such commitment, programs often fail to be fully implemented, and, even when implemented, fail to continue over time (Shapiro and Levine 1999).[5]

The history of higher education is marked by short-term efforts. Institutions will start a program, often with external funds, but fail to provide it continuing support. The program will last for several years and then fade away. The process is repeated with another innovative effort, perhaps involving some of the same people. Start, stop, start, stop. The resulting cycle of sporadic action generates cynicism among faculty and staff about the nature of institutional improvement and the commitment of institutions to student success. Little wonder, then, that faculty and staff are often reluctant to become involved with new efforts.

Since benefits accrue to the institution from retention-increasing initiatives, a particularly effective form of incentive is that which returns at least some of the benefits to the individuals, programs, or departments responsible for those initiatives. Such incentives can do much to encourage faculty and staff members to collaborate with others in developing new strategies and to become involved with one, once started, or to continue with an initiative over time.[6]

Staying the course, however, is not easy. There are many competing interests that drive institutional action, and many factors—financial, political, and so forth—that constrain them. The recent impact of state budget deficits on higher education is only one instance of external forces constraining the ability of institutions to pursue desirable goals. Nevertheless, an institution that wishes its students to succeed must find ways to support retention-enhancing initiatives over the long term. There are no secret formulas or quick fixes, no easy path that does not require commitment to continuing incentives and rewards. Substantial increases in the rate of student retention and graduation simply take time and the willingness to invest in a range of actions.

Take as an example the development of learning communities. More than most other types of educational reforms, the success of learning communities depends on the willingness and capacity of faculty and, in some cases student-affairs professionals, to work collaboratively, often across departmental lines, developing the materials and activities that make up linked courses (Smith, MacGregor, Matthews, and Gabelnick 2004). Planning and preparation typically requires up to a year of effort prior to the start of the learning community. Such levels of involvement require faculty and staff to add additional time and effort to their already full workloads, or else to reallocate their effort among often competing domains of work (e.g., teaching and research). Unfortunately, incentives and rewards to do so are not common. The promotion and tenure systems of most institutions are not geared to such efforts. Nor are the professional norms of many fields particularly conducive to collaborative activities or interdisciplinary curricular that take faculty outside their own fields (Umbach and Porter 2002). It is for these reasons that many learning communities end up being little more than co-registration programs in which faculty are only tangentially involved.

Although substantial increases in student retention and graduation are not common, some institutions have achieved sizable gains. Between 1997 and 2002, three public institutions and one small private institution increased their graduation rates quite dramatically: Louisiana Tech, a "competitive" doctoral institution, from 35% in 1997 to 55%; Weber State University, a "noncompetitive" institution, from 31% to 45%; Troy University, a "competitive" institution whose undergraduate student body is approximately 33% minority, from 40% to 57%; and Maryville College, from 41% to 65% (Carey 2004). Some institutions have been able to graduate a higher proportion of their students than would be expected by student and institutional attributes alone, or what is referred to as their expected graduation rate (Astin 2005). These can be identified in the *U.S. News and World Report* annual college rankings and a variety of online resources.

A fair number of colleges achieve graduation rates higher than others of similar size, institutional mission, and the like and with similar student bodies and funding (Carey 2005a). Using the data from the Education Trust's College Results Online, Carey (2005b) studied a number of these institutions—specifically Alcorn State University, Elizabeth City State University, St. Mary's University in Texas, Syracuse University, the University of Northern Iowa, and the University of Notre Dame—in order to learn about what actions they took that would account for their higher graduation rates. Each institution identified somewhat different approaches, which arose out of their specific circumstances: Alcorn State University, for instance, worked to improve the freshman and sophomore years; Elizabeth State University stressed the importance of having everyone, in particular the faculty, work to improve retention and graduation; Syracuse University and the University of Northern Iowa pointed to their focus on teaching and student research and the long-term use of assessment data on student retention. But a number of common themes underlay their efforts. First and foremost, each institution was marked by a long-term commitment by campus leaders to make increasing student retention and graduation an institution-wide priority. Moreover, each focused on getting students engaged, especially during the critical first year; and each emphasized the importance of undergraduate teaching and learning, and the need for continuous monitoring and utilization of data on student progress, both to help students and to make needed changes in institutional practices and policies (Carey 2005b, p. 2).[7]

■ Investing in Faculty Development

Since student success is primarily a function of success in the classroom and the ability of the faculty to promote that success, it follows that any long-term strategy to enhance student retention must involve long-term investment in faculty development. Colleges already invest in a range of development activities. What matters, however, is their effectiveness in promoting faculty skills and the degree to which faculty avail themselves of such activities. The fact is participation in faculty development on many campuses is spotty. This reflects the many demands on faculty and the limited time faculty have to devote to development activities. Recall that community college faculty typically teach fifteen or more hours per week and have three if not more preparations. Furthermore, many faculty in four-year institutions are under increasing pressure to carry out research and publish.

Outside of making participation in development activities a requirement (as do those institutions noted in chapter 5), participation can be enhanced by a variety of incentives, such as salary increases, promotions and tenure considerations. Reduced teaching or workloads are particularly useful when faculty and staff are asked to initiate new courses or programs. Without some form of relief, most faculty simply cannot spare the time and energy needed for the development of new or redesigned initiatives.

■ Implementation of Institutional Action

Knowing what actions or programs in which to invest is one thing. Knowing how to successfully implement a program is another. Here we deal with program implementation, first, in ways that promote their effectiveness; second, in ways that enable programs to endure over time; and third, in ways that enhance the possibility that they can be scaled up over time. In this instance we will use the example of learning communities since effective learning communities require substantial restructuring of both curriculum and pedagogy and a good deal of collaboration among faculty and often between faculty and student-affairs professionals (Hurd and Stein 2004; Knight 2003; Shapiro and Levine 1999; Levine-Laufgraben and Shapiro 2004).[8] As a result, they often pose some of the most difficult challenges in being effectively implemented. Nevertheless, what applies to the implementation of learning communities can be said to apply to programs generally.

Implementing to Succeed

Successful programs do not occur overnight. They often take three to four years to become fully effective. Typically, the establishment of a learning community requires up to a year of planning, in which faculty, together with staff where appropriate, build the curriculum and deal with other issues, including the recruitment and training of faculty and staff, course selection and timing, schedules, registration of students, and publicity and marketing (Shapiro and Levine 1999). The first year of implementation is typically one of learning how to deal with administrative issues, matters of coherence, curriculum changes, and the like—all characteristic of starting a new effort. Presuming some form of formative as well as summative assessment, the second year is one of modification and fine-tuning. By the third year, faculty and staff have learned what works best, and it is possible to say the program has been implemented.

The developmental period of program implementation is characteristic of virtually all new initiatives. Reading about a program and talking to other people about it is no substitute for the experience that comes from trying to implement the program in a specific context with a specific group of faculty, staff, and students. In the case of learning communities, the developmental period reflects the many issues surrounding collaboration among individuals from different fields of study and areas of responsibility. Groups seeking to implement a new program, therefore, should plan for that developmental period and make it clear to the sources of their funding that making judgments about the program's effectiveness must wait until the end of that period.

Successful implementation also requires that the stage be set in ways that are sensitive to campus culture and politics. The first questions one must ask are where and how a program should begin. Regarding the "where," those administering the program should pick a location in the program map of the institution or in a curriculum that will provide the most receptive context for the program in its initial implementation. At the same time, the program or action should be located in the temporal part of student experience most likely to yield the greatest benefit. For learning communities, indeed for most programs whose goal it is to enhance student retention, that location is typically in the first year. Where in the first year depends on the specific goals of the program. Supplemental instruction, for example, is located either in key gateway or foundational courses of the first semester or in those introductory/foundational courses that exhibit high failure rates. For learning communities, much depends on the intended audience. If the audience consists of students who enter academically underprepared, learning communities are commonly located both in basic skills and, where possible, in one or more content courses to which those basic skills can be applied.

As to "how" of starting a program, the best advice is to start small. Begin it as a demonstration or pilot program. Finding support for such a program is easier than for larger initiatives, because such support does not commit the institution to permanent funding. In small programs, there are relatively few administrative and logistic problems, which often overwhelm larger programs. A small program is much easier to manage in its early stages, while those involved are still figuring out how to make it work well. It is also less intrusive, perhaps less challenging to the existing structure and forms of practice. As a result, a small program is less likely to generate the sorts of resistance that new actions sometimes encounter. This is particularly true of initiatives like learning communities that call for substantial curricular reform. Hence, the ability of a program to demonstrate its effectiveness at the end of the pilot period is of prime importance, as subsequent funding depends on evidence of the benefits accrued to the institution by its initial investment and the likelihood of further benefits from continuing investment.

This last observation leads to another rule of effective implementation, namely, assess and use the resulting data to improve. All programs, however well planned, can improve with experience. But to learn from experience one needs to invest in formative assessment, or what is often referred to as assessment to improve. This can take on a variety of forms, from survey questionnaires to focus groups, interviews, and observations.[9] An assessment, regardless of its specific form, should reveal what was not known beforehand and what needs to be improved. Qualitative forms of assessment are particularly useful in this regard because they allow those in charge of a program to hear from the students to whom the program is directed (Chism and Banta 2007; Harper 2007). Those voices are most powerful when they represent what students would say to each other when no one else is around, as they might in ethnographic focus groups. This is especially important when the program serves minority students (O'Neil Green 2007; Perna 2007). When matched with other data that confirm the relationship of those experiences to outcomes, qualitative assessment provides a powerful tool for program improvement (St. John 2006).

All this leads to a simple rule: the goal of initial implementation is to succeed. Programs are unlikely to garner the support they need to continue if they are unable to demonstrate early success and, by implication, the value of added investment to promote greater success for more students. That is why, among other issues already discussed, it is wise to recruit the initial participants carefully. People make programs succeed, and no participants

are more important to program success than those who take on the responsibility of initiating the program.

A word about the recruitment and training of faculty and staff. Learning
communities, in particular those that adopt collaborative learning pedagogies, require that faculty not only know the "rules" that govern learning
communities (e.g., linked syllabi, common grading procedures) but also acquire a range of pedagogical and assessment skills they may not otherwise
possess. For this reason, as we saw in chapter 5, a number of institutions
invest in development programs for faculty and staff who will be participating in a learning community. Almost any new program, of course, requires
recruitment and training of those who will be in charge. The effectiveness
of any program ultimately reflects the commitment and skills of those
charged with implementing it.

Implementing to Endure

Clearly, there is little point in beginning a program if it does not endure.
Effective implementation must enhance the likelihood that the program
will endure beyond not only its initial pilot phase but also when those who
first initiated the program or action are no longer involved. Among relevant
steps to this end are determining where the program is to be located; how
others can be encouraged over time to participate in the program and share,
or even take over, responsibility for the program; and how it can be demonstrated that the program is worth supporting over the long term.

A common reason for the failure of programs to endure is that they have
been unable to locate themselves, administratively or instructionally, in a
place that matters. They remain at the margins of institutional life and can
easily be cut when resources are limited. It is therefore in the program's
long-term interest to be located in the center of institutional life or at close
to it as possible. Administratively this means that the program should fall
within the purview of a central office or line of responsibility, whether in
academic or student affairs. Instructionally, it should normally be located
in the academic mainstream of the institution where its impact is likely
to be most strongly felt and therefore of greatest benefit to the institution.
As regards student retention, it follows that programs are more likely to
endure when they are located in the first year and are directed to issues
or student populations that are central to the mission of the institution
(e.g., low-income students, underserved students, honors students).

But location alone is not enough. Too often, a programs folds because only one or two persons are responsible for it, and when those persons leave the institution or tire of running the program, no one else steps in. As suggested above, the initial participants need to bring in other faculty or staff and allow them to gradually take over responsibility. It is often difficult for the initiators of a program to cede control, if only because they feel particularly responsible for both the character and direction of the program and may be unwilling to let others modify it. Yet this sharing and eventually turning over responsibility to others is precisely what is required for programs to endure.

A program's ability to endure ultimately resides in its ability to demonstrate its value to the institution and the various audiences it serves and therefore to prove itself worthy of long-term support. Here, summative assessment, or assessment to prove, is critical. Unlike assessment to improve, which is directed specifically to the staff responsible for a program's operation, assessment to prove is directed to a range of audiences whose support or participation is needed for the program to continue. These audiences may include administrators, faculty, staff, students, and sometimes parents. Since different audiences often use different criteria in judging a program's benefits, the assessment evidence each receives should also differ in both content and type.

Clearly the most important audience for program survival is the administrative one, in particular the leadership of an institution. The evidence of program success that matters most to that audience is typically determined by student satisfaction, and increased retention and graduation. But even that evidence may not be enough. It is sometimes necessary to also provide evidence of a program's financial returns to the institution's investment. One approach is to translate increased retention into projected increased direct and indirect revenue, which should result from increased rates of graduation (Center for Student Success 2007, pp. 139–45). The information received by the administrative audience must include easily interpreted quantitative evidence of program effectiveness that is seen as representative and reliable. Though qualitative data may be useful, in this case numbers matter more.

Faculty and staff audiences require somewhat different information to be convinced of the value of a program or course of action. While they also want to know whether the program improves student success, what they take success to mean may differ. For instance, it may mean increased learning or greater course success as well as increased retention. Faculty and staff concerns may also center on the degree of work entailed in becoming part of a program. Do they have time to participate in the program, given their current obligations? Many may also want to know whether their participation is intrinsically beneficial. Is it personally worth doing? All these concerns affect the likelihood of other faculty and staff becoming involved in the program over time. Unless they see their participation as both feasible and beneficial, a program is unlikely to endure beyond those who initiate it. Some faculty and staff may decide to participate because of perceived intrinsic benefits, but for a program's long-term success, institutional incentives and support are essential.

Faculty and staff require both quantitative and qualitative data. Beyond the numbers, they need to hear firsthand the experiences of those already participating in the program. It is therefore useful to host workshops, lunches, and the like, where interested faculty and staff can meet and talk to current program participants. Held consistently (e.g., once a year) in an environment of institutional support, such events are important to the recruitment of new faculty who can assume responsibility as the initiators of the program step aside.

In some cases, the audience for a program's assessment may be students whom the program seeks to attract. As in the case with faculty and staff, the data one needs to convey to students should be varied in both type and character. Is the program beneficial? Is it fun? Is it too hard? These are but a few of the questions students may have about the program. Again like faculty and staff, students need to hear that information from other students either directly, through meetings, or indirectly through printed or visual means. In this regard, encouraging students to participate in a program is very much akin to what college admission staff do in encouraging people to apply for admission to the institution. This is clearly true of first-year programs, whose likely participants are prospective students who may be undecided either about attending the institution or participating in the program. The audience for this kind of information may also include parents or guardians who want to know whether program participation is beneficial to their child. In any case, no program can endure without a sufficient number of student participants.

Implementing to Scale Up
Even if a program endures, it does follow that it will be able to scale up to a level where it substantially improves the overall retention rate of an institu-

tion. Too often, certain programs endure but have a relatively minor impact on the overall rate of institutional student retention and graduation. Some programs, of course, are focused on very specific and quite small student subpopulations; others may respond to particular issues that only affect a few students. But those that are intended to have broader impact often fail to do so.

The ability of a program to scale up depends on a variety of factors, not the least of which is the character of the setting in which it is housed. Smaller, more homogeneous settings, such as small private colleges, are generally more conducive to program scalability than are more diverse institutions, such as large research universities. In large institutions it is often more difficult to find common agreement among a wide range of members or units that would facilitate scalability. The multiple missions in such an institution sometimes reflect quite different views of appropriate action, which are represented in a particular field of study or functional unit.

If there is one temporal location, one point in the student college career, where program scalability is more likely to occur, it is the first year of college, when students are taking a relatively common set of introductory or core courses, regardless of major. So programs like freshmen seminars, supplemental instruction connected to introductory courses, and, to some degree, first-year learning communities have scaled up more successfully than other initiatives. After the first year, students often part ways into their separate majors with their own requirements and associated cultures. The logic of location applies as well to different majors. Programs are then more likely to scale up if located where they can be reached by most if not all students who major in a particular field of study. Whether for beginners or more advanced students, programs should be located in the mainstream, not at the margins, of institutional academic and social life.[10]

Another way to think about location is to ask where, in an institution a program or course of action will most likely connect with and influence other parts of the institution. These connections and the networks of affiliation they provide enable a program to directly and indirectly affect other parts of the institution and therefore other students not immediately served by a program. Much like intersecting streets in a city, networks in a college or university provide wide-ranging access to other students, faculty, and staff. First-year programs such as freshman seminars, interdisciplinary learning communities, and introductory gateway courses are good locations for such networks. By contrast, programs located in the academic side streets of an institution often find themselves isolated.

Scaling up a program, though never easy, is considerably less difficult when it becomes a continuing and normal part of institutional operation and thus qualifies for financial support. An academic program is most likely to achieve this status when it becomes a required part of student experience. This, however, typically requires that ownership of the program be shared by many, not just those who initiated the program. Others must also buy into it. Invariably, shared ownership means that compromises have to be made in the character of a program or in its being differentiated in ways that various stakeholders perceive as serving their specific needs. Failure to make such compromises not only hinders a program's ability to scale up but also threatens to undermine its very existence. As a general rule, effective implementation is more likely to occur when those responsible perceive themselves as having a voice in the program and the way it is implemented.

The ability to scale up depends as well on the effort required by faculty, staff, and departments to adopt a program. Programs that require a substantial effort rarely, if ever, expand beyond a limited number of faculty and academic programs. Here is where technology matters. Take, as an example, the use of early warning systems within classrooms to identify students who are struggling and in need of assistance. Most strategies require a good deal of effort on the part of individual faculty, not all of whom have either the time or the disposition to use those strategies. This is but one reason why a web-based program like the Signals Project at Purdue University is so promising. Once faculty place their quizzes or one-minute papers online, the work entailed in using them is greatly diminished. Furthermore, the technology can be employed in a great many courses regardless of content.

In the final analysis, the ability of a program to scale up depends on assessment data that proves the worth of the program to its stakeholders and to the institution writ large. Without acceptable evidence of worth, it is very difficult, if not impossible, for programs to scale up beyond the setting in which they are first established.[11] The learning communities at Iowa State University, for example, were able to grow over time in part because they were able to garner a portion of the additional revenue they generated for the university from the proven gain in persistence of learning community students.[12]

Implementing the University College at Indiana
University—Purdue University Indianapolis

The University College (UC) is the academic unit at IUPUI that provides a common gateway to the academic programs available to entering students. Begun in 1997 following a Faculty Council vote establishing the college, it was seen as a way to address the low rate of retention and graduation at the university. The college faculty are recruited from senior faculty throughout the university. Over the years, the college has instituted a variety of programs, including mandatory placement testing and orientation before classes begin, and a first year seminar required of all entering students, which forms the basis of a learning community linking the seminar to another course such as writing, speech, or math. Emphasis is placed on collaboration and shared learning. Begun with five learning communities, the college now includes more than 120, involving nearly all first-year students. Each seminar is team-taught by a faculty member, a librarian, an academic adviser, and a peer mentor. The peer mentors, now numbering over 200, are an important component of the college. They are required to take a four-semester sequence of four courses, taught by faculty, in mentoring, collaborative learning, leadership development, and research. At the same time, faculty who teach courses in the UC can participate in a faculty development program (Gateway Program), geared to the teaching of new students. In addition, academic advisers meet with the students in their learning community over the sixteen weeks of the semester. Finally, the college maintains a web-based early warning system that calls for faculty to alert support staff of student difficulties at the third week of the first semester and again at the midpoint of the semester. A range of support is provided. Some students, for instance, choose to participate in a Summer Bridge Program, based on a model developed at Brooklyn College, before entering the UC. Others, whose first-year performance is marginal, can participate in a structured learning-assistance program (a modified form of Supplemental Instruction developed at Ferris State University) in their second year and possibly even in their third. The effectiveness of the UC is clear: at its outset, only 50% of first-year students continued to the second year, whereas over 70% do so currently. Over the same period, the six-year graduation rate from the university doubled.

Successfully implementing the UC, however, took time, patience, and the considerable skills of the dean, Scott Evenbeck, and the faculty of the college. First, they established the principle that the UC would offer very few classes on its own but would organize the curriculum, with courses taught by IUPUI faculty, and coordinate college activities. In doing so, it avoided the problems of marginalization that sometimes affects separate first-year colleges in university settings. Second, the UC stresses the importance of assessment to monitor, modify, and improve. Assessment is ongoing, multifaceted, systematic, and mandatory, reflecting a culture of evidence that pervades the way the college goes about its business. The faculty do not leave assessment to chance or leave data unused. They continually ask how programs can be improved, and make improvements when these are called for. Third, data are shared with all levels of the university—faculty, staff, and administration—not only to document the college's effectiveness and but also to generate the ongoing support that it requires to succeed, endure, and scale up. As a result, the college has grown and has ongoing funding that is integrated into the university budget.

■ Timing of Institutional Action

To what point in the student career should institutions direct their actions? Here the answer is clear. Actions should be directed primarily to the first year of college, indeed to the first semester or quarter of that year and, if possible, to the period just before entry to college.[13]

The First Year of College

The first year, as noted earlier, has long been recognized as a key period in student learning and retention (e.g., Barefoot et al. 2005; Upcraft, Gardner, and Barefoot 2004). Yet it is the period in which student attrition is typically the highest. Even when students continue, their experiences during the first year almost always influence the attrition that follows. Therefore, investments in that year are most likely to yield the greatest gains in retention and in turn the largest returns to the institution. One such return is the revenue that results from increased retention beyond the first year and the consequent reduction in costs associated recruiting students.[14]

It is therefore more than a bit disappointing that Upcraft, Gardner, Barefoot, and Associates (2005), in their review of the landscape of first-year programs, found that retention rates of first-year students are still too low, and that many institutions still fail to give sufficiently high priority to the first year. Too many institutions, especially the larger universities, invest in ways that appear to undermine instructional and academic activities. This is most evident in the hiring of part-time or adjunct faculty for first-year classrooms or the assignment of the least experienced junior faculty to those classrooms (Eagan and Jaeger 2008, 2009; Jaeger and Eagan 2009; Jaeger and Hinz 2008). It can also be seen in the frequency of large lecture classes during the first year, even when evidence suggests that those settings are not very effective in promoting student engagement, learning, or retention. Though there are more than a few exceptions, investment in instructional and academic support is too often neither consistent nor systematic. More important, it often runs counter to what we know about the attributes of an effective first year of college. Simply put, the conditions in which too many first-year students are placed are not particularly conducive to student success.[15] First-year classes are not challenging enough, are poorly connected to existing academic and social support, do not provide sufficient and timely feedback to students and faculty about student performance, and fail to actively involve students in learning.

An increasing number of institutions, however, are not only instituting first-year seminars such as those described by Upcraft, Gardner, and Associates (1989), but also paying attention to the many gateway courses whose successful completion plays a major role in subsequent student success. Some institutions focus on those courses that have high failure, withdrawal, or drop rates. Some, as noted earlier, invest in faculty development programs to enhance the pedagogical and assessment skills faculty bring to first-year classrooms. In these and other cases, institutions often redesign courses, connect them to support services, or include them in first-year learning communities (Twigg 2005; Tinto, Goodsell, and Russo 1993; Tinto and Goodsell 1994; Tinto and Russo 1994; Tinto 1997). John Gardner's Foundations of Excellence program works with two- and four-year colleges to redesign the first year. Like the Lumina Foundation for Education's Achieving the Dream initiative, it asks institutions to analyze institutional data as a beginning point of reform. Carol Twigg's National Center for Academic Transformation explores the effective use of information technology to improve student learning in first-year introductory courses (Twigg 2005).[16]

Beyond the widespread use of orientation programs, institutions are more commonly instituting summer bridge programs, which reach out to high-school students. Syracuse University's Haudenosaunee Promise program and the University of Southern California's Neighborhood Academic

Initiative are two examples. The second of these, established in 1989, is a six-year program designed to prepare low-income middle- and high-school students from the surrounding neighborhood for admission to the university. Its Pre-College Enrichment Academy provides helps students to acquire the academic skills they need to succeed in higher education.[17]

The College Now program in New York pursues the same goal by developing partnerships between New York City public high schools with one or more of the seventeen City University of New York (CUNY) colleges. Eligible students are offered a number of ways to improve their high-school performance and get a jump start on college. These involve taking CUNY courses; campus-based tours and cultural events, such as theater or dance performances; and even scholarship offers. Students who participate in College Now are reported to do better, on average, than their counterparts once they're in college.[18] In California, several colleges provide support for high-school students whose Early Assessment Program results indicate the need for additional academic work. The Long Beach Promise program brings together faculty and staff of Long Beach Unified School District, Long Beach City College, and California State University–Long Beach to reach out to potential students and their families and help students gain access to either the college or the university. Its strategies include courses taught in the senior year of high school, summer bridge programs for those not yet ready for college-level work, targeted academic advising and counseling, and faculty professional development.[19]

Going Beyond the First Year
The emphasis here on the first year of college should not be taken to suggest that there is little institutions can do to promote student retention beyond that year. Enhancing student retention requires that institutions consider all phases of student experience, from entry to completion (Bowen, Chingos, and McPherson 2009; Gardner, Van der Veer, and Associates 1997; Hunter et al. 2010; Schreiner and Pattengale 2000; Tobolowsky and Cox 2007).[20] But before we consider what institutions can do to address retention beyond the first year, several caveats are called for. First, the very notion that students progress through an institution in yearly blocks of time or curriculum is problematic, at least as it applies to many low-income students and those attending community colleges. For those students, there is no sophomore year, junior year and so on, but a series of courses to be completed as they work toward a degree or certificate; their college years

are commonly measured one course at a time. Consequently, to frame a discussion about student retention in terms of years is, in effect, to limit our thinking about what is possible. Second, even if we begin the conversation about retention with the sophomore year, we should not lose sight of the fact that not all second-year students have reached the same level. Some have not earned enough credits to be classified as a sophomore (Adelman 2006). They begin their second year as sophomores in name only.[21] Their not having completed the requirements is clearly a reflection of what happened or did not happen during their first year of college. Adelman (2006, 2007) refers to this situation as the "qualitative" aspect of retention. Third, one cannot effectively address the needs of students beyond the first year without knowing what they experienced and achieved during that year. Experience and achievement are necessarily linked.[22] Finally, though the term "sophomore slump" has become part of the popular lexicon of student experience in college, it is not clear that all or even most students experience a slump in their second year. The slump appears to reflect the experience of traditional-aged students, especially those attending four-year institutions, rather than that of older students and those who have multiple obligations beyond the campus. Even among the former, the sophomore slump probably reflects a number of different issues including the developmental challenges students face as they mature; the need to choose a major field of study and, by extension, a possible career; and the increased academic demands of the second year of study (Freedman 1956; Gahagan and Hunter 2006; Graunke and Woolsey 2005; Lemons and Richmond 1987; Richmond and Lemons 1985; and Schaller 2005). In response, institutions such as Beloit College, Brandeis University, Bridgewater State College, Colgate University, Emory University, Kennesaw State University, McPherson College, Rensselaer Polytechnic Institute, Southern Arkansas University, Stony Brook University, Stanford University, Syracuse University, Texas Christian University, the University of Cincinnati, and the University of Washington, among many others, have offered academic support, advising, counseling, and career counseling for students in their second year of college.[23]

Perhaps the most pressing issue facing sophomores is that of selecting a major (e.g., Kramer 2000; Gardner 2000; Gordon 2007, 2009). For that reason many institutions focus their efforts for second-year students on academic advising; among these are Beloit College, Harvard University, Macalester College, McPherson College, the University of Central Florida, the University of Michigan, the University of Tennessee Knoxville, and the University of Washington.[24] The University of Washington's Individualized Second-Year Advising Program helps students develop an educational plan to guide their studies throughout their stay at the university. At McPherson College, students take a Sophomore Seminar that stresses developing college life skills, with specific emphasis on leadership, networking, mentoring, and ethics. The seminar deals with career planning, including resume and letter writing, interviewing, job searching, and exploring internship opportunities; and it includes service learning, with significant time in the course spent participating in a service project. In the Stony Brook University Sophomore Seminar, students are required to attend the Academic and Pre-Professional Advising Center's "Major Decisions Week," which includes workshops, activities, and events focused on selecting a major. Through this week, every academic department, as well as special-interest departments, converge in one forum to connect with students.[25]

Advising, however, is not merely helping students select a major. It also involves changing a major. As best we know, about 50% to 60% of college students change their major at least once, more than a few of them several times over the course of their college career. A sampling of transcripts of those students who leave without completing their degree, even though they are well into their third or even fourth year, often reveals that many have changed their majors more than once but have insufficient degree credits to graduate. When this is the case, it is likely that the underlying issue is one of ineffective advising, whether for students seeking to change their major or those who began college undecided about their choice of study. In any case, effective advising is essential for students throughout their journey through college. Advising carried out within an advising center staffed by professional advisers must be aligned with the advising that takes place within programs of study. Similarly, students who seek to transfer between institutions, as well as those who take courses from more than one institution (known as "swirling") need consistent advice. Too often, advising between programs or between institutions is a hit-or-miss affair. Alignment of advising matters.

For students who have not fared well academically in the first year, some institutions have established first-to-second-year bridge programs, targeted academic assistance, and other support. These programs, such as the Student Success Initiative at Syracuse University provide additional academic support to promote student success beyond that provided in the first year.

Unlike those programs that rely on pre-college records or entry assessment tests to predict the likelihood of academic difficulty, first-to-second-year bridge programs rely solely on academic performance in the first year, thus capturing students whose academic struggles were not predicted earlier. In this way, they resemble early warning systems, which rely on classroom performance to trigger academic support. Northeastern State University and other institutions provide additional academic support during the sophomore year. Students on academic probation are required to meet regularly with an Academic Commitment Specialist, who works with them to analyze transcripts, explore major options, and interpret the institution's academic forgiveness policy. Students receive personalized attention and are directed toward issue-specific campus resources as needed.

Institutions such as Colgate University, Colorado College, Duke University, and Stanford University take a somewhat different tack to enhance students' academic engagement in the second year. Stanford University's Sophomore College, for instance, offers sophomores the opportunity to study intensively in small groups with Stanford faculty for several weeks before the beginning of the fall quarter. Each Sophomore College course enrolls twelve to fourteen students, who receive two units of credit for the course. In addition to faculty instructors, each section has two upper-class Sophomore College Assistants, who work with the faculty and serve as peer advisers to the participants. Students and staff live together in a Stanford residence hall and participate in morning classes, required field trips, and other course activities.

Another issue shaping student retention beyond the first year has to do with the alignment of courses within programs, in particular how the acquisition of knowledge and skills in one course is a necessary condition for success in the following courses to which it is linked. The common specification of course prerequisites and the listing of course numbers suggest a logical sequence of course taking. Yet programs of study rarely make explicit the way courses within a program are related to each other, empirically document the degree to which they are associated with success in those courses, or restructure those courses to better promote student progress through the program. The courses are rarely aligned, either in content or in pedagogy, in ways that promote the successful completion of sequential courses in the first year and beyond. This lack of integration occurs not only within programs of study but within developmental course sequences as well. It is still too often the case that students will success-fully complete their developmental course sequence only to struggle and fail in the course to which the successful completion of that developmental sequence is a requirement.[26]

A related issue concerns the experience of those students who transfer to a four-year institution. Several issues that shape the experience of trans-fer students have already been noted. To address their needs, a number of institutions, such as Richard Stockton College of New Jersey, Sacred Heart University, the University of South Carolina, and the University of Texas at Dallas have turned to transfer student centers, transfer student semi-nars, and a variety of programs designed to assist transfer students' move-ment into and through the institution. Universities such as Cleveland State University work with nearby community colleges to establish structured programs within the community colleges that would automatically lead to admission to the university.[27] Similarly, a number of states, including Arizona, New Jersey, Ohio, and Washington, have engaged in systematic transfer and articulation reform; the resulting legislation requires two-year institutions to offer transfer associate degrees, which allow students both to earn an associate degree and to transfer seamlessly into a state university with junior status (Kisker, Wagoner, and Cohen 2011).

■ Organizing for Student Retention

Studies of effective institutions tell us that improvement in rates of stu-dent retention and graduation is achieved not merely by the actions taken but also by the way those actions are organized (Carey 2005a, 2005b; Jen-kins 2006; Kuh et al. 2005). It bears repeating that effective institutions are intentional, structured, and proactive in their pursuit of student success. They collect and utilize data on student success, develop plans of action to enhance success, and actively pursue that goal. They assess their efforts, monitor their progress in promoting student success, and adjust their ac-tions accordingly. Rather than wait for students to avail themselves of ser-vices, effective institutions make programs such as freshman seminars and first-year learning communities a required part of student experience when such participation has been shown to benefit students (Zeidenberg, Jen-kins, and Calcagno 2007). At the same time, they institute systems such as early warning that enable them to take action early enough to make a differ-ence in the success of their students.[28]

Systematic Action

Effective institutions are systematic in their approach. Their actions are not piecemeal but encompass the full range of actions that demonstrably assist students in their pursuit of a college degree or certificate. As argued in chapter 1, student retention and graduation are most likely to occur when four conditions are met: that students experience high and clear expectations; that they find needed academic and social support; that they are assessed and provided with frequent feedback about their progress; and that they are socially and academically involved in the life of the institution, especially in the classrooms of the campus. Establishing these conditions requires, in turn, a range of actions, many of which are described in chapters 2–5. To ensure significant gains in student retention, all those conditions must be present on campus for all students. Regrettably, institutions tend to invest more in some actions than in others and do so in ways that are more likely to involve student affairs than academic affairs. Often it is the classroom that is neglected, even though there is more than enough evidence to support the claim that it is the one place in which all four of those conditions must apply.

Alignment of Action

Just as learning communities require coherent alignment of its courses, effective institutional action requires alignment of its actions, so that those actions and the persons and offices responsible for them work together in a coherent manner. The total effect of various actions should be as great if not greater than the sum of the individual actions. Unfortunately, it is often less, because programs may act in discordant or even contradictory ways.

A study of over 150,000 students in three cohorts of first-time Florida community-college students who enrolled in 1998, 1999, and 2000 provides concrete evidence of the importance of alignment (Bailey and Alfonso 2005; Bailey et al. 2005; Jenkins 2006). Among the community colleges studied, several were identified as performing better than one would expect, given their attributes and the students they served, while several others were identified as performing less well than expected. These colleges were compared on a variety of measures in order to ascertain what management practices distinguished the better from the worse performing groups. To quote Jenkins (2006), "the key to a college's effectiveness is not whether it adopts particular policies or practices, but how well it aligns and manages all of its programs and services to support student success" (Jenkins 2006, p. vi).

The need for alignment is one reason why institutions establish offices, positions, committees, or teams to oversee their student success actions. Ensuring alignment and interconnectedness between various actions requires working with representatives from all areas of a college whose actions impact student success. Some institutions also establish subcommittees, offices, or positions within each functional area of the institution to guide the actions within that area. In this instance, the campus-wide committee becomes a steering committee that coordinates the work of those other committees. Unfortunately, though a recent study of retention practices among four-year institutions found that nearly 60% of campuses surveyed had a designated retention coordinator, an average of only one-third full-time equivalent was allocated to that role, and most coordinators were "given little to no authority to implement new program initiatives" (College Board 2009, p. 1; see also Hossler et al. 2010).

Another important function of a committee or office is to oversee research and assessment activities related to student success. In some cases, a committee or office will direct or carry out research on the nature of student success on campus, construct a detailed inventory of actions on campus directed toward student success, and oversee the assessment of those actions. In other cases, they will also serve as a center for sharing information about student success and actions that can be taken to enhance it. In this latter regard, some offices or committees will sponsor workshops on campus for various audiences as a way of advancing awareness of the issue and also generating willingness to initiate or join others in relevant actions.

Whatever their specific function, student success committees and the like are most effective when given some authority to initiate actions. Not all have such authority. Recently, the Indiana University Project on Student Success reported results of a College Board–sponsored survey of 275 four-year institutions in the states of California, Georgia, Indiana, New York, and Texas; the survey sought to ascertain how four-year institutions organized themselves around retention efforts and to determine what sorts of policies and practices they had implemented (Hossler, Ziskin, and Orehovec 2007). Though more than 70% of the institutions reported having a retention committee that attempted to coordinate various efforts on campus, barely more than 40% of such committees had at least some authority to implement new initiatives, and only 25% had the authority to fund new initiatives.

But the authority to initiate action should not take the place of actions initiated by others. Since individuals nearly always support what they create, an organizing committee, office, or team should see its work as facilitating the actions of other offices and persons. Its ability to take or initiate action should generally result from the way it provides targeted incentives or resources that promote the actions of others.

Alignment in the First Year of College

At no time is alignment more important than during the first year of college. But achieving alignment is often difficult because of the various functional units and programs of study who each make a claim on determining the direction of particular first-year actions. For this reason, a number of institutions, mostly four-year, have established committees to oversee first-year initiatives; in some cases a position such as dean of the first year has been created. Other institutions, such as North Carolina State University at Raleigh, have taken the logic of a first-year program one step farther, placing it within a separate organizational structure, a first-year college, which is charged with overseeing all activities within that year.

One of the many virtues of such an organizational structure is that decisions about first-year programs fall within that structure and are therefore amenable to integration and alignment. Whereas most conversations about the first year start with questions such as whether or not to have a freshman seminar or a first-year learning community, the existence of a separate college enables the institution to ask a more fundamental question, namely, what is the purpose or mission of the first year of college? Having answered that question, one can then ask how the first year should be organized to achieve its mission. Few institutions, however, begin conversations about the first year in this manner, so discussions about possible first-year initiatives are decontextualized, and subsequent initiatives typically end up as add-ons to existing modes of practice that do little to change that practice. Such initiatives often run into considerable resistance from established patterns of academic practice and, even when established, have less impact than they might.

This is true as well for students who are the object of those initiatives. To the degree that they perceive a first-year initiative as merely an add-on, whether it be a freshman seminar or some other program, they will tend to discount its value and therefore invest little energy in it, especially if it does not yield credits toward the completion of a program or degree. Beginning with the foundational question of mission, by contrast, leads to a much richer conversation, in which possible actions can be discussed within the context of the broader mission of the first year and, in turn, of the college experience generally. Having answered the question of mission and decided how the first year should be organized to achieve it, one can then ask, for instance, whether a freshman seminar is necessary. If the answer is yes, one then asks the contextualized question, how the freshman seminar should be organized.

The point of the preceding conversation is not simply to ask whether a first-year seminar or any other initiative should be part of the first year of college. Rather, it is to argue that all such questions should emerge from more fundamental questions about the first year that are too rarely asked on most campuses. Treating the first year as a distinct educational and organizational unit enables those sorts of questions to be more easily posed and answered and, more important, greatly facilitates the integration and alignment of actions.

A number of institutions have indeed taken the first-year seminar or, more specifically, the ideas that inform it to restructure the freshman year. The Foundations of Excellence project by the Policy Center on the First Year of College, through a process of institutional self-study and guided inquiry, has worked with over three hundred colleges, both two- and four-year, to rethink their first year in order to enhance student learning and retention.[29]

The growing popularity of first-year learning communities suggests that in their own way, when fully integrated and connected to existing academic and support services, they act like a mini-first-year college. This is particularly true of living-learning communities, when participating students share a residence. Some programs, indeed some institutions, have implemented learning communities over the entire first year course of study. In effect, they have used learning communities as the organizational structure for first-year course alignment. Perhaps even more important, such learning community programs also provide a curricular vehicle for the development of more effective interdisciplinary programs of study.

Wagner College—Redesigning the First Year of College Experience around Learning Communities

The Wagner Plan for the Practical Liberal Arts, begun in 1998, incorporates learning communities at three points in the undergraduate curriculum: in the first semester, at an intermediate point (between spring of the first year and the senior year), and during the senior year in conjunction with the major. The first-year program is unique in that it incorporates many features that are seen as optimal practices in higher education. First, three courses are linked with an interdisciplinary theme, taught by two full-time faculty from two different disciplines. All courses meet General Education requirements. Second, students in each learning community engage in an experiential learning component, which is designed by the faculty members and incorporates the theme of the learning community (minimum of 30 hours). These components may take the form of service learning, community-based learning, community research, field trips, or a mixture of these. Third, one of the courses is a writing-intensive reflective tutorial, in which students are asked to reflect on, and write about, the connections between what they are learning in the classroom (theory) and what they are seeing and doing in the community/field (practice). Fourth, the faculty members serve as academic advisers for the students until the students declare a major.

Focusing on faculty development has been an important element in the creation and sustainability of the First-Year Program, as faculty shape the experiential component of each learning community, and are responsible for a writing-intensive course. Faculty participate in a two-day retreat in May of each year, and in monthly meetings to share best practices during the fall semester. Two meetings are held each spring semester to focus on an aspect of pedagogy and plan for the fall semester. These allow for vital communication across departments and disciplines, and among experienced faculty and those who are new to the program. A faculty leader of the program coordinates with administrators, who provide support for locating experiential learning sites (such as community agencies, schools, museums, and city offices) and building partnerships with them, and for student advising. As it takes time for the experiential learning component to gel, faculty teams are expected to teach together for three years, learning from their own experiences and refining their procedures each year. The First-Year Program Review Committee, comprising faculty and administrators, assists in selecting and forming learning communities, plans agendas for meetings and retreats, allocates funds for expenses associated with experiential learning components, and reviews syllabi to determine that the goals of the program are met.

In addition to the courses in each learning community, a goal of the First-Year Program is to "support the College's commitment to citizenship, inter-culturalism, and service to society by promoting discussion of issues related to diversity" (Wagner College 2010). All first-year students attend Theater Night, a theatrical production by students in the Theater Department. The show and topics change each year, but the production always includes a talk-back session with the cast, director, or writer, so that reactions and ideas can be discussed in a large-group setting, then followed up later in individual learning communities.

First-Year Academies at LaGuardia Community College
The first-year program at LaGuardia Community College seeks to improve student success by fostering seamless transitions between developmental courses, English-language learning, and discipline-area work, and by creating a sense of community and heightened engagement with the college, student peers, faculty, and staff. It does so through its First Year Academies, which function as "schools-within-a-school," combining various activities including discipline-specific New Student Seminars, a newly developed second-semester career development course titled Fundamentals of Professional Advancement, student electronic portfolios, and an array of discipline-relevant co-curricular activities. These serve a range of new students, from those who require additional basic-skills instruction to those for whom English is a second language. All the academies use learning communities to contextualize skills development within disciplinary coursework and to integrate a variety of support services for first-year students. Non-ESL students enroll in one of three learning communities in Business/Technology, Allied Health, and Liberal Arts. Each academy provides students with a college-level course in their major, as well as basic-skills instruction as applied to that major. These are followed up by a Gateway to the Workplace course, tailored to the specific field served by the learning community. All the learning communities include a new-student seminar, whose activities are tailored to the needs of the students in the learning community.

Key to the success of the First Year Academy is the willingness of faculty to coordinate their courses around a common theme that connects the content and activities of the individual courses and the New Student Seminar. This coherent, integrative learning experience furthers students' learning and promotes their success. The ePortfolios that students are required to create—longitudinal electronic portfolios—deepen their learning and help them make meaningful connections between coursework, community, and career.

While these programs continue to expand and evolve, early results are quite positive. For academy learning-community students, semester-to-semester retention rates are 75.6% versus 71.7% for the college as a whole; and pass rates average 77.1% versus 72.0% for the same courses offered as "stand-alones." For the learning communities' basic writing course, the pass rate is 69.5% versus 63.6% in stand-alone sections.

Aligning Institutional Action to Student Needs

While speaking of the importance of alignment, we should note that institutions sometimes maintain practices whose misalignment inadvertently sets up barriers in the way of students. Removing these barriers can help promote success as much as can other actions. One such barrier has to do with the misalignment between the availability of required courses and the need for students to take those courses to complete their degrees in a timely manner. In this regard, several institutions have gotten their faculty to offer required courses at frequencies, times, and with sufficient seats so that full-time students in a particular major can finish their degrees within the standard time frame, which for most fields of study is four years. At the University of Florida, for example, faculty in each discipline develop curricular tracks for students to follow, so that once they have declared a major, they can complete their degrees in the shortest possible time (Capaldi, Lombardi, and Yellen 2006). Tied to their degree-audit system, both students and their advisers can then clearly identify the sequences of courses being offered that will enable them to finish their degrees. The results have been striking. Four-year graduation rates increased from 43% in 1995 to 51% in 2000, five-year rates from 65% to 71%, and six-year rates from 70% to 76%.[30]

A related issue concerns the timing of registration. On average, students who enroll after the deadline are less likely to complete the course in which they enroll and less likely to graduate than students who register by the required date (Smith, Street, and Olivarez 2002; Johnston 2006). Not only are late registrants less motivated, on average, than those who enroll on time; they also begin coursework behind their classmates and as a result tend, without support, to be less successful than the others. Late registrants can also undermine the success of those who enroll on time, because faculty who are faced with large numbers of late-start students will sometimes delay the real work of the course and/or spend time repeating material. In response, an increasing number of colleges have instituted late-start classes, which, with adjusted hours, still result in the same credits as do regular-start classes. This relatively simple policy of aligning class times to student needs can positively impact student success, especially when those classes are linked to institutional support services.

Another facet of aligning action to student needs is the physical location of services. In too many institutions, students are required to travel across campus to access differing services, in particular those involving registration and support services. Given the many demands on students time, in particular for those who work and commute to college, it is not surprising that some students get frustrated and fail to access the services that might help them succeed. It is for this reason that an increasing number of colleges, two- and four-year, have reorganized their services around the "one-stop" shop model. Locating various services in the same place facilitates the integration and alignment of those services.

The alignment of action can also come about through the analysis of institutional functioning and patterns of student progression, as well as the assessment of student experience based on student surveys and student transcript data. Transcript data, for example, can identify the existence of curricular barriers to student progress, such as courses with high failure rates, and in turn serve to direct institutional efforts to those courses. The use of momentum point analysis can be used in a similar manner to identify critical intermediate points of achievement (e.g., earning a specific number of credits within a given period of time) and therefore direct institutional action to help students achieve those points in a timely fashion.

University of Texas, San Antonio—Aligning Institutional Action to the Needs of First-Year Students

The University of Texas, San Antonio, a Hispanic-serving institution, first established learning communities for first-year students in fall 2000 with a Title V grant from the U.S. Department of Education. They were subsequently expanded and became a division of the Tomas Rivera Center for Student Success in 2005. During the 2008–9 academic year, a total of seventy-two learning communities were offered to all freshmen. These include traditional learning communities serving students in good academic standing; residential learning communities; basic-skills learning communities, which are required of all for students who are undecided about their major; and access learning communities, a special scholarship and retention program aimed at incoming freshmen from specific high schools.

All learning communities include a 3-hour, 3-credit college-level freshmen seminar, which is part of the university's core curriculum. As the common anchor to all learning communities, the seminar serves a variety of purposes, from providing peer mentors to engaging students in the university's required Summer Common Reading program. A yearly Summer Teaching Institute for all learning-community instructors is offered not only to promote faculty teaching but also to recruit new faculty into the program.

Aligning the Actions of Faculty and Staff

Alignment of actions requires more than just an organizing office or committee. It requires that functional units, offices, programs, and faculty and staff collaborate to ensure that their work is directed toward the same end. Collaboration and coordination, the underpinnings of alignment, are critical to the success of institutional actions. Nowhere is this collaboration more important than in the classroom and, therefore, among faculty and between faculty and staff. It is the key to constructing classrooms that fully engage students in learning, provide support for learning, and connect students to other services that promote their success. This is particularly evident in basic-skills learning communities and supplemental education programs. In the former, collaboration among faculty is essential to the building of a coherent learning environment that aligns the content and activities of the courses that constitute the learning community (Krellwitz, Pole, and Potter 2005). When the learning community serves academically underprepared students, that collaboration also includes faculty and/or staff who are responsible for basic-skills courses. As in supplemental instruction, the effectiveness of basic-skills learning communities depends, in part, on the careful alignment of the activities of the basic-skills courses to those in the other courses of the learning community.

Such collaboration is not easily achieved if only because of the heavy time demands it entails and the competing demands on faculty and staff time. Here again, institutional support matters, especially as it addresses the issue of faculty and staff workloads. Typically this support has centered on initiatives such as freshman seminars, learning communities, supplemental instruction, and first-year courses (Stevenson, Duran, Barrett, and Colarulli 2005). In these cases, as in others, collaboration is often most successful when it involves actions that have concrete goals and outcomes and is supported by the institution in visible ways.

The benefits of collaboration accrue to faculty and staff as well as to students (Albrecht 2003; Austin and Baldwin 1991; Shapiro and Levine 1999). Faculty who have worked together in a learning community report that although it was hard work, it was one of their best teaching and learning experiences. It not only changed their pedagogy but also renewed their sense of excitement about teaching (Reumann-Moore, El-Haj, and Gold 1997). In the same way that students learn better together, so do faculty. That is probably why learning communities as well as teaching academies have gained acceptance on both two- and four-year campuses.

■ Administrative Action for Student Retention and Graduation: A Comment

Without institutional commitment, which springs from institutional leadership, to the goal of increasing student success, the actions described in the preceding chapters are unlikely to yield the gains to which most colleges aspire. Leadership matters. Just paying attention to the importance of student retention and graduation can make a difference. But good intentions on the part of institutional leadership, however sincere, are not sufficient to ensure gains in student retention and graduation as described in the preceding chapters. What is required is knowledge of the way institutions should act and the policies they should pursue to translate their commitment into meaningful outcomes.

This is but one reason why the initiative of the Governance Institute for Student Success is so promising. By offering trustees and presidents of community colleges a leadership model that identifies key policy decisions, actions, and levers they can employ to support innovation within their campuses to improve student success, it opens up the possibility of engaging in campus-wide conversations about how all members of an institution can work together to promote greater student success.[31]

7

■ **Reflections on a Framework for Institutional Action**

Institutions that ask what they can do to increase student retention will find that there are many possible answers to that question and thus many possible courses of action they can take to achieve that end. Some recommendations are the result of sound research; others are based on anecdotal evidence; and still others are claims made by various organizations, groups, and individuals, including the increasing number of retention consultants who offer the "secret" of student retention. In this book, I have not sought to replicate that universe of possible action or to reiterate the claims of others. Rather, I have attempted to provide a research-based framework for institutional action that argues that whatever actions an institution chooses to take, it must eventually address the four conditions that are known to promote student retention, namely expectations, support, assessment and feedback, and involvement. At the same time, I have identified the major types of action that institutions can take to establish these conditions and the sorts of institutional policies they should pursue to ensure that those actions are successfully implemented over time in ways that endure and scale up.

As readers will have seen, the framework proposed here places the classroom at the center of a student's educational life and in turn at the center of institutional action for student success. For most institutions, especially those that are nonresidential, the classroom is the one place, perhaps only place, where students meet each other and the faculty and engage in formal learning activities. For the great majority of students, success in college is most directly shaped by their experiences in the classroom. Furthermore, for the many students who attend part-time or begin college academically underprepared, success in college is measured one course or even one class at a time.

Several implications for institutional action follow. First, all institutions, especially community colleges, must carefully align and sequence their courses and the support services for those courses such that success in one course leads to success in those that follow. The result should be a series of coherent pathways that students can follow to completion of their programs of study in a timely manner. Second, the actions of faculty in the classroom, the skills and knowledge they possess to engage students there, are critical to student success. Third, and in consequence, faculty development must be part and parcel of institutional efforts to promote student retention. Just as colleges must take seriously the task of enhancing student retention and completion, so too must they take seriously the task of enhancing the skills and knowledge that faculty bring into the classroom.

Aside from requiring development activities on the part of faculty, as is the case in some institutions for new faculty, institutions must provide meaningful incentives and rewards for faculty to engage in those activities. To do so, institutions must address several issues. Four-year institutions must address the frequently discussed conflict between teaching and research and provide incentives and rewards for being involved in faculty development efforts. Though teaching and research need not be in conflict, on many campuses they are not given equal weight, either by faculty or by administrators. This is certainly the case in the leading research universities and increasingly so in four-year institutions concerned about their ranking in national ranking systems. Faculty are under ever greater pressure to carry out research and publish, if only for job security. Among two-year institutions, however, the issue is not so much teaching versus research than finding the time to engage in professional development activities. The typical course load is such that few faculty have time for activities beyond the classroom. Rewards and incentives, therefore, must be measured not only in resources but also in time.

■ Taking Student Success Seriously: Moving beyond Add-Ons

Many colleges speak of the importance of increasing student retention. Indeed, quite a few invest substantial resources in programs designed to achieve that end. Yet few institutions take student retention seriously. Most treat it as one more item to add to the list of issues to be addressed. They adopt what Parker Palmer calls the "add a course" strategy. Need to address the issue of diversity? Add a course in diversity studies. Need to address the issue of student retention, in particular that of new students? Add a freshman seminar or perhaps a freshman mentoring program, but leave untouched the essential educational character of student experience. Furthermore, in seeking to address the issue of student retention, too many institutions exhibit what can be referred to as a form of programitis. They invest in many programs in the hope that doing so will somehow translate to sizable gains in retention, that more programs will translate into more gains in retention. While it is true that more programs are better than fewer, the number matters less than where the programs are situated in the educational life of the institution and how they are organized and aligned one to another. Merely investing in retention programs does not mean taking student retention seriously. Added programs have often sat on the margins of institutional life and have done little to change the prevailing character of student educational experience, especially in the classroom, and thus little to address the deeper roots of student attrition. Consequently, most efforts to enhance student retention have had limited impact.

What would it mean for institutions to take student retention seriously? It would mean that institutions would stop tinkering at the margins of institutional life and make enhancing student retention the linchpin about which they organize their activities. They would move beyond the provision of add-on services and establish those educational conditions that promote the retention of all students, in particular in the classroom, the one place most actions have failed to touch. And they would act to align the actions of its various units so that each is directed in the same direction, namely the success of their students, especially during the first year of college.

To retain and graduate their students, institutions must also take seriously the task of faculty development. They must establish, as several institutions have done, required programs to help new faculty acquire the skills and knowledge they need to help their students succeed in the courses they teach—skills and knowledge that are not typical of faculty new to higher education. It is simply unacceptable that faculty in higher education are the only teachers from kindergarten to university who are literally not trained to teach their students.

■ Success Does Not Arise by Chance

Student success does not arise by chance. Nor does substantial improvement in institutional rates of student retention and graduation. It is the result of intentional, structured, and proactive actions and policies directed toward the success of all students. Effective institutions provide a clear template for the actions of all its members: students, faculty, and staff alike. They establish structures within which various parts of the organization relate to each other and together impact student success. They address systematically each of the conditions shaping student success and do so over the full course of student progression through the institution. Finally, they are proactive: they take action to control events shaping student success rather than merely responding to events. Given evidence of effectiveness, they will often require action rather than leave it voluntary.

Not surprisingly, the conditions for student success described in the preceding chapters are no different from those for institutional success. Every institution needs to set clear and high expectations for itself and its members, provide support for its members, assess and provide feedback about their performance, and actively involve its members with others in determining how the institution as a whole should act to meet those expectations. The source of an institution's success, like a student's success, is its ability to learn and improve over time. Effective institutions employ evidence of student experiences and outcomes in their decision-making. They assess their actions and policies, modify them when necessary, carefully align them to the same end, and invest resources over the long term to achieve that end. An institution following such practices may be described as a "learning centered college" (O'Banion 1997) or a "learning paradigm college" (Tagg 2003). In a very real sense an effective institution is as educative of its faculty, staff, and administrators as it is of its students.

Unfortunately, too many decisions are made without evidence of whether one course of action would yield a better outcome than another, or whether an action already taken has produced its intended outcome. It is telling that while institutions will add new programs in the hope that they will increase retention, rarely do they eliminate existing programs. They may talk about the need for data, but often fail to use the data they already have as the basis for institutional change.[1]

■ Access without Support Is Not Opportunity

On the surface, America's public commitment to provide access to any individual who seeks a postsecondary education seems to be working. Our system of higher education has one of the highest participation rates in the world. More than 20 million students are currently enrolled in undergraduate study in public and private two- and four-year colleges and universities, an increase of over 44% between 1990 and 2009 (Snyder and Dillow 2010, table 205). The proportion of high-school graduates entering college immediately after high school has increased from about 49% in 1980 to 68% in 2008 (Snyder and Dillow 2010, table 200). As overall enrollments have grown, so too have the number of economically disadvantaged students who attend college (National Center for Education Statistics 2005; Chen and Carroll 2005).

But scratch beneath the surface of this apparent achievement and the news about access and opportunity in American higher education is much more complex and a lot less hopeful. Despite gains in access, the gap between high- and low-income students in college completion remains, especially for four-year degrees.[2] The facts are unavoidable. Although access to higher education has increased, greater equality in the attainment of four-year college degrees has not followed suit. This is the case for a variety of reasons, not the least of which is that many low-income students begin higher education without the requisite academic skills to succeed.[3] There is little question that differences in preparation among students continue to challenge our ability to translate the opportunity access to college provides to the attainment of a degree (Adelman 2007; Bowen, Kurzweil, and Tobin 2005).

Addressing this issue will not be easy. In addition to efforts in elementary, middle, and high school, it will require of states, the federal government, and foundations a substantial and continuing investment in higher education reform, especially in the community colleges of our nation where the problem of academic underpreparedness is most pressing.[4] Just as important, states will have to take seriously their obligation to provide colleges, especially two-year colleges, with adequate support so that they can give their students the academic support they need to succeed. But adequate institutional support, though necessary, will still be insufficient to address the challenges we face. Institutions must also be willing to reconsider how they go about providing academic support for students and institute a range of changes in their practice, especially in their developmental education courses.[5] And they must provide faculty and staff with the support they need to effectively respond to the academic needs of their students.

■ The Limits of Institutional Action

There are limits to what institutions can do to increase student retention and completion. A student's decisions to stay or leave, to transfer to another institution, or to leave higher education altogether are shaped by a variety of forces, not all of which are amenable to institutional action. Even when a student's experiences within an institution are entirely satisfactory, external forces can lead to departure. Clearly, this is more often the case among two- and four-year institutions that serve large numbers of students who commute, work, or attend part-time, in particular those from low-income backgrounds, than it is for residential institutions serving full-time students from more affluent backgrounds. Unlike the latter, for whom college attendance is their sole or principal obligation, most of the former attend college in addition to other obligations that compete for their time and energies. At the same time, more than a few students, in particular but not only in community colleges, enroll with no intent to complete a degree or certificate. Others begin with the often unstated intent of transferring to another institution. Many will do so regardless of their experiences. As a result, institutions serving these students are more limited in their capacity to increase student retention, at least in the short term. Furthermore, one of the challenges they face in implementing effective action is to fine-tune such action to students' lives beyond the campus as they seek to negotiate the pathway to completion.[6]

Gains in retention and completion also depend in part on an institution's existing rates and on how much has already been done to address retention. A campus with low rates of retention and graduation that has yet to invest in systematic actions can reasonably expect a considerable gain in rates, since almost any action will, if properly implemented, yield sizable results. For a campus that has already addressed most of the major forces on campus shaping student success, a ceiling effect may be operative. In this case, additional actions, while desirable, will have more limited impact, and the returns to those actions will likely be smaller.

Recognition of the limits of institutional action also influences the projections or goals institutions set for themselves as they plan their actions. Though expectations should never be set too low, expecting too much of a course of action or assuming that it can be achieved in too short a time may lead people to become disheartened and give up when they should not. Just as student success is best measured one course at a time, so should institutional success be measured by the achievement of reasonable action plans, one at a time, over a longer period of time. The simple fact is that substantial improvements in student success, whether measured by retention, the attainment of particular momentum points, or graduation, take time and a not inconsequential investment of energy and resources. As noted earlier, the willingness to invest in a long-term process of improvement, one achievable goal at a time, is a necessary condition for improvement in student retention and graduation.

Setting reasonable expectations is especially important when issues of accountability are at stake. Too often external agencies, in particular those in the public sector, expect too much of institutions or are impatient for improvements to occur. The political timetable that shapes expectations is typically shorter than that which would reasonably apply to individual institutions. Nevertheless, to the degree that an institution must attend to those expectations, it is important that they be reasonable and sensitive to what is achievable in different contexts.[7]

■ A Call to Action

This book began with a question: What can institutions do to enhance student retention and completion? In answering that question, a range of actions were described that institutions can take to achieve that goal. But knowing what institutions *can* do is not the same as knowing what they *should* do. What set of actions *should* institutions take to enhance student success? It is to this important question that we now turn.

It bears repeating that my recommendations for institutional action do not absolve students of responsibility for their own success. No actions will ensure the success of students who are themselves unwilling to expend the effort needed to succeed in college. By the same token, student effort may prove futile in settings that are not conducive to success. In admitting a student, a college enters into a contract— indeed, takes on a moral obligation—to establish those conditions on campus, especially in the classroom, that enhance the likelihood that students who are willing to expend the effort will succeed.

What then should institutions do if they are serious in their pursuit of increased student retention and graduation? Although the answers to this question will differ according to context, the following actions represent what any institution should do to enhance the likelihood that substantially more of its students will stay and graduate.

* *Institutions should establish a cross-functional team of faculty, support staff, and administrators whose task it is to oversee institutional planning and action for student success.*

Whether under the direction of an individual or of an office authorized to oversee institutional action, the team must represent the key persons and offices within the institution whose involvement is needed to drive systematic action. All voices in the institution whose actions impact student retention and graduation must be represented. It is a matter not simply of representation and the team's legitimacy in the eyes of members of the institution, but of the capacity of the team to work together to guide a campus-wide effort. Though the team can serve a variety of purposes and may take action when and where agreement exists to do so, it should see its role as facilitating the actions of other offices and persons. As noted earlier, faculty and staff will support what they create, not necessarily what others create for them.

- *Institutions should assess student experience and analyze patterns of student progression through the institution.*

Institutions should continually assess student experience, especially in the classroom, and monitor how changes in institutional action impact student experience. They should carry out detailed analyses of student progression that distinguish between patterns of progression of those who complete their programs of study and those who do not, and should do so in ways that describe progression for specific groups of students, especially those who enter underprepared, with major undeclared, from low-income backgrounds, and for differing programs of study. The institution should develop flow models that indicate how different groups of students progress through different programs within the institution and the points along those paths where students' progress is most at risk. Identifying these critical points enables the institution to think in more practical terms about how different institutional actions should be timed and sequenced so as to move students to and beyond them as quickly as possible to degree completion. Such longitudinal tracking and analyses of student progress should be the norm, not exception, of institutional practice.

- *Institutions should invest in long-term program development and ongoing assessment of program and institutional functioning.*

Institutions should invest in forms of practice that enhance student success, in particular those that impact success within the classroom. Funding should be provided for a period of at least three years in order to allow programs to move beyond the start-up stage, and should carry with it the proviso that funded programs assess themselves, demonstrate their effectiveness, and share the results of their work with the campus community. The goal of investment should be to establish programs that are not only effective, but also able to be sustained and scaled-up over time.

- *Institutions should coherently align institutional actions one to another and to the key progression points identified by its analysis of institutional data.*

Having identified the key points of attainment, institutions should align their actions to create a longitudinal series of actions whose common goal is to enable differing students to successfully navigate the various stages of attainment to degree completion. Institutional actions should serve to enhance the likelihood that students will complete their courses and their differing stages of attainment, one course and one stage at a time. They should result in a series of "model pathways to completion," designed to help students complete their journey in a timely fashion.[8]

- *Institutions should change the way they attend to the task of developmental education.*

Institutions should begin by carrying out a detailed analysis of existing developmental education courses and the sequence of courses that lead to college-level work. In addition to changes in pedagogy and assessment, institutions should contextualize and/or integrate basic-skills instruction into college-level courses and accelerate, through mainstreaming, the movement of developmental education students through the curriculum. This can be achieved by placing some students referred to developmental education directly into college-level courses where they receive additional instruction through companion classes (e.g., learning communities), labs, or other supports such as supplemental instruction.

- *Institutions should align academic support to key first-year courses.*

Academic support should be aligned to key first-year courses, which are considered foundational to different programs of study, and to basic-skills courses where accelerated learning is possible. Wherever feasible, academic support should be embedded in key first-year courses, so that it is contextualized to the content of the course and the students' learning of that content. Institutions should promote collaboration between those who teach courses and those who provide support and do so in ways that lead to a seamless blend of teaching and support.

- *Institutions should establish early warning systems for key first-year courses.*

Institutions should establish early warning systems for key-first year courses in ways that not only provide feedback to faculty about student performance but also trigger the provision of support when it is needed. Such systems should be proactive and provide academic support as early as possible in an academic term.[9] Wherever possible, institutions should utilize technology to facilitate the wider adoption of early warning systems across campus.

- *Institutions should ensure that all first-year students have the experience of learning in community with others.*

Whether it takes the form of learning communities that link at least two courses in which students enroll, of learning academies in which students, faculty and staff come together for particular fields of study, or of courses that utilize pedagogies of engagement such as cooperative or project-based learning strategies, institutions should ensure that every first-year student has the experience of learning in community with others. Where feasible, institutions should establish learning communities for all first-year students in ways that provide for interdisciplinary, contextualized learning. Institutions must provide the faculty and staff with the support and time they need to ensure that the content and activities of the individual courses constituting a learning community are coherently linked and designed to foster shared learning experiences among students. Wherever possible, learning communities should also be made available to those who enter academically underprepared, in ways that link one or more basic-skills courses to a college credit-bearing course.

- *Institutions should provide advising to all new students and to those who change majors.*

Institutions should provide a blend of individual, group, and online advising to all new students to ensure the greatest possible use of advising resources. They should require, whenever possible, developmental advising to those who are undecided in their field of study. Special attention should be paid to the needs of students who are the first in their families to attend college, especially those from low-income backgrounds. An advising center should be staffed by professional advisers working in liaison with faculty. Once students enroll in a specific program of study, they should be advised by faculty members in the program. A separate office should be established to advise students who change their major. Wherever possible, institutions should utilize technology to ensure that students can access advising whenever the need arises.

- *Institutions should invest in faculty development, especially for new faculty and those who teach the key first-year courses.*

Institutions should require all new faculty who have not otherwise received training to participate in a two-year faculty development program, preferably one that takes the form of a faculty learning community. Such a program should place particular emphasis on the use of classroom assessment techniques and pedagogies of engagement that actively involve students in learning with others. Special attention should be paid to those who teach first-year courses that are foundational to different programs of study, and those that make up the basic-skills course sequence. Whenever possible, adjunct faculty members should be included along with full-time members in faculty development activities.

Three observations about these recommendations: First, they focus primarily on the first year of college and the classrooms of that year. It is in that beginning part of the student career and in those places where students and faculty meet that institutions should initially direct their actions. The point of doing so is not only to establish a sound foundation upon which subsequent learning is built, but also help students develop sufficient momentum (e.g. credits hours) to propel them forward to program and degree completion. Second, given the centrality of the classroom to institutional action, these recommendations highlight the importance of the faculty to institutional efforts to enhance student success and, in turn, the need for institutions to attend to faculty development. Third, they point up the need for an organizational structure that coherently aligns institutional actions, so as to promote student retention systematically from entry to completion. Just as student success does not arise by chance, neither does institutional success.

■ Closing Comment

The classroom is the building block upon which student retention is built and the pivot around which institutional action for student retention must be organized. But while institutions have invested for years in retention programs, they have yet to significantly reshape the college classroom and student experience within the classroom. If we hope to make significant gains in retention and graduation, institutions must focus on the classroom experience and student success in the classroom and align classrooms one to another in ways that provide students a coherent pathway that propels them to program completion. In doing so, institutions must also focus on the acquisition of knowledge and skills students require for life after college. Lest we forget, the goal of retention is not only that students stay in college and graduate, but that they learn while doing so.

■ Defining Retention and Persistence

To describe what we know about the scope and character of student retention in higher education requires that we first define what we mean by the terms *student retention* and the associated term *student persistence*. A convenient point of departure is to distinguish between that way of thinking about student progress which asks whether the student continues in higher education, and that of the institution, which asks whether students are progressing through the institution. For the student's view, we use the term *persistence*; for the institutional view, we use the term *retention*. In the former case, *persistence* and *completion* refer to the rate at which students who begin higher education at a given point in time continue in higher education and eventually complete their degree, regardless of where they do so. In the latter case, *retention* and *graduation* refer to the rate at which an institution retains and graduates students who first enter the institution as freshman at a given point in time. The difference between the two is not trivial, because many students persist to degree completion even though they do not do so in the institution in which they initially enrolled. In the case of *transfer* to another institution, the terms *student persistence* and *student completion* are synonymous with the terms *system retention* and *system completion*, which refer to the rate at which the higher education system writ large retains students until degree completion, regardless of where they first entered the system. It follows that measures of student persistence and completion are higher on average than institutional rates of student retention and graduation.

The picture is made more complex because student persistence is sometimes discontinuous. Some students will temporarily suspend college attendance, sometimes for a considerable period of time.[1] In other words, they *stop out*. In some cases, students will return to their initial institution (*discontinuous institutional retention*). In other cases they will enroll in another institution (*delayed transfer* or *discontinuous student persistence*). The challenge researchers face in these cases is knowing whether and when to classify a student a *dropout* or a *stopout*. Though it can be logically argued that any student can return at some point and therefore can be considered a stopout, researchers set a time limit after which a student who does not re-enroll is considered a *dropout*, that is has ceased enrollment without completing a degree program or certificate. From the system perspective, that time period is typically set at nine years. In this case, with respect to a cohort of entering students, I use the term *student attrition* to describe the rate at which students terminate college without completing a degree. From the perspective of a particular college, I use the term *institutional attrition*. I sometimes use the term *system attrition* to designate departure from the higher educational system.

The time limit by which one judges institutional retention and graduation depends not only on the nature of the institution (two- versus four-year) or the nature of the program (e.g., engineering programs), but also on the fact that not all students enroll full-time or are consistent in their enrollment patterns. Many, indeed an increasing number, enroll part-time or vary between full- and part-time. This, together with transfer, helps explain why the average time to complete a four-year college degree is now more than five academic years.[2] It is one reason why the U.S. Department of Education currently sets the time period to assess four-year institutional graduation and two-year institutional graduation at six years and three years respectively, or 150% of the time normally required to complete a degree with full-time continuous enrollment. For a variety of reasons, such as large numbers of part-time students, more than a few observers argue that even the three-year time period for two-year colleges is too short and therefore underestimates the eventual rates of graduation among those institutions.[3]

■ Student Retention and Persistence in Higher Education

Several caveats are necessary before we turn to the data on retention and persistence. First, different data sources are used to describe retention and persistence. Sources vary not only in character (e.g., which students are included) but also in the time period covered. Some provide data on all beginning students, others do not. Some are more recent, others somewhat dated. It is important to understand these differences in order to make sense of what these data tell you.

Second, not all students who begin higher education do so with the intent of gaining a degree or certificate (Polinsky 2003). For instance, among students who began higher education in the 1995–96 academic year, nearly 3% indicated that they did not plan for either a degree or certificate. Understandably, such students are more common in two-year colleges than in four-year ones, if only because the former institutions serve a range of interests and needs, not all of which require the completion of a degree or certificate. That institutions serving large numbers of such students have lower retention and graduation rates than other institutions is not surprising nor a sign of institutional failure. At the same time, more than a few students, especially in the public sector, begin with the intent of transferring to another institution to complete their degree.

Third, though students may enroll in a degree program and indicate their intent to obtain a degree, not all are equally serious in their pursuit of that goal. As Adelman (1998) observed, more than a few entering students attempt only six or fewer credits during their first academic year.[4] Many, but by no means all, do not persist beyond that year.

Fourth, current measures of institutional graduation, for instance those based on the Integrated Postsecondary Education Data System (IPEDS), count only those students who begin in the fall semester of an academic year. Yet we know that some students delay their entry until later, typically in the spring semester, and that such delayed entry is more frequent in some institutions than others (e.g., large urban public institutions as compared to selective private ones). Since delayed entrants are somewhat less likely to complete their degrees than fall entrants, it follows that current measures of institutional graduation rates, as presented here, will be somewhat biased.

My point is quite simple. As we consider the data on retention and persistence, we must be wary of rushing to judgment. In interpreting differences in institutional rates of retention and graduation, we should carefully consider not only the attributes of students (e.g., skills, backgrounds), but also the nature of students' intent and the seriousness of their pursuit of a degree or certificate. We must also keep in mind the different types of institutions that students attend.[5] Some, like community colleges, serve a multitude of students whose interests vary considerably, while others have more specific missions. Some welcome students who are only exploring college, while others are much more particular in whom they are willing to admit. What is a strength of our higher educational system, that it is multifaceted and diverse in its missions and in the students it serves, also makes it difficult to draw any generalizations about differences between institutions in retention and graduation.

The following analysis focuses on public and private, not-for-profit, four-year institutions and public two-year institutions, since the overwhelming

Table A1. Graduation and retention from first institution among 1995–96 beginning four- and two-year students, as of spring 2001 and spring 1998 (in percentages)

First institution type	Attained at first institution				
	Bachelor's degree	Associate's degree	Certificate	Still enrolled at first institution	Total
Four-year:					
Public	45.5	1.9	1.0	8.3	56.7
Private not-for-profit	61.0	1.0	0.6	3.2	65.8
Total	50.7	1.7	1.0	6.4	59.8
Two-year public	—	6.0	6.5	31.6	44.1

Source: National Center for Education Statistics 2003, table 3.1a; and National Center for Education Statistics, 2000, table 3.1a.

majority of students attend those types of institutions. Though for-profit, less-than-two-year institutions have grown significantly over the past two decades and now serve increasing numbers of students, in particular those from low-income backgrounds, the data on their retention and graduation rates are not of sufficient quality to permit useful comparisons. Although we need to know about the effectiveness of those institutions, the analysis of their effectiveness is beyond the scope of this book.

Turning first to student retention and graduation, we draw on the data from Beginning Postsecondary Students (BPS) 1995–96 that describe rates of institutional retention and graduation at the initial institution of entry for students who first entered four-year public and private, not-for-profit institutions and two-year public institutions in 1995–96 (table A1). Rates of institutional retention and graduation are calculated for the standard 150% of "normal" time to degree completion as determined by the federal government, namely, six years for four-year institutions and three years for two-year institutions.

Among public four-year institutions, 45.5% of students earned their bachelor's degree within six years from their initial institution of entry, while

61.0% did so among private four-year institutions. In both cases, a small percentage of students earned certificates or associate degrees while others are still enrolled in their initial institution after six years, specifically 8.3% in public institutions and 3.2% in private ones. Among public two-year colleges, only 6.0% earned their associate's degrees and 6.5% their certificates from their initial institution of entry within three years. But another 31.6% or almost a third of all beginning public two-year college students are still enrolled in their initial institution after three years.

But not all students graduate at the same rate. Table A2 describes the six-year institutional graduation rates at public and private four-year institutions of different groups of students by defined by academic merit, parents education, and family income, who began in 1995–96. In this case, academic merit is a composite measure that includes SAT or equivalent ACT scores, rigor of high school curriculum, and high-school grade-point average. Students are classified by quartiles of academic merit: high, middle-high, middle, and low. Parents' education is classified as first-generation college status (yes or no) and income (low-income vs. not low- income as defined by Pell eligibility). In both cases table A2 uses the definitions of first-generation college status and low-income established by the U.S. Office of Education, namely: a first-generation college student comes from a family in which no one has earned a bachelor's degree, and a low-income student has an annual dependent income of less than $25,000. These two attributes are central to student eligibility for TRIO services. As such they allow us to compare TRIO-eligible students to non-TRIO students of comparable ability.

Several points warrant mention. First, institutional graduation rates are uniformly higher in private, not-for-profit, four-year institutions than in public ones. Second, differences in students' ability yield the largest differences in retention and degree completion in both public and private not-for-profit institutions. Third, first-generation college students do not fare as well as non-first-generation college students, even after controlling for income and ability. Differences between the two are of roughly the same magnitude as differences between low- and non-low-income students. Fourth, among four-year institutions there were too few first-generation college and low-income students of middle-high or high ability to be included in the data. That fact alone is a telling reminder of the association between social status broadly understood and the ability of students to acquire academic skills prior to college.

Table A2. Graduation and retention from first institution among 1995–96 beginning four-ye[ar] students, as of spring 2001 (in percentages)

Institution type First-generation college status, income, and academic merit index	Highest degree attained at first institution				To
	Bachelor's degree	Associate's degree	Certificate	Still enrolled at first institution	
Public:					
First generation, low-income					37
Low merit	23.1	2.0	1.2	11.2	55
Middle merit	37.4	3.2	0.0	15.0	—
Middle–high merit	—	—	—	—	—
High merit	—	—	—	—	
Not first generation, low-income					61
Low merit	41.0	3.5	0.0	16.9	61
Middle merit	45.6	0.0	2.1	13.7	—
Middle–high merit	—	—	—	—	
High merit	—	—	—	—	—
First generation, not low-income					42
Low merit	30.2	2.3	0.8	9.0	54
Middle merit	45.7	1.6	0.7	6.9	75
Middle–high merit	65.7	1.1	0.0	9.0	74
High merit	67.1	0.0	1.4	5.5	
Neither first generation nor					45
low-income	34.8	1.5	0.4	8.4	67
Low merit	60.1	0.3	1.0	6.0	82
Middle merit	73.9	1.5	0.0	6.6	77
Middle–high merit	73.5	0.0	0.0	3.6	
High merit					
Public total	45.5	1.9	1.0	8.3	56
Private not-for-profit:					
First generation, low-income					
Low merit	37.0	0.4	2.2	5.9	45
Middle merit	46.8	1.0	0.0	1.7	49
Middle–high merit	—	—	—	—	—
High merit	—	—	—	—	—
Not first generation, low-income					
Low merit	—	—	—	—	—
Middle merit	56.4	0.0	0.0	4.6	49
Middle–high merit	70.1	0.0	0.0	3.8	73
High merit	75.4	0.0	0.0	0.0	75

le A2. *(continued)*

titution type st-generation ege status, income, academic merit index	Highest degree attained at first institution				
	Bachelor's degree	Associate's degree	Certificate	Still enrolled at first institution	Total
irst generation, low-income					
Low merit	44.0	2.1	0.8	1.3	48.2
Middle merit	57.5	1.5	0.3	3.7	63.0
Middle–high merit	71.9	0.0	0.0	3.5	75.4
High merit	79.1	0.0	0.0	1.3	80.4
Neither first generation nor low-income					
Low merit	54.2	0.6	0.6	1.4	56.8
Middle merit	69.9	0.4	0.0	3.0	73.3
Middle–high merit	79.1	0.0	0.3	0.9	80.3
High merit	81.4	0.0	0.0	1.7	83.1
ate total	61.0	1.0	0.6	3.2	65.8

rce: National Center for Education Statistics 2003.

■ The Timing of Student Retention and Graduation

Knowing the rate at which institutions graduate their students is only one part of the puzzle. We also need to know how long it takes students to do so. To answer this question, we considered the institutional rates of bachelor's degree completion from the initial institution of entry among beginning bachelor's degree-seeking students who first entered higher education in 1995–96 (table A3). Several observations should be made about these data. First, the percentage of beginning students who left their initial institution follows the well-established finding that institutional attrition is generally highest in the first year and declines thereafter.[6] After the first year, 13.8% of beginning students who began in four-year institutions with the intent of earning a bachelor's degree left their first institution. Subsequently, 10.6%, 5.6%, 3.4%, 2.0%, and 1.0% did so in the following years (marginal increments year to year in total dropout rates). As a proportion of the total six-year institutional attrition rate of 37.9% of leavers departed their initial institution before the start of the second year, 29.1% before the

Table A3. Bachelor's degree graduation and attrition from first institution among 1995–96 beginning four-year college students, as of spring 2001 (in percentages)

Time frame	Completed BA/BS	Left initial institution	Proportion of all leavers
End of first year	—	13.8	37.9
End of second year	—	10.6	29.1
End of third year	2.3	5.6	15.4
End of fourth year	33.5	3.4	9.3
End of fifth year	51.4	2.0	5.5
End of sixth year	55.3	1.0	2.7

Source: National Center for Education Statistics 2003, tables 7.1–7.6.

start of the third year, 15.4%, 9.3%, 5.5%, and 2.7% respectively in subsequent years. From the perspective of the four-year institution, then, attrition is greatest during the first two years (67% of all leavers).[7]

Second, these data tell us that the so-called four-year degree is anything but that. Of the approximately 55% of students who complete their bachelor's degree from their initial institution, only a little over 33% (or 60% of all degree earners) do so within the standard four-year time frame (see NCES 2003–151, tables 7.1–7.6). The remaining 22% (or 40% of all degree earners) do so in the following two years.

■ **Long-term Student Retention and Graduation**

Some students remain enrolled in their initial two- and four-year institution after three and six years respectively. As a result, rates of institutional graduation for both two- and four-year colleges, especially the former, are likely to be higher, perhaps considerably higher, than those indicated by use of the standard 150% time to degree graduation metric.[8] For four-year institutions, that rate can be estimated by making the conservative estimate that 60% of students still enrolled after six years will eventually complete their bachelor's degree. It follows that longer-term graduation rates for four-year public institutions will be at least 50%, and for private ones more than 60%. For public two-year colleges we can use the BPS 1995–96 six-year data to determine the six-year graduation rates, and from those who are still enrolled we can estimate the longer-term rate of degree or certificate completion. We find that while the percentage of students who earn a certificate does not increase over six years, the percentage that earn an associate's degree from their initial institution more than doubles, from a little more than 6% to 16%. It is likely that that figure will increase over time to around 19%.

For two-year institutions then, more so than for four-year ones, the metric typically used to measure time to degree completion is seriously flawed. In the case of associate's degrees, it captures less than a third of estimated long-term institutional degree completion. Furthermore these data do not take into account the likelihood that some students who stop out may return to their initial institution sometime in the future to finish their degrees.

■ Variability of Institutional Graduation Rates

The above data represent national averages. The retention and graduation rates of individual institutions vary, with some private universities graduating over 90% of their beginning students, and some public ones less than 30%. The Education Trust, for instance, maintains an online database entitled College Results Online that enables one to compare overall institutional graduation rates as well as the graduation rates of various groups of students within the institution (race, ethnicity, and gender) for virtually any four-year college and university.[9] Institutions that enroll more middle- and high-income students, students from college-educated families, and students who have higher test scores have, on average, higher rates of institutional retention and graduation (Astin and Oseguera 2005; Gold and Albert 2006; Horn and Carroll 2006).

The relationship between whom the institution admits and graduation rates is, however, less than perfect. Take, for instance, the often discussed relationship between institutional selectivity and graduation rates. A report by Hess, Schneider, Carey, and Kelly (2009) examined data for six-year graduation rates for the 2001 incoming class from over 1,800 colleges and universities whose data were reported to IPEDS. It was found that while rates of graduation were directly related to selectivity (ibid., figure 2), there was considerable variation in graduation rates across institutions within the same selectivity categories, namely noncompetitive, less competitive, competitive, very competitive, and highly competitive (ibid., tables 1–2). In the "competitive" category, for instance, the top ten institutions had an average six-year graduation rate of more than 75%, while the bottom ten graduated just 20%. These figures held, even controlling for other factors such as institutional resources (Hamrick, Schuh, and Shelley 2004). The upper and lower bounds of mean graduation rates for each of the eight Carnegie categories (research I and II, doctoral I and II, master's I and II, bachelor's I and II) were such that some institutions in lower categories had higher mean graduation rates than those in the next higher category (ibid., table 2).[10]

While the above studies considered categories of selectivity, Astin's (2005) research looked at variations in graduation rates among individual institutions of similar selectivity. Though he found that slightly "more than two-thirds of the variation in degree attainment rates among institutions can be attributed to differences in the students who enroll" (p. 14), differences remained that are not entirely accounted for by student attributes.

Institutions also vary in their capacity to retain and graduate students of different backgrounds. Horn and Carroll (2006), for instance, looked at the relationship between institutional selectivity and the size of low-income enrollment (proportion of Pell grant recipients) and between overall six-year graduation rates and those of different racial groups and gender enrolled in institutions granting doctoral, master's, and bachelor's degrees. They found that graduation rates, both for all levels of selectivity and for all three degree-granting levels, varied inversely with the proportion of low-income students enrolled. At the same time, more selective institutions at all degree-granting levels graduated higher proportions of all racial groups and higher proportions of both men and women at all levels of low-income enrollment from small to large (see Horn and Carroll 2006, tables 8 and 10). In other words, attending a more selective institution appears to benefit all those who attend.

■ Student Persistence and Completion

The rate at which institutions graduate their students is only part of a more complex picture. Another part is the rate at which students persist and complete their degrees whether it is from their initial institution or another to which they transfer. Many students continue their studies elsewhere, while others may quit for a while and later continue their studies in another institution. As a result, as seen in table A4, student persistence and completion rates are higher than institutional rates of retention and graduation. The six-year rate of bachelor's degree completion among beginning public and private four-year students is 53.0% and 68.8% respectively, or 7.5% and 7.8% higher than that reported by institutions (table A1). Among public two-year students, associate's degree and certificate completion is 16.7% and 9.7%, or 9.7% and 3.2% higher than that reported by institutions.

Table A4. Completion and persistence among 1995–96 beginning students, as of spring 2001 (in percentages)

First institution type	Attained bachelor's degree	Attained associate's degree	Attained certificate	No degree; still enrolled four-year	No degree; still enrolled two-year	No degree; Not enrolled
Four-year						
Public	53.0	4.4	2.8	14.5	2.8	22.5
Private, not for profit	68.8	2.8	1.8	7.1	2.3	17.2
						20.5
Total	58.8	3.8	2.5	11.8	2.6	
Two-year public	10.3	16.7	9.7	8.4	9.1	45.9

Source: National Center for Education Statistics 2003, table 2.0A.

What is particularly striking about these data is that nearly 80% of students who begin in public and private four-year institutions either earn a degree or certificate or remain enrolled after six years. Among students who begin in public two-year colleges, more than half, or 54.1%, do so. Slightly more than 10% transfer to a four-year institution and earn a bachelor's degree within six years, while another 17.5% remain enrolled in either a four-year or a two-year institution. Clearly, student persistence and completion are higher than typically described in the popular media.

■ Estimating Long-Term Student Persistence and Completion

Rates of two- and four-year degree completion are likely to be higher still if we expand our time horizon beyond the standard three- and six-year time frames normally used to assess student completion. To estimate how much these rates are likely to change, we make the conservative estimate that half of the students who remain enrolled after six years will eventually complete their two- or four-year degrees. It follows from table A4 that long-term four-year degree completion will be at least 60% for those who begin in public four-year institutions and at least 72% for those who start in private ones. We can therefore expect the long-term four-year degree completion rate to reach approximately 65%. Another 9% and 5% respectively will have earned an associate's degree or certificate. Some will do so while earning a four-year degree. Assuming that 50% do not, it is likely that degree and certificate completion will range from 65% for public four-year college entrants to 75% for private four-year entrants. Among public two-year college entrants, approximately 15% will earn a bachelor's degree and about 30% will earn an associate's degree or certificate.

These estimates of long-term completion rates prove to be similar to estimates by a National Center for Higher Education Management Systems' study of eight- and nine-year graduation rates in four- and two-year colleges.[11] Utilizing data from the National Student Clearinghouse (NSC) files on first-time, full-time students who began college in fall 1998 and 1999 in five states (Kentucky, Minnesota, Nevada, New York, Washington), each of which had high NSC participation rates, the researchers found that eight- and nine-year total degree completion rates for four-year college entrants ranged from 56% to slightly more than 78%. Of particular interest is their finding that much of the increase in longer-term completion rates was the result of students earning their degrees out of state.

■ Variation in Student Persistence and Completion

Individuals, like institutions, differ in persistence and completion. Consider, for instance, table A5, which compares six-year completion rates at public and private four-year institutions, defining students who began in 1995–96 by academic merit, parents' education, and family income. When the numbers are contrasted to those in table A2, it is evident that student persistence and six-year completion rates are higher for all groups of students, as is the percentage still enrolled in higher education after six years. First-generation, low-income students show the greatest relative gain in continued enrollment in both public and private institutions. This is especially true among public institutions, where approximately 24% are still enrolled after six years.

A study by Attewell and Lavin (2007a, 2007b) provides yet another estimate of long-term completion, which suggests that over a much longer period of time, rates of student persistence and completion of four- and two-year degrees will continue to rise. Their study focused on the thirty-year attainment of more than eighteen thousand women who were admitted to the City University of New York under their open-admission policy. On the basis of their academic performance in high school, some were admitted to the four-year institutions of the university, others to the community colleges. For women who entered CUNY's four-year degree programs in 1970, more than 70% had earned a degree of some kind by 2000. Over 55% had earned a bachelor's degree or more (over 25% had earned a master's and/or an advanced degree), and another 15.5% had earned an associate's degree. Among those who began in a CUNY community college, slightly more than 30% had earned a bachelor's or higher degree (Attewell and Lavin 2007a, table 2.2, p. 23). While the mean number of years to earn a bachelor's degree among those who started in a four-year institution was about seven, among those who started in a two-year college the mean was slightly more than eleven (Attewell and Lavin 2007a, table 2.4, p. 329). Strikingly, the mean number of years to earn an associate's degree among two-year college entrants was slightly more than five, a considerably longer period than that used by IPEDS. The mean number of years to earn a bachelor's degree was more than eleven.

Attewell and Lavin also compared the completion rates of women of different race or ethnicity. Among those who began in a four-year college, African American and Hispanic women took an average of 8.1 and 7.9 years respectively to complete their bachelor's degree, while white students took

Table A5. Persistence and completion among 1995–96 beginning four-year students, as of spring 2001 (in percentages)*

Institution type First-generation college status, income, and academic merit index	Highest degree attained at first institution				To
	Bachelor's degree	Associate's degree	Certificate	Still enrolled at first institution	
Public:					
First generation, low-income					
Low merit	27.9	5.0	6.7	25.9	65
Middle merit	46.0	4.6	1.1	22.5	74
Middle–high merit	—	—	—	—	—
High merit	—	—	—	—	—
Not first generation, low-income					
Low merit	50.5	5.2	0.0	28.3	84
Middle merit	60.5	5.9	2.1	17.8	86
Middle–high merit	—	—	—	—	—
High merit	—	—	—	—	—
First generation, not low-income					
Low merit	37.6	4.5	3.0	19.6	64
Middle merit	55.4	4.6	2.6	17.9	80
Middle–High merit	71.8	2.8	0.4	11.8	86
High merit	70.3	0.0	1.9	13.5	85
Neither first generation nor low-income	42.3	7.4	4.2	23.2	77
Low merit	68.9	1.7	2.0	14.4	87
Middle merit	80.7	1.8	0.5	8.3	91
Middle–high merit	80.4	0.0	0.0	8.1	88
High merit					
Public total	53.0	4.4	2.8	17.3	77
Private not-for-profit:					
First generation, low-income					
Low merit	40.8	3.1	7.8	15.3	67
Middle merit	51.4	3.0	1.4	15.3	71
Middle–high merit	—	—	—	—	—
High merit	—	—	—	—	—
Not first generation, low-income					
Low merit	—	—	—	—	—
Middle merit	70.3	3.7	0.0	13.1	87
Middle–high merit	81.9	0.0	0.0	9.7	91
High merit	87.4	0.0	0.0	0.0	87

le A5. *(continued)*

titution type st-generation lege status, income, academic merit index	Highest degree attained at first institution				
	Bachelor's degree	Associate's degree	Certificate	Still enrolled at first institution	Total
First generation, not low-income					
Low merit	50.8	6.7	3.7	10.3	71.5
Middle merit	69.9	3.7	0.6	8.4	82.7
Middle–high merit	78.5	2.5	0.8	8.0	89.9
High merit	89.4	0.0	0.0	4.1	93.4
Neither first generation nor low-income					
Low merit	64.7	4.8	0.6	8.3	78.4
Middle merit	77.3	2.3	0.3	9.3	89.1
Middle–high merit	88.3	0.1	0.3	5.4	94.1
High merit	89.6	0.0	0.0	4.2	93.8
rate total	68.8	2.8	1.8	9.4	82.9

rce: National Center for Education Statistics 2003.

an average of 6.4 years. Among community college entrants, African American and Hispanic women took an average of 11.5 and 14.9 years respectively to complete their bachelor's degree and 6.7 and 6.3 years to complete an associate's degree, while white students took an average of 10.2 years to earn their bachelor's degree and 4.3 years to earn their associate's degree. Combined, African American and Hispanic women took between three and four years longer to earn their bachelor's degree.[12]

If we now ask, as Attewell and Lavin did, about the difference in bachelor's degree completion over the six-year time span used by BPS and the longer span of thirty years, we find that the difference in completion rates between white women and African American and Hispanic women diminished markedly (Attewell and Lavin 2007a, table B-3, p. 217). These authors maintain that "one would erroneously classify as dropouts 25% of the white women who in fact eventually graduated; 56% of Black BA's and 53% of Hispanic ones would erroneously be classified as having fallen by the wayside" (Attewell and Lavin 2007a, p. 30).

■ Changes in Institutional Retention and Graduation

Having described what we currently know about the scope of retention and persistence in higher education, we can ask whether rates of institutional retention and graduation have changed over time. The issue is of more than academic interest. Given that colleges, states, and the federal government have invested a good deal of money since the early 1990s in efforts to increase degree completion, they have reason to ask whether that investment has made any appreciable difference.

To answer this question, we turn to data on three- and six-year graduation rates for two- and four-year institutions respectively, provided by the NCHEMS Information Center for Higher Education Policy Making and Analysis.[13] These are presented in table A6. Each year noted represents the year at which completion is measured for those who started three or six years earlier. For four-year institutions, the cohorts for whom data are provided are those that began in 1995 through 2001; for two-year institutions, those that began in 1998 through 2004. In each instance, data are for all Title IV institutions, including private for-profit as well as private nonprofit institutions.

Two observations: First, the six-year completion rates reported are higher than the latest cohort reported in BPS, namely that which began in 1995–96. The same is true, but even more so, for three-year completion rates among two-year college students (table A1). This probably reflects the fact that the data in table A6 are drawn from the NCES IPEDS Graduation Rate Surveys, which represent all first-time degree-seeking students who returned in the following fall as either full- or part-time students. Indeed, completion rates from BPS 1995–96 for similar students, namely first-time, full-time degree-seeking students, are very similar (National Center for Education Statistics 2003, tables 3–2A, 3–3A, and 4–2A). Second, rates of six-year graduation show a small but consistent rise over time, while three-year graduation rates for two-year institutions show the reverse. The latter finding is particularly troubling since community colleges serve as an important point of access to higher education for many low-income and first-generation students. A different and more recent measure of six-year graduation rates comes from the NCHEMS utilization of the National Student Clearinghouse data files (Ewell and Kelly 2009). Graduation rates are calculated from the student records provided to the National Student Clearinghouse by the more than 2800 colleges and universities that participate in its enrollment and degree-

Table A6. Three- and six-year graduation rates for full-time, first-time, degree-seeking students

Institution type	2001	2002	2003	2004	2005	2006	2007
Four-year	54.0	54.3	54.3	55.3	55.8	56.4	56.1
Two-year	29.8	29.1	30.6	30.0	29.3	29.1	27.8

Source: NCHEMS Information Center for Higher Education Policy Making and Analysis. Data are drawn from the NCES, IPEDS Graduation Rate Surveys.

verification services; these institutions represent over 91% of total higher education enrollments in the United States. All first-time, full-time entering undergraduate students who began anytime during an academic year are tracked over time to ascertain whether they graduated from their initial institution or elsewhere, within the same state or in another state. The result is a somewhat more representative portrait of institutional graduation than that provided by the Graduation Rate Surveys alone. Of the four-year degree-seeking students in the 2000 cohort shown in table A6, a total of 63.0% completed college within six years. Of these, 55.0% graduated from their initial institution, 4.5% from another institution in the same state, and 3.5% from an out-of-state institution (Ewell and Kelly 2009, table 1).

Compared to the data in table A6, these data point, as one would expect, to somewhat lower rates of six-year institutional graduation. If part-time students were included, it would be lower still, well within range of the BPS 1995–96 data. Beyond reminding us that students persist and complete their four-year degrees at a higher rate than that suggested by institutional data alone, the National Student Clearinghouse data suggest that there has been little, if any, substantial change in institutional graduation rates over the period studied.[14]

The same conclusion appears to apply as well to retention from the first to the second year (table A7). The NCHEMS data also provide evidence of changes in first-to second-year institutional retention. Again, there is little if any change over the period covered.[15]

That being said, the data for a six-year follow-up of the entering 2003–4 cohort indicate that some changes have taken place in the last decade (Radford, Berkner, Wheeless, and Shepherd 2010).[16] As indicated in table A8, it appears that the rate of completion in the public four-year sector has, rela-

Table A7. Freshman to sophomore retention among beginning first-time, full-time degree-seeking students (in percentages)

Institution	2004	2005	2006	2007
Public	76.8	76.2	76.1	76.5
Private, Not-for-Profit	79.1	78.9	78.3	78.6

Source: Higher Center for Education Management System Information Center for Higher Education Policy Making and Analysis. Data are drawn from the NCES, IPEDS Graduation Rate Surveys.

Table A8: Completion from first institution among 2003–4 beginning four- and two-year students, as of spring 2009 (in percentages)

First institution type	Attained at first institution				
	Bachelor's degree	Associate's degree	Certificate	Still enrolled at first institution	Total
Four-year:					
Public	51.5	1.5	0.5	5.9	59.4
Private not-for-profit	57.0	2.2	0.6	2.8	62.6
Two-year public	—	15.5	5.9	8.9	30.3

Source: Radford, Berkner, Wheeless, and Shepherd. 2010, table 4.

tive to the 1995–96 cohort, increased from 45.5% to 51.5%, while the completion rate at private four-year institutions has declined somewhat from 61.0% to 57.0%.[17] At least a portion of these differences seems to reflect the fact that fewer students in the public sector are still enrolled in their initial institutions, whereas in the private four-year sector more students remain where they first enrolled. What might explain these preliminary data has yet to be explained, though one possibility is the increasing cost of higher education in a period of economic decline. Notably, little change is seen among those entering public two-year colleges. As in the earlier cohort, only between 21.5% and 22.5% are completing their associate degrees or certificates in six years.

■ Changes in Student Persistence and Completion

Even though the most recent data suggest that overall rates of institutional retention and six-year graduation have improved, it does not follow that rates of student persistence have similarly improved. To ascertain whether they have, we turn to two sources. The first is a recent NCES study of changes in five-year degree completion and persistence rates between 1994 and 2000 (Horn, Berger, and Carroll 2004). In this case, the authors used data from the 1990–94 and 1996–2001 Beginning Postsecondary Students Longitudinal Studies, which are representative of all full-time, first-time students who enrolled in a national sample of institutions. Their analysis, captured in table A9, compares data for the two BPS cohorts, namely those who began in the 1989–90 and 1995–96 academic years.[18]

These data tell us that the changes in five-year institutional graduation rates are not necessarily indicative of similar changes in the rates at which students eventually obtain their degrees. Not only are rates of student persistence and completion higher than for institutions, as one would expect, but the percentage who earn their degrees anywhere and are still enrolled has increased over the period studied.

ⅉle A9. Completion and continued enrollment after five years at first or other institutions, ong 1989–90 and 1995–96 beginning students (in percentages)

titutional Type:	Bachelor's degree	Associate's degree	Certificate	No degree; still enrolled at four-year	No degree; still enrolled at two-year	Total
ɔlic four-year:						
ɪ9–90	46.9	4.7	3.2	16.1	2.3	73.2
ɪ5–96	46.6	4.1	2.6	20.9*	3.7*	77.9*
ʲate four-year:						
ɪ9–90	66.6	3.0	2.3	7.4	1.2	80.4
ɪ5–96	65.3	2.9	1.6	10.7*	2.2*	82.7
ɪal four-year:						
ɪ9–90	53.3	4.2	2.9	13.3	1.9	75.6
ɪ5–96	53.4	3.7	2.3	17.2*	3.2*	79.6*

ᵣrce: Horn, Berger, and Carroll 2004, table 5A.

dicates a statistically significant difference at the p.05 level.

Table A10. Completion and continued enrollment at first or other institutions, among 2003–4 beginning students, as of spring 2009 (in percentages)

First institution type	Bachelor's degree	Associate's degree	Certificate	No degree; still enrolled four-year	No degree; still enrolled two-year	Tot
Four-year						
Public	59.5	3.8	1.6	9.7	3.2	77.8
Private, not for						
profit	64.6	3.8	1.5	7.9	3.2	81.0
Two-year public	11.6	14.4	8.5	6.7	12.9	54.0

Source: Radford, Berkner, Wheeless, and Shepherd 2010, table 1.

Nonetheless, rates of student persistence for the 2003–4 beginning-student cohort appear to have slowed, such that the projected rate of total degree completion remains unchanged from the earlier cohort (table A10). Though the proportion of students entering public four-year institutions who earn a bachelor's degree within six years from any institution has increased from 53% among the earlier cohort (table A4) to 59.5%, the proportion that remain enrolled has declined from 14.5% to 9.7%. This suggests that the increase in overall four-year degree completion seen in table A8 is due in large measure to the increase in the number of students who finish within the six-year time span, not to any significant increase in overall student persistence, which remains at about 78%. Among those who enter private four-year institutions, however, the overall rate of completion has declined slightly. This is also the case among those entering the public two-year college sector.

■ **Assessing Student Retention and Graduation**

Current measures of institutional graduation rates, such those based on IPEDS, count only those students who begin in the fall semester of an academic year. Yet we know that some students delay their entry until later in the academic year; that delayed entrants are somewhat less likely to complete their degrees than fall entrants; and that when they do persist, they are likely to take longer to graduate. Therefore, current measures of rates of institutional retention and graduation that look only at fall entrants and use a six-year time frame for graduation will be somewhat inaccurate (Adelman 2007). For institutions that serve relatively large numbers of late entrants—urban community colleges, for instance—the inaccuracy can be considerable.[19]

Adelman (2007) further argues that a more accurate picture of institutional effectiveness in promoting student graduation would not count as enrolled those students who are "incidental" in their attendance, that is, those who do not earn at least six credits during the first academic year. Such students, data reveal, are considerably less likely to complete their degrees than are students who are more fully engaged. Consequently, institutions that serve relatively large numbers of such students will appear less effective than they would have appeared if those students had not be included in the institution's rates of retention and graduation. The same can be said for those institutions that serve many students who enter with no intention of completing a program of study. In a system of accountability that employs retention and graduation rates, institutions that are willing to serve incidental students and those who wish to acquire knowledge and skills but not necessarily degrees or certificates may be penalized.

But not to count or at least monitor the retention of incidental students, for instance, is shortsighted. Students who attempt six or fewer credits in a given academic year are more likely to be from low-income backgrounds, to be older, and to have other responsibilities. Their level of participation does not necessarily reflect lack of seriousness. Even though excluding such students from estimates of institutional graduation rates may yield a more accurate picture of institutional effectiveness, institutions ought to track those students, ascertain what happens to them, and attempt to more fully engage them in the educational life of the institution.

■ The Quality of Student Retention

A final note regarding student retention: These data, though helping us better understand the scope of institutional retention, do not tell us about its quality. We may know the number of students who continue to their second year, but we do not know about the credits they earned or the grades they obtained in the first year. These qualitative aspects of retention, as Adelman (2006, 2007) demonstrates with the National Education Longitudinal Study (NELS) 88/2000 data, are significant determinants of subsequent retention and degree completion. Our ability to help students stay in college and graduate depends not just on our being able to help them continue to the second year, but to do so with the credits, knowledge, and skills required for success beyond the first year. In other words, their success depends on their education, not merely their retention. By extension, their success depends on our capacity to build effective first-year programs that foster student learning and enable students to develop sufficient momentum (credits earned) to continue onto program and degree completion.

The issues surrounding accountability are complex and much debated. Take, for instance, the seemingly simple measure of graduation rates as applied to the assessment of institutional effectiveness. Given the increasing incidence of part-time enrollments, multiple enrollments (sometimes within the same time spell), stopouts or interrupted enrollments, and transfers between and within sectors, it is becoming more difficult to decide how to measure college completion (Chen and Carroll 2007; Bailey, Crosta, and Jenkins 2006; Adelman 2004; Burd 2004). The currently accepted measure of 150% of "normal" time to degree completion, three years for a two-year degree and six years for a four-year degree, though reasonable for many four-year institutions, substantially underestimates rates of completion among two-year colleges. Furthermore, it fails to accurately capture the effectiveness of institutions that serve large numbers of lower-income and adult students, who tend to take longer than other students to complete their degrees. Institutions that serve those students will inevitably appear less effective when standard measures of graduation are used in accountability systems.[1] Moreover, as more students complete their degrees by compiling course credits from multiple institutions ("swirling"), it becomes less clear which institution should be held accountable for degree completion.

This is especially true for community colleges. In these, some students intend to complete a degree or certificate, while others do not. Many attend just to take additional courses or acquire additional skills for work, while many others plan to transfer, typically to a four-year institution. In judging the effectiveness of two-year colleges, one would presumably take account of transfer. But doing that is no simple matter. A study of transfer from community colleges in the state of California found that estimates of transfer can vary substantially, depending on who is counted as transfer eligible (Horn and Lew 2007a, 2007b). At the same time, a majority of students in California who transfer from community colleges to four-year institutions do not meet the minimum state-specified requirements for transfer, and nearly one-third of those who did meet those requirements had not transferred to any four-year institution within six years of their first enrollment. As with graduation rates, the measurement of transfer rates as part of an accountability system is fraught with complexities.

This is one reason why a number of researchers have used what are referred to as expected and actual graduation rates as a way of assessing institutional performance for four-year institutions. Expected rates are calculated by employing regression analysis that takes account of student and institutional factors, such as expenditures per student and student attributes, which also influence graduation rates (Astin 2005; Astin and Oseguera 2005). These analyses seek to "predict" what an institution's expected graduation would be if it behaved like other institutions of similar characteristics and expenditures and that admit similar students. The comparison between its actual graduation rate with that "expected" of it if it behaved like the average institution of its type would then indicate whether the institution's impact on graduation rates was positive, that is to say, whether its actions added to the rate of graduation that one would expect if it were merely a reflection of the students it enrolls.

Though estimates of expected graduation rates are useful, estimation is based on a regression technique that uses what amounts to a linear average of a scattergram of the graduation rates of similar types of institutions. In other words, the predicated-versus-actual graduation rate comparison is based on the assumption that an institution's predicted graduation rate can be based on what is known about the average contribution of student attributes and institutional attributes to an institution's graduation rate. Some institutions, however, lie above the average, others below. And other institution-specific factors, reflecting an institution's local context and particular student body, are not included in these calculations (e.g., the percentage of first-generation college students or part-time students). The net result is that expected-versus-actual calculations are better than simple graduation rates alone, they are less than satisfactory when used in an accountability system.

A variant of this form of analysis was developed by the Education Trust (Carey 2004). These analysts compared an institution's actual graduation rate with those of a set of peers defined by similarity in a range of attributes including SAT/ACT scores, institutional mission, and financial resources. In addition to yearly graduation rate analysis, they also looked for institutions that were effective in serving minority students and those that had made rapid gains over five years.[2] Though this analysis goes farther than the analyses noted above, since it seeks to take account of institutional mission, it is susceptible to problems arising out of the construction of an institutional peer group.

RETENTION AND ACCOUNTABILITY   151

Another suggested alternative, which follows that of the Education Trust in concept, employs production frontier analysis (Archibald and Feldman 2008). This form of analysis does not employ linear regressions that average the impact of inputs on expected graduation rates. Instead it uses data from institutions in the immediate vicinity of the scattergram of institutional inputs (i.e., student attributes and institutional resources) and outputs (i.e., graduation rates) to determine which institutions outperform others in the same vicinity. In other words, the analysis compares institutions to the "best practice" of institutions like their own, which allows institutions to improve their own practice by learning from others.[3]

Regardless of methodology, most analyses rely on the Graduation Rate Survey data, which examine only first-time, full-time students whose graduation is measured over a six-year period. Consequently they do not capture the full range of students served by institutions of higher education or the significant variation among institutions in students' mode (full- and part-time) and pattern of attendance (stopout, transfer, etc.). Noting these problems, the Joint Commission on Accountability Reporting (JCAR) of the American Association of State Colleges and Universities (AASCU), the American Association of Community Colleges (AACC), and the National Association of State Universities and Land-Grant Colleges (NASULGC) proposed a more elaborate form of reporting that would enable the states to obtain a much more contextualized picture of how effective institutions are in promoting student progress on a variety of measures (American Association of State Colleges and Universities 2006).

As applied to public four-year colleges and universities, AASCU and NASULGC are working together to develop a Voluntary System of Accountability, designed to provide information to the public about the performance of their member institutions. The so-called College Portrait is intended to provide "consistent, comparable, and transparent information on the characteristics of students, cost of attendance, student engagement with the learning process, and core educational outcomes"—especially student retention, persistence, and graduation.[4] The National Association of Independent Colleges and Universities (NAICU) is developing a similar, but less complete, system of reporting for private institutions.[5] Though such systems enable the public to compare the performance of similar institutions, important questions remain about the accuracy and comparability of data drawn from institutional and national databases. We are still some distance from having a truly national database that accurately tracks the movement of differing students in higher education within and between public and private two- and four-year institutions (see Ewell and Boeke 2007).

In the meantime, rather than comparing institutions to one another, a more straightforward approach to the issue of accountability that gets at the heart of institutional effectiveness is to compare an institution's performance with its own previous performance (American Association of State Colleges and Universities 2006). What matters is not so much a college's performance in any one year as its performance over time. The critical issue is not simply whether an institution's graduation rate is higher than that of its peers or greater than what one might expect, but whether it is improving over time.

All the above presumes, however, that the primary mission of the institution is to promote student graduation. Yet most institutions serve multiple missions, not all of which focus on completing a program of study. Consequently, a more reasonable way of measuring institutional effectiveness would be to employ multiple measures of institutional performance. As regards retention and graduation, it would be more useful to monitor changes over time, not only in institutional graduation rates (in this case program completion rates), but also in the rates at which students move from the first to second year and the rate at which students are earning credits toward their degrees or certificates.

Here is where the utilization of momentum points to assess institutional performance proves its worth, as it breaks down the process of retention and graduation into units that are more easily addressed by institutional action (Prince, Seppanen, Stephens, and Stewart 2010; Pettit and Prince 2010). Momentum point analysis sharpens an institution's focus not only on the critical first year of college but also on its ability to move students through their programs in a relatively timely manner. In all cases, an institution must take account of the changing mix of students who enroll and track the freshman year retention, credit progress, and graduation rates of different types of students. This is necessary if only because institutions may be tempted to change their admission criteria so as to reduce entry to those students they feel would lower their graduation rate.[6] Another virtue of this form of analysis is that by tracking the changing rates of retention, credit progress, and graduation of different student populations, the state maintains the capacity to target its policies to increase the graduation rates of populations whose success it deems to be in the public interest. Furthermore, this sort of analysis can be done now.

Taking a different approach to measuring institutional performance, the University of Alaska at Anchorage, which serves large numbers of students who would not be counted under the federal guidelines (i.e., full-time, first-time), has developed a Student Learning Progress Model (see Brown 2011). The model tracks all entering first-time students each fall for ten years, including those who enter as non-degree-seeking, and monitors not only whether they graduate during that period, in the same institution or elsewhere, but also their academic performance and enrollment history. For degree-seeking students, full- or part-time, it includes data on the number of semesters of enrollment, the number of courses passed, and the achievement of intermediate goals such as earning an associate's degree. Institutional performance is determined by the number of certificates and degrees awarded to all students over ten years, and by levels of successful learning performance of students measured by the ratio of courses successfully completed with a passing grade to total courses attempted. Currently, eighteen institutions, both two- and four-year, are now piloting the model.

A group of nineteen college systems in sixteen states and Puerto Rico have voluntarily joined "Access to Success," an initiative sponsored by the National Association of System Heads in partnership with the Education Trust.[7] The initiative aims, by 2015, to reduce by 50% the gaps in access and success that separate low-income and minority students from others, while also improving overall student success rates. Participating systems have agreed to collect and analyze a common set of data metrics on the extent to which they are meeting their goals, and to have those data reported on an annual basis by the Education Trust. It is hoped that the use of such data, together with the public disclosure of annual measures of progress, will be sufficient to spur institutional action without having to resort to more formal accountability systems. It is a data-intensive project, which mirrors, in a number of ways, the Achieving the Dream initiative funding by the Lumina Foundation for Education.

Unfortunately, all these measures, even that which tracks changes in graduation rates over time, ignore the existence of student swirling, double-dipping, and transfer. Though estimates of multiple attendance varies, it is estimated that over 50% of all bachelor's degree recipients have attended more than one undergraduate institution, and over 20% have attended at least three (McCormick 2003). Transfer aside, it is evident that a sizable and increasing number of students enroll in more than one college over the course of a year (swirling), sometimes in multiple colleges at the same time (double-dipping). Among other reasons, they do so in order to take courses unavailable or more expensive at their initial institution. Beyond the impact on program coherence, multiple enrollment raises the nontrivial question of who should be held accountable for what. For the purposes of discussion, let us say students take 25% of their courses at institutions other than that in which they are matriculated. Since the learning in any one course can influence success in subsequent courses, it is entirely possible that students may do poorly in a program of study at their second institution because of what they did not learn in their first. Who then shall be held accountable for the failure of these students to graduate? The same question can be asked when transfer to another institution is part of an intended course of action. If the quality of learning in the initial institution is such as to lessen the probability of graduating from second one, should the second institution be penalized for what has occurred before the student enrolls?[8] There are other complications. But the issue remains the same: graduation rates as a measure of institutional performance should be used with care.

Nevertheless it is evident that the public conversation about graduation rates and institutional accountability has produced a climate in which states will soon require all institutions, two- and four-year alike, to demonstrate their ability use public resources in promoting the retention and graduation of their students. In such a climate, no institution can ignore the need to assess itself and to hold itself accountable for the success of its students.

NOTES

1. Ironically, as more individuals enter college and graduate, the absolute value of a college degree for future occupational attainment diminishes, since graduates are competing with more persons with similar credentials. At the same time, the penalty for not earning a degree increases as nongraduates are increasingly distinguished from graduates. Thus the pressure individuals face to obtain a degree increases even though its absolute value diminishes. By extension, as the importance of simply going to college and earning a degree diminishes, the importance of going to particular, high-prestige colleges increases, as does the pressure to earn additional degrees.

2. A recent study by Attewell and Lavin (2007a) demonstrates that a substantial portion of the benefits of increased education, even if it does not result in the completion of a four-year college degree, consists in its impact on the next generation's social and economic attainment. A number of observers have correctly argued that for many students, especially those from low-income backgrounds, the earning of an associate's degree is an important first step in that family's upward mobility across generations.

3. In community colleges in particular, many students enroll with no intention of completing a certificate or degree. Some begin with the intent of transferring to another institution while others enroll to improve their skills for job advancement.

4. The early data from the recently completed six-year study that followed the entering cohort of 2004 indicate only minor changes in differences in completion among varying types of students (Radford, Berkner, Wheeless, and Shepherd 2010, tables 1–7).

5. The federal Pell grant, unlike a loan, does not have to be repaid. It is intended to help needy students cover the cost of college attendance. Though students with a total family income up to $50,000 may be eligible for Pell grants, most Pell funding goes to students with a total family income below $20,000. A large proportion, or about 83%, of Pell-eligible students begin higher education in the two-year sector and therefore would not be expected to earn a four-year degree within six-years.

6. At first glance this runs counter to Bowen, Chingos, and McPherson's (2009) claim that "nearly half of all withdrawals occur after the second year" (p. 236). That claim is based, however, not on a nationally representative sample but on data drawn from twenty-one "prestigious research-intensive flagship universities" (p. 10).

7. The Education Trust, for instance, maintains an online database entitled College Results Online, which enables one to compare overall institutional graduation rates as well as the graduation rates of various groups of students within the institution (race, ethnicity, and gender) for virtually any four-year college or university. Visit http://www.collegeresults.org/.

8. Bound, Lovenheim, and Turner (2009), comparing completion rates of the high school cohorts from 1972 and 1992, found that the eight-year college completion rate

had declined, with the greatest decline among men beginning college at less-selective public four-year colleges and students of either sex entering community colleges.

9. There are now a number of projects whose goal is to increase college completion. These include Achieving the Dream, Complete College America, College Completion Toolkit, The College Completion Agenda, Completion Matters, Completion by Design, and Pathways to College Network.

10. Though the early work of Astin (1984, 1993) and Pace (1984) and, more recently, Kuh (2003) and Kuh, Kinzie, Schuh, Whitt and Associates (2005) has done much to operationalize the concept of academic and social engagement in ways that can be reasonably measured and in turn used for institutional assessment (e.g., National Survey of Student Engagement), that work does not yet tell institutions how they can enhance engagement. While recent studies, such as those by Engstrom and Tinto (2007, 2008), Kuh et al. (2005), Tinto (1997), Zhao and Kuh (2004), have looked into practices that enhance engagement, there is a great deal more to do.

11. A number of reports argue, for instance, that financial aid policies and curricular alignment between high school and college are central to student success in college (Advisory Committee on Student Financial Assistance 2006; Kirst and Venezia 2004).

12. More than a few institutions, especially those labeled "selective," see this issue as one of recruitment, of attracting more able and motivated students who are more likely to graduate. Thus the oft-heard phrase "recruit graduates."

13. The U.S. Department of Education reported that at least 28% of all beginning college students in the 2000 academic year enrolled in at least one basic-skills or "remedial" course in reading, writing, or mathematics. That percentage was twice as high in two-year than four-year institutions (42% and 20% respectively). But even these percentages may substantially underestimate the number of students in college who should take such courses, since not all students who are referred to those courses actually take them.

CHAPTER 2

1. This is not to say that the actions of other people on campus do not also influence student expectations. It is well established that student peer groups also influence student expectations (Berger and Milem 2000; Bonous-Hammarth 2000; Oseguera and Rhee 2009). Persons or groups beyond the campus (e.g., family and friends) can also influence student retention. Nevertheless, for the purposes of the present discussion we treat those expectations as beyond the direct influence of institutions. Furthermore, we assume that responding to the needs of individual students will, in aggregate, improve the retention climate of the institution as expressed by the expectations of other students.

2. Much of the research on social capital derives from Pierre Bourdieu's (1986) use of the concept as it is applied to the tendency of social structures to reproduce themselves over time. Like economic capital, social capital can be acquired by individuals

and used to further their attainment. Social capital can arises from various sources, including the knowledge and contacts that are embedded in the networks of affiliation to which the individual has access (see Calhoun 1992; Portes 1998).

3. As described in a report by the Center for Community College Student Engagement (2009).

4. Effective orientation is more than just information sharing. Though such sharing is necessary, experience tells us that effective orientation serves two other goals: the formation of social affiliations and the establishment of a context in the year that follows in which students will know whom to approach with their questions and, just as important, be willing to do so (see Ward-Roof 2010).

5. Each year since 1984 at its annual meeting, the National Academic Advising Association (NACADA) has selected for recognition a number of advising programs. The selection process includes evidence of program effectiveness. To learn more about these institutions, visit http://www.nacada.ksu.edu.

6. The assets of Miami University's DARS system are now part of redLantern LLC (visit http://www.redlanternu.com/).

7. Personal correspondence from Margaret King.

8. See the LifeMap website, http://www.valenciacc/lifemap/.

CHAPTER 3

1. This fact runs counter to what many faculty believe is the case, namely that mathematics is the major barrier to student success.

2. A recent study by Museus (2009) suggests that the impact of loans may vary for different racial groups.

3. The reader is encouraged to read the report of the Advisory Committee on Student Financial Assistance (2010), as it provides an up-to-date detailed analysis of the impact of changing financial aid on student access and completion.

4. A recent study for the Bill and Melinda Gates Foundation suggests that the impact of monetary problems upon persistence is at least partially due to the stress that results from trying to attend to multiple obligations while attending college (Johnson and Richkind 2009).

5. It is noteworthy that a number of elite universities have recently decided to fund the entire cost of attendance for students whose income falls below a certain level, typically set somewhat higher than that established by the Pell grant program.

6. For more information on summer bridge programs, visit the website of the National Center for Summer Learning, http://www.summerlearning.org/. The center's Excellence in Summer Learning Awards has periodically recognized outstanding university programs.

7. The interested reader should visit the website of the National Resource Center for the First Year Experience and Students in Transition at the University of South Carolina, http://sc.edu/fye/.

8. Visit the residential learning community website, http://pcc.bgsu.edu/rlcch/.

9. Visit the website of the International Center for Supplemental Instruction at the University of Missouri, Kansas City, http://web2.umkc.edu/cad/SI/si-programs .html.

10. Data provided by Luis Barrueta, supplemental instruction program coordinator, El Camino Community College.

11. Taken from a story in *Inside Higher Education*, July 15, 2011.

12. The study involved the following four-year institutions: California State University at East Bay, Temple University, Tennessee State University, Texas State University–San Marcos, and the University of Texas at El Paso; and the following two-year colleges: Camden County College, Cerritos College, Community College of Baltimore County, DeAnza College, Grossmont College, Holyoke Community College, LaGuardia Community College, San Jose City College, Sandhills Community College, Santa Fe Community College, Seattle Central Community College, Shoreline Community College, and Spokane Falls Community College. Several of these served as case study sites.

13. Case studies were carried out at California State University at East Bay, Cerritos College, DeAnza College, LaGuardia Community College, and the University of Texas at El Paso.

14. The interested reader should visit the I-BEST Resource website, http://flight line.highline.edu/ibest/.

15. It is also true that more than a few students who are referred to a basic-skills course do not enroll in the course (Bailey, Jeong, and Cho 2009b).

16. Interested readers should visit the project website at the Carnegie Foundation for the Advancement of Teaching, http://72.5.117.129/programs/.

17. A detailed description of the Patrick Henry Community College initiative can be found in Zachry (2008).

18. Visit the Basic Skills Initiative website at www.cccbsi.org.

19. Visit the website of WestEd at www.wested.org/SLI.

20. For more information about TRIO and Student Support Services, visit the U.S. Department of Education, http://www.ed.gov/about/offices/list/ope/trio/index.html.

21. Data for this case study were drawn from Jenkins et al. (2010) and Jenkins, McKusick, and Adams (2011).

22. Visit http://www.carnegiefoundation.org/statway.

23. Taken from the website of the peer-mentoring program Buffalo State College, http://www.buffalostate.edu/firstyearprograms/x521.xml.

24. For research and policy issues, visit the websites of the Council of Opportunity in Education (http://www.coenet.us) and the Pell Institute for the Study of Opportunity in Higher Education (http://www.pellinstitute.org).

25. Personal correspondence from John Schuh, June 14, 2007.

26. The FWS Program provides funds that are earned through part-time employment to assist students in financing the costs of postsecondary education. Students can receive FWS funds at approximately 3,400 participating colleges. Institutional

financial aid administrators at participating institutions have substantial flexibility in determining the amount of FWS awards to provide to students who are accepted or already enrolled. Hourly wages must not be less than the federal minimum wage. (Quoted from the webpage of the Federal Work Study Program, http://www2.ed.gov/programs/fws/index.html.)

27. For more information, visit http://www.unc.edu/carolinacovenant/.

28. Students are still expected to cover some of their own expenses from their summer income, part-time work during the school year, and their own savings.

29. See the Performance-Based Scholarship Demonstration at MDRC.

30. For more information, visit http://www.in.gov/ssaci/2345.htm.

31. For more information, visit http://supa.syr.edu/promise/.

32. For more information, visit http://www.syr.edu/financialaid/.

33. For more information about College Goal Sunday, visit http://www.lumina foundation.org/newsroom/news_releases/061705.html.

CHAPTER 4

1. Because I have drawn from so many studies in this introductory paragraph, I list them here rather than as parenthetical references within the text: Angelo 1991, 1998; Banta 2001; Becker and Haugen 2001; Boud 2001; Braxton and McClendon 2001; Cohen and Kugel 1994; Cross and Steadman 1996; Ewell 1997; Guskin 1994; Cottell and Harwood 1998; Haugen and Becker 2005; Hodges 2010; Kuh et al. 2005; McKeachie 1986; Nulden 2000; Rucker and Thomson 2003; Sorcinelli 1991; Steadman 1998; Steadman and Svinicki 1998; Wholey, Hatry, and Newcomer 1994.

2. For California's Early Assessment Program, see the website of the California State University system at http://www.calstate.edu/eap/.

3. The interested reader should visit the early assessment program website at http://www.csulb.edu/divisions/students/eap/.

4. California State University announced a new Early Start policy, to begin in 2012, that requires students who fail proficiency tests to take CSU-sponsored courses during their senior year in high school or in summer school before the start of the first year of college.

5. Accuracy of assessment, however, is difficult to achieve, not only because of the complexity of the knowledge and skills required for college success, but also because of the inevitable cultural issues that impinge upon assessing the knowledge and skills of students of different ethnicity, race, income, language, and nationality. For this reason, some institutions employ multiple forms of entry assessment or use alternative indicators of knowledge and skills. Some will also ask students to assess their own level of knowledge and skills, for students may be sensitive to issues impacting their performance that are not directly related to knowledge and skills as normally measured.

6. Unfortunately, not all students who are recommended for course placement take the course or courses so recommended. This is particularly noticeable among students who are assessed as requiring basic-skills courses.

7. There is increased interest in developing entry assessments that are diagnostic in nature to help colleges decide whether students' learning needs would be better served by specific modules rather than an entire course.

8. The interested reader should visit the Noel-Levitz website at https://www.noellevitz.com/.

9. Cited in Bowen, Chingos, and McPherson 2009, p. 227.

10. Interested readers should visit http://www.achieve.org/adp-network.

11. E-portfolios have also been employed in student affairs (Garis and Dalton 2007).

12. The reader is encouraged to visit the ePortfolio Project at LaGuardia Community College at http://www.eportfolio.lagcc.cuny.edu, and that at Kalamazoo College at http://www.kzoo.edu/pfolio/. In addition, the ePortConsortium at Indiana University / Purdue University Indianapolis brings together institutions from across the country and individuals from around the world to collaborate on developing software to enable effective e-portfolios for both students and faculty (visit http://www.eportconsortium.org/).

13. Portfolios are also being used in the job application process. Juniors and seniors typically employ their portfolio to present themselves professionally via an electronic résumé as they apply for work and graduate opportunities.

14. Classroom difficulties may sometimes reflect other issues that students are struggling with, which, if left unattended, lead students to withdraw from college.

15. In residential campuses, early warning systems are also employed in dormitories to alert residential staff to student struggles.

16. Visit http://www.thencat.org/PCR.htm.

17. Visit the website of the program at http://ctl.utexas.edu/programs-and-services/course-transformation-program/.

18. Taken from Twigg 2005, p. 31. Other case studies can also be found in that document.

19. Taken from the 2010 Community College Survey of Student Engagement Annual Report. For more information, visit http://www.ccsse.org/.

CHAPTER 5

1. Though used as if they were identical in meaning, the concepts of integration and engagement are different in at least one important way. *Integration*, as used by this author (Tinto 1973, 1987), refers to the degree to which a person integrates the values and norms of a community into his or her own value system. *Engagement* implies no such internalization. Rather, it speaks to the person's interaction with those values and norms and the individuals who share them. Though internalization may follow, it is not a given. Nevertheless, both concepts necessarily imply a level of interaction with others in a community that can lead to an individual perceiving him- or herself as being included in that community as a valued member. In a somewhat different manner, Astin defined the term student involvement as "the amount of physi-

cal and psychological energy that the student devotes to the academic experience" (1984, p. 297). So defined, involvement refers primarily to student behaviors instead of what meanings they make of those behaviors. As contrasted to engagement, and certainly to integration, involvement implies no internalization whatsoever; it implies only that an individual interacts with others. For a thoughtful discussion of engagement in higher education, see Harper and Quaye (2008).

2. Also see Astin (1993); Berger and Braxton (1998); Billson and Terry (1987); Borglum and Kubala (2000); Braxton and McClendon (2001); Braxton and Mundy (2001–2); Braxton, Vespar, and Hossler (1995); Carini, Kuh, and Klein (2006); Elkins, Braxton, and James (2000); Fischer (2007); Kuh et al. (2005); Malaney and Shively (1995); Nicpon et al. (2006); Pascarella and Chapman (1983); Pascarella and Terenzini (1980, 1983); Polewchak (2002); Sand, Kurpuis, and Rayle (2004); Terenzini, Lorang, and Pascarella (1981); Tinto (1975, 1987).

3. The impact of such involvements on academic involvement depends in part on social and academic orientation of individuals who are members of the organization. Some research on sororities, for instance, indicates a positive impact on academic outcomes (DeBard and Sacks, 2010).

4. This is analogous to Bowen, Chingos, and McPherson's (2009) finding that "black male students who went to more selective institutions graduated at a higher rate . . . than did similarly prepared black students who went to less selective institutions" (p. 228).

5. See Attinasi (1989); Fries-Britt and Turner (2001); Gonzales (2002); Hausmann, Ye, Schofield, and Woods (2009); Hurtado and Carter (1996, 1997); Hurtado, Carter, and Spuler (1996); Nora (1987); Nora and Cabrera (1996); Ostrove and Long (2007); Pavel (1991); and Suen (1983).

6. The same may also apply, but perhaps in a somewhat different manner, to any group of students who see themselves at odds with others on campus, or to any individual student, regardless of racial, ethnic, or other forms of identification (Donaldson 1999; Harris 2006).

7. The University of Delaware has an excellent center for problem-based learning; it was the 1999 recipient of Hesburgh Certificate of Excellence. Interested readers should visit http://www.udel.edu/pbl.

8. See Bonwell and Eison (1991); Cooper et al. (1990); Cooper, Robinson and McKinney (1994); Garth (1999); Johnson and Johnson (1994); Johnson, Johnson, and Smith (1991, 1998); Millis (2010); and Millis and Cottell (1998).

9. Also see Allen, Duch, and Groh (1996); Duch (1995); Duch, Gron, and Allen (2001); Major and Palmer (2001). There are a number of centers on problem-based learning at both two and four-year institutions, for instance at Maricopa Community College, Samford University, and the University of Delaware.

10. Also see Amador, Miles, and Peters (2006); Cooper and Robinson (1995); Major and Palmer (2001); Ravitz (2009); Strobel and Barneveld (2008); Springer, Stanne, and Donovan (1999); and Wilkerson and Gijselaers (1996).

11. In a different, but related manner, see Steele (1999) and Steele and Aronson (1998). These authors show how students' own sense of self relative to other students also influences their performance, in this case on standardized tests of ability.

12. For more information, visit the Center for Problem Based Learning, http://www.udel.edu/pbl.

13. For more information on any of these projects, contact Judith Kamber at jkamber @necc.mass.edu or visit http://cit.necc.mass.edu/ofsd/index.php.

14. For more information, contact Kathleen Langan Pusecker, director of the Office of Educational Assessment, University of Delaware, klp@udel.edu.

15. Also see Baker and Pomerantz (2001); Castro-Cedeno (2005); Engstrom and Tinto (2007, 2008); Hoffman, Richmond, Morrow, and Salomone (2003); Johnson (2000); Pike (1999); Pike, Schroeder, and Berry (1997); Scrivener (2007); Tinto (1997); Tinto, Goodsell, and Russo (1993); Tinto and Russo (1994); Rocconi (2010); Wathington, Pretlow, and Mitchell (2010–11); Zhao and Kuh (2004).

16. Much of the material is taken from information provided on the LinC webpage, http://www.deanza.edu/linc.

17. Interested readers should visit the National Service-Learning Clearinghouse website, http://www.servicelearning.org/. A listing of service-learning programs can also be found at http://evergreen.loyola.edu/.

18. More information about the program can be found at http://www.raritanval .edu/academics/servlearn/program.html.

19. See http://www.hofstra.edu/faculty/ctse/cte_links.cfm for links to a wide range of teaching and learning centers across the nation. Also see http://www.cte .ku.edu/.

20. A valuable resource on faculty learning communities can be found at the Miami University of Ohio Center for the Enhancement of Learning and Teaching (http://www.units.muohio.edu/celt/flcs/).

21. Ibid. That website also provides access to an international list of institutions that have faculty-learning communities as part of the faculty development program.

22. Interested readers should visit the website of the Professional and Organizational Development Network in Higher Education (POD), http://www.podnetwork .org.

23. Visit the website of Preparing Future Faculty Program at http://www.preparing-faculty.org.

CHAPTER 6

1. This is precisely the position taking by the Lumina Foundation for Education's Achieving the Dream Initiative and the Foundations of Excellence in the First College Year Program headed by John Gardner. For more information visit www.luminafoun-dation.org and www.fyfoundations.org/.

2. The recent MDRC evaluation of Achieving the Dream indicated that while participating institutions had developed a "culture of evidence" and had instituted

a range of retention programs, those efforts, on average, had not yet scaled up sufficiently to make substantial improvements in rates of student retention and graduation (Rutschow et al. 2011).

3. The interested reader should visit http://www.sbctc.edu/college/e_student achievement.aspx. Also contact Tacoma Community College Office of Institutional Effectiveness.

4. For more information, visit http://regents.ohio.gov/hei/success_points.html.

5. As regards learning communities, experience teaches us that most programs typically take three to four years to become fully effective.

6. Collaboration and sharing across the borders of institutional life remains, however, a continuing hurdle in the ability of institutions to promote wider change and innovation. Too frequently, faculty and staff are unaware of actions to enhance student retention taken by others in the institution. The issue is not so much lack of interest as it is the challenge of communicating across the borders and fiefdoms that mark institutional life, the paucity of opportunities for faculty and staff from across campus to meet together to learn from each other and share what they know. Without incentives, such meetings and the unanticipated learning that arises from them are difficult to sustain.

7. Since it has been established that differences in student selectivity account for a large measure of differences in graduation rates, one might reasonably ask if any of the gains were primarily the result of changes in recruiting practices. Though this may have been partly true of two of the three private institutions studied by Carey (2005a, 2005b)—Syracuse University and the University of Notre Dame—it is unlikely to be true of the public institutions, in particular Alcorn State University and Elizabeth City State University, since both remain "less selective" institutions, which admit 70%, if not more, of all applicants whose high-school grade-point averages are about 2.8. In any case, even among the private institutions, the relationship between student selectivity and actions to enhance retention and graduation is complex. In many cases, but by no means all, institutional actions that are effective in enhancing student experience and, consequently, retention and graduation will lead to a heightened ability to attract more able students, which in turn feeds continued improvement in retention.

8. For a fuller discussion of the implementation of learning communities, see Levine-Laufgraben and Shapiro (2004).

9. In some cases, often the most effective, multiple forms of assessment are employed (see Upcraft and Schuh 1996).

10. The issue of scalability can also apply to specific fields of study. Here the issue is how a program can be scaled up within the field of study and the department in which it is located so that it impacts the department generally. As with an institution as a whole, one has to ask when, in the life of a department, scalability is most likely. The answer is the same, namely: it is most likely at that point in time when the students within a department are sharing relatively common experiences.

11. What constitutes worth is not one-dimensional. In some cases it may mean improving rates of student success; in others, generating revenue from increased persistence that more than offsets costs; and in still others, enhancing the institution's reputation by giving it a distinctive signature that in turn attracts more students to it in the future.

12. Increased persistence generates a number of revenue outcomes. In addition to the revenue that results from more students enrolling for longer periods, revenue comes from more student expenditures in other institutional services and from decreased costs of recruitment, since fewer students are needed to replace those who leave.

13. For many students and many institutions, the first year of college begins before the start of the fall semester. Besides the summer bridge programs, typically directed toward students who need additional academic support, a number of programs encourage students to get a head start on their academic programs. These range from The City University of New York College Now program (discussed in chapter 6) to Syracuse Universities Project Advance. Students who participate in College Now are reported to do better, on average, than their counterparts once they're in college. Project Advance, one of the largest of its kind, involves over 170 high schools, more than 500 teachers, and more than 8,000 students in Maine, Massachusetts, New Jersey, and New York. High schools offer qualified seniors the opportunity to enroll in Syracuse University courses for credit. Courses are offered in high-school classrooms during the regular school day and are taught by high-school teachers who have completed graduate seminars in their subject areas and been named adjunct instructors at Syracuse University. Courses are the same as those taught to freshmen and sophomores on the main Syracuse University campus but are considerably less expensive than those offered on the main campus.

Unlike programs that originate from colleges, the Early College High School program, sponsored by the Bill and Melinda Gates Foundation, originates in high schools and is targeted at low-income youth, first-generation college goers, English-language learners, students of color, and other young people underrepresented in higher education. Its goal is to enable students to earn a high-school diploma and an associate's degree or up to two years of credit toward a bachelor's degree—tuition free. Begun in 2002, the program has involved over 160 high schools in twenty-four states.

14. One of the consequences of high rates of first-year attrition is that many programs of study (majors) find themselves with too few upper-classmen to remain sustainable.

15. The recent study of learning in college by Arum and Roksa (2010) makes essentially the same point.

16. Visit the website of the Center at http://www.center.rpi.edu/.

17. For more details, visit the website http://communities.usc.edu/education/nai .html.

18. The interested reader should visit the CUNY website of College Now at http://collegenow.cuny.edu/.

19. For more information on the Long Beach Promise, visit the websites http://www.lbusd.k12.ca.us/Main_Offices/Superintendent/Success_Initiative/college_promise.cfm, and http://www.csulb.edu/misc/inside/archives/v60n7/stories/4.htm.

20. The book edited by Hunter et al. (2009) is especially useful, as it speaks to a range of ways in which colleges and universities can address the needs of students beyond the first year.

21. Adelman (2006) found that 16% of the students in his survey began the second year of college either in poor academic standing or having failed to make satisfactory progress toward their degrees.

22. In this context, it should be observed that the use of momentum point analysis avoids these problems, since it makes no assumption about years in college but measures concrete forms of progress, regardless of year.

23. For more detailed listing of sophomore-year programs, the reader should visit the website of the National Resource Center for the First-Year Experience and Students in Transition at http://www.sc.edu/fye/resources/soph/school.html.

24. The National Academic Advising Association (NACADA) annually awards outstanding advising programs. Some awards are given for those that focus on second-year students. Visit http://www.nacada.ksu.edu/Programs/Awards/index.htm for more information.

25. Program descriptions taken from the website of National Resource Center for the First-Year Experience and Students in Transition at http://www.sc.edu/fye/resources/soph/.

26. Clearly, alignment of courses here is in substance no different from that of the alignment of high-school courses to those in higher education (Kirst and Venezia 2004). As part of the broader K-16 movement, high-school and college faculty and administrators in a number of states, such as California, Georgia, Illinois, Maryland, Oregon, and Texas, have entered into conversations about how they can better align their courses so as to promote greater success in the transition between high school and college.

27. The interested reader should visit the website of National Resource Center for the First-Year Experience and Students in Transition, at the Foundations of Excellence in the First College Year website: http://www.fyfoundations.org/transfer.aspx.

28. It should be observed, however, that in more than a few cases, institutions require things of students even though there is little evidence that doing so makes a difference. Take, for instance, the common use of prerequisite courses for a program of study. With few exceptions, most institutions have not demonstrated that students who do not follow stated prerequisites fare any less well than those who do. This does not mean that prerequisites do not matter, only that many institutions have failed to demonstrate that they do. By contrast, one can ask why institutions do not require, within reason, particular courses, programs, or experiences when evidence exists that they benefit students.

29. For more information on the Foundations of Excellence Project please visit http://fyfoundations.org/index.aspx.

30. Some institutions have employed software programs, such as ASTRA, that enable them to compare supply and demand for courses and in turn better schedule courses to meet existing demand.

31. This initiative is a project of the Association of Community College Trustees and the Community College Leadership Program at the University of Texas at Austin, with support from the Bill and Melinda Gates Foundation. Interested readers should visit http://www.governance-institute.org.

CHAPTER 7

1. This is one of the goals of the Lumina Foundation for Education's multiyear national initiative Achieving the Dream: Community Colleges Count. For more information visit http://www.achievingthedream.org.

2. While more than 56% of students from families earning over $70,000 earn a four-year degree within six years of entering higher education, only 26% of those from low-income backgrounds—family incomes of less than $25,000—do so.

3. Whereas nearly six in ten four-year college entrants earn a bachelor's degree within six years, only a little over one in ten public two-year college entrants do so (National Center for Education Statistics 2003, table 2.1A).

4. A number of foundations, most notably the Lumina Foundation for Education and the Bill and Melinda Gates Foundation, have invested in programs to enhance college graduation, especially among community college students. At the same time, the federal government has recently proposed a $2.5 billion College Access and Completion Fund, directed to the same end.

5. A recent report by the Lumina Foundation for Education argues that states should take a variety of steps to improve student outcomes, such as improving their assessment and placement policies; fostering program innovation, implementation, and evaluation; and the development of performance measures that inform the use of incentives to promote greater student success (Collins 2009). The same can be said of foundations. A number of foundations—the Bill and Melinda Gates Foundations, the Lumina Foundation for Education, the William and Flora Hewlett Foundation, and the Carnegie Foundation for the Advancement of Teaching, among others—have invested in a range of programs directed to the improvement of developmental education.

6. As noted in chapter 4, such institutions often have to reach out beyond the borders of the campus to find ways of addressing or at least taking account of the external forces that may limit the impact of actions taken within the institution.

7. Here is where the use of momentum point analysis can be useful, for it breaks down the longitudinal process of college completion into a series of intermediate steps that can be more easily addressed in a relatively short time by the institution.

8. Completion By Design is a multistate initiative funded by the Bill and Melinda

Gates Foundation that seeks, among other things, to facilitate the development among participating community colleges of coherent, longitudinally aligned pathways that students would follow to complete their certificate or degrees.

9. Much can be learned from the increasing number of institutions that employ action-analytical procedures to help students succeed in college (Norris et al. 2008). Among these are Capella University, Century College, Irving Valley College, Rio Salado College, Saddleback College, and Sinclair Community College, which have employed a variety of commercial programs including GPS LifePlan, Starfish, MAP-Works, and Design2Learn, as well as locally developed programs such as Signals and SHERPA.

APPENDIX A

1. In measuring persistence, it is very difficult to discern the difference between forms of stopout that vary in duration and may result in returning to one's institution, in enrolling in another institution, or in terminating all forms of participation (Porter 2003).

2. Another major reason for increased time between entry and degree is transfer, which often entails changes in major or loss of some prior academic credits.

3. Though these time spans may be reasonable on the average, a number of undergraduate degree programs (e.g., engineering degrees) require more than four years of continuous enrollment to complete. At the same time, in many urban two-year colleges, where enrollments are increasingly part-time, a three-year time span is unrealistically short.

4. Some of these students may have been forced by events to leave college before the first semester or year is completed. Others may have begun part-time and therefore could attempt few credits.

5. Take, for instance, low-income students in higher education. Relative to other income groups they are differentially enrolled in the public two-year sector and in certain four-year institutions. Academically, they tend to be disproportionately underprepared for college. Thus their overall four-year degree attainment rate is lower than that of many other groups, and the institutions that serve them tend to have lower rates of student retention and graduation.

6. This does not necessarily apply to the issue of student persistence and attrition.

7. These estimates differ strikingly from Adelman's (2007) claim that 90% of students persist until the second year. The difference reflects the fact that Adelman is using the NELS data that track high-school students who enter college and takes persistence to mean the enrollment of students regardless of institution. Here we estimate the institution's retention of all entering students into their second year, not just those who enter immediately after high school.

8. Not all students, however, who begin in four-year institutions aim at a bachelor's degree. In BPS 1995–96, nearly 10% do not. Not surprisingly, rates of completion are

somewhat higher for degree-seeking students, specifically 50.0 percent among public four-year colleges and 65.3 percent among private ones.

9. The interested reader should visit http://www.collegeresults.org/.

10. The same conclusion follows from analysis of the ACT data (ACT 2005, tables 7 and 8). Among the public four-year institutions it surveys, five-year graduation rates vary from a high of 74% for highly selective institutions to 32% for open-enrollment ones. The corresponding five-year graduation rates among private institutions, are 84% and 48%. What is telling about the ACT data, however, is that rates of institutional completion can vary considerably within different categories of selectivity. The standard deviations that measure variation in graduation rates within each category are such that some lower-selectivity institutions have higher rates of graduation than institutions in the next higher category of selectivity.

11. A copy of a paper entitled "Creating State-Level Degree Completion Rates from a National Database: Results of an Exploratory Analysis" can be found at http://www .nchems.org/c2sp/ . . . /ClearinghouseProjectReport_June2008.pdf.

12. Presumably some of these differences are related to aggregate differences in social status between white, African American, and Hispanic women.

13. For more detailed information on NCHEMS (National Center for Higher Education Management Systems), as well as complete data files, visit the website of the Center at http://www.higheredinfo.org/.

14. Though from a different set of institutions, ACT data from annual surveys of institutional retention, since 1983 also point to little or no change in completion rates.

15. The same conclusion arises from analysis of the ACT data, in this case over a much longer time frame, 1986–2007.

16. Like the 1995–96 survey, the most recent survey tracks a nationally representative cohort of beginning postsecondary students over six years. As a result, it provides, even in a preliminary form, the most direct test of possible changes in rates of graduation in the United States.

17. The researchers point out that while the t-test of the means for the public four-year colleges is significant, that for the private four-year colleges is not (personal correspondence).

18. Special thanks to Laura Horn of MPR Associates Inc. for supplying the data for table A9.

19. Take the case of the University of Alaska at Anchorage. Using federal guidelines that count only full-time students who graduate from the institution within six years results in a graduation rate of only 24.6%. But nearly nineteen out of every twenty students the university serves are not included in the official numbers: many attend part-time and consequently take longer than six years to graduate, some transfer to other institutions, and others never intended to earn a degree. At Black Hills State University, many students are military personnel at the nearby Ellsworth Air Force Base. Given how often military personnel move, it is not surprising that the six-year graduation rate of the university is only 30%.

APPENDIX B

1. Horn and Carroll's (2006) study of six-year graduation rates at four-year colleges and universities across the nation shows that graduation rates dropped in a systematic fashion as the size of the low-income freshman student population increased, even within Carnegie classification and selectivity level of the institution.

2. The results of the Education Trust's analysis can be found on line so as to enable consumers to obtain comparative and longitudinal data not easily obtained elsewhere. Visit http://collegeresults.org.

3. Current measures that compare institutional effectiveness are typically cross-sectional in nature; that is, they measure graduation rates at one point in time, and compare institutions one against another at that point. In doing so, these analyses ignore the fact that there may be sizable year-to-year variations in institutional graduation rates that may have little to do with the issues that shape institutional effectiveness generally (e.g., characteristics of enrolled students). In one year the institution may seem more effective, in another year less so.

4. The interested reader should visit http://www.voluntarysystem.org.

5. The interested reader should visit http://www.ucan-network.org.

6. A report in *Inside Higher Education* dated June 8, 2007, describes the debate in the state of Kansas about the desire of the University of Kansas to increase admission standards in part because its six-year graduation rate did not compare well with similar state flagship universities (Redden 2007).

7. See the Education Trust website: http://www2.edtrust.org/.

8. These patterns of student attendance emphasize the role of academic advising in student success and raise some fundamental questions about the responsibility of the home institution. For instance, are students getting accurate information about courses they wish to take at other institutions and the extent to which taking those courses will affect program completion? Are they getting information that is consistent across institutions? An even more fundamental question concerns the role of the state: How can the state ensure that information about courses within the state are accurate and easily available to all students, regardless of their institution of enrollment?

REFERENCES

ACT. 2005. *National Collegiate Retention and Persistence to Degree Rates 2005.* Iowa City: American College Testing Program.

Adelman, C. 1998. "What Proportion of College Students Earn a Degree?" *AAHE Bulletin* 51 (2): 7–10.

———. 1999a. *Answers in the Toolbox: Academic Intensity, Attendance Patterns, and Bachelor's Degree Attainment.* Washington, DC: U.S. Department of Education, Office of Educational Research and Improvement.

———. 1999b. *The New College Course Map and Transcript File: Changes in Course-Taking and Achievement, 1972–1993,* 2nd. ed. Washington, DC: U.S. Department of Education, Office of Educational Research and Improvement.

———. 2004. *Principal Indicators of Student Academic Histories in Postsecondary Education, 1972–2000.* Washington, DC: U.S. Department of Education, Institute of Educational Sciences.

———. 2006. *The Toolbox Revisited: Paths to Degree Completion from High School through College.* Washington, DC: U.S. Department of Education.

———. 2007. "Do We Really Have a College Access Problem?" *Change* 39 (4): 48–51.

Advisory Committee on Student Financial Assistance. 2006. *Reflections on College Access and Persistence.* Proceedings and papers from a symposium held in Washington, DC, September 8, 2005.

———. 2010. *The Rising Price of Inequality: How Inadequate Grant Aid Limits College Access and Persistence.* Washington, DC: U.S. Office of Education.

Albrecht, N. 2003. "University Faculty Collaboration: A Transformational Model." International Learning Conference, University of London, UK.

Allen, D., B. Duch, and S. Groh. 1996. "The Power of Problem-Based Learning in Teaching Introductory Science Courses." In *Bringing Problem-Based Learning to Higher Education: Theory and Practice: Teaching and Learning,* no. 68, edited by L. Wilkerson and W. Gijselaers, 43–52. San Francisco: Jossey-Bass.

Allen, E., and M. Madden. 2006. "Chilly Classrooms for Female Undergraduates: A Question of Method?" *Journal of Higher Education* 77 (4): 684–711.

Allen, M. 2003. *Assessing Academic Programs in Higher Education.* San Francisco: Jossey-Bass.

Altschuler, G., and I. Krammick. 1999. "A Better Idea has Replaced 'In Loco Parentis.'" *Chronicle of Higher Education,* November 5.

Amador, J., L. Miles, and C. Peters. 2006. *The Practice of Problem-Based Learning: A Guide to Implementing PBL in the Classroom.* San Francisco: Jossey-Bass.

American Association for Higher Education. 1998. *Powerful Partnerships: A Shared Responsibility for Learning.* A Joint Report of the American Association for

Higher Education, the American College Personnel Association, and the National Association of Student Personnel Administrators. Washington, DC.

American Association of State Colleges and Universities. 2005. *Student Success in State Colleges and Universities: A Matter of Culture and Leadership*. Washington DC.

———. 2006. *Graduation Rates and Students Success: Squaring Means and Ends—Perspectives*. Washington, DC.

Anderson, J., and R. Ekstrom. 1996. "Improving the Retention of African-American Undergraduates in Predominantly White Colleges and Universities: Evidence from 45 Institutions." Paper presented at the American Educational Research Association, New York, April.

Angelo, T. 1991. "Ten Easy Pieces: Assessing Higher Learning in Four Dimensions." In *Classroom Research: Early Lessons from Success*. San Francisco: Jossey-Bass.

———, ed. 1998. *Classroom Assessment and Research: An Update on Uses, Approaches, and Research Findings: Teaching and Learning*, no. 75. San Francisco: Jossey-Bass.

Angelo, T., and P. Cross. 1993. *Classroom Assessment Techniques: A Handbook for College Teachers*. 2nd ed. San Francisco: Jossey-Bass.

Archibald, R., and D. Feldman. 2008. "Graduation Rates and Accountability: Regressions versus Production Frontiers." *Research in Higher Education* 49 (1): 80–100.

Arum, R., and J. Roska. 2011. *Academically Adrift: Limited Learning on College Campuses*. Chicago: University of Chicago Press.

Astin, A. 1975. *Preventing Students from Dropping Out*. San Francisco: Jossey-Bass.

———. 1984. "Student Involvement: A Developmental Theory for Higher Education." *Journal of College Student Personnel* 25 (4): 297–308.

———. 1993. *What Matters in College? Four Critical Years Revisited*. San Francisco: Jossey-Bass.

———. 2005. "Making Sense Out of Degree Completion Rates." *Journal of College Student Retention: Research, Theory and Practice* 7 (1–2): 5–17.

Astin, A., and L. Oseguera. 2002. *Degree Attainment Rates at American Colleges and Universities*. Revised edition. Los Angeles: Higher Education Research Institute, University of California Los Angeles.

———. 2005. *Degree Attainment Rates at American Colleges and Universities*. Revised edition. Los Angeles: Higher Education Research Institute, University of California Los Angeles.

Astin, A., L. Vogelgesang, E. Ikeda, and J. Yee. 2000. *How Service Learning Affects Students*. Los Angeles: Higher Education Research Institute, University of California Los Angeles.

Attewell, P., and D. Lavin. 2007a. *Passing the Torch: Does Higher Education for the Disadvantaged Pay Off Across the Generations?* New York: Russell Sage Foundation.

————. 2007b. "Distorted Statistics on Graduation Rates." *Chronicle of Higher Education*, July 7.

Attewell, P., D. Lavin, T. Domina, and T. Levey. 2006. "New Evidence on College Remediation." *Journal of Higher Education* 77 (5): 886–924.

Attinasi, L., Jr. 1989. "Getting in: Mexican Americans' Perceptions of University Attendance and Implications for Freshman Year Persistence." *Journal of Higher Education* 60 (3): 247–77.

Austin, A., and R. Baldwin. 1991. *Faculty Collaboration: Enhancing the Quality of Scholarship and Teaching.* San Francisco: Jossey-Bass.

Bahr, P. 2008. "Cooling Out in the Community College: What is the Effect of Academic Advising on Students' Chance of Success?" *Research in Higher Education* 49 (8): 704–32.

Bailey, T. 2009a. *Rethinking Developmental Education in Community College.* CCRC Brief, no. 40. New York: Community College Research Center, Teachers College, Columbia University.

————. 2009b. "Challenge and Opportunity: Rethinking the Role and Function of Developmental Education in Community College." In *Policies and Practices to Improve Student Preparation and Success. New Directions for Community Colleges,* no. 145, edited by A. Bueschel and A. Venezia, 1–106. San Francisco: Jossey-Bass.

Bailey, T., and M. Alfonso. 2005. *Paths to Persistence: An Analysis of Research on Program Effectiveness at Community College.* New York: Community College Research Center, Teachers College, Columbia University.

Bailey, T., J. Calcagno, D. Jenkins, G. Kienzl, and T. Leinbach. 2005. *Community College Success: What Institutional Characteristics Make a Difference?* New York: Community College Research Center, Teachers College, Columbia University.

Bailey, T., P. Crosta, and D. Jenkins. 2006. *What Can Student Right-to-Know Graduation Rates Tell Us about Community College Performance?* New York: Community College Research Center, Teachers College, Columbia University.

Bailey, T., D. Jeong, and S. Cho. 2009a. *Referral, Enrollment, and Completion in Developmental Education Sequences in Community Colleges.* Presentation given at the 89th Annual Convention of the American Association of Community Colleges. Phoenix.

————. 2009b. *Referral, Enrollment, and Completion in Developmental Education Sequences in Community Colleges.* CCRC Brief, no. 45. New York: Community College Research Center, Teachers College, Columbia University.

————. 2010. *Student Progression through Developmental Sequences in Community Colleges.* CCRC Working Paper, no.15. New York: Community College Research Center, Teachers College, Columbia University.

Baker, S., and N. Pomerantz. 2001. "Impact of Learning Communities on Retention at a Metropolitan University." *Journal of College Student Retention: Research, Theory and Practice* 2 (2): 115–26.

Baldridge, V. 1971. *Power and Conflict in the University; Research in the Sociology of Complex Organizations*. New York: John Wiley.

Bandura, A. 1986. *Social Foundation of Thought and Action: A Social Cognitive Theory*. Englewood Cliffs: Prentice-Hall.

Bank, B., R. Slavings, and B. Biddle. 1990. "Effects of Peer, Faculty, and Parental Influences on Students' Persistence." *Sociology of Education* 63 (3): 209–25.

Banta, T. 1993. *Outcomes of Decade of Assessment in Higher Education*. Boulder: National Center for Higher Education Management Systems.

———. 2001. *Assessment Update: Progress, Trends and Practices in Higher Education*. San Francisco: Jossey-Bass.

Banta, T., E. Jones, and K. Black. 2009. *Developing Effective Assessment: Principles and Profiles of Good Practice*. San Francisco: Jossey-Bass.

Banta, T., J. Lund, K. Black, and F. Oblander. 1995. *Assessment in Practice: Putting Principles to Work on College Campuses*. San Francisco: Jossey-Bass.

Barefoot, B. ed. 1993. *Exploring the Evidence: Reporting Outcomes of Freshman Seminars*. Monograph, no. 11. Columbia: National Resource Center for the Freshman Year Experience, University of South Carolina.

———. 2005. "Current Institutional Practice in the First College Year." In *Challenging and Supporting the First-Year Student: A Handbook for Improving the First Year of College*, edited by M. Upcraft, J. Gardner, and B. Barefoot. San Francisco: Jossey-Bass.

Barefoot, B., J. Gardner, M. Cutright, L. Morris, C. Schroeder, S. Schwartz, M. Siegal, and R. Swing. 2005. *Achieving and Sustaining Institutional Excellence for the First Year of College*. San Francisco: Jossey-Bass.

Barkley, E. 2010. *Student Engagement Techniques: A Handbook for College Faculty*. San Francisco: Jossey-Bass.

Barkley, E., P. Cross, and C. Major. 2005. *Collaborative Learning Techniques: A Handbook for College Faculty*. San Francisco: Jossey-Bass.

Barnett, E. 2011. "Validation Experiences and Persistence among Community College Students." *Review of Higher Education* 34 (2): 193–230.

Barr, R., and J. Tagg. 1995. "From Teaching to Learning: A New Paradigm for Undergraduate Education." *Change* 27 (6): 12–25.

Barton, J., and A. Collins, eds. 1997. *Portfolio Assessment: A Handbook for Educators*. Menlo Park: Addison-Wesley.

Baum, S., and K. Payea. 2004. *Education Pays 2004*. New York: The College Board.

———. 2005. *Education Pays Update*. New York: The College Board.

Baum, S., and J. Ma. 2007. *Education Pays: The Benefits of Higher Education for Individuals and Society*. New York: The College Board.

Baxter Magolda, M. 1999. *Creating Contexts for Learning and Self-Authorship: Constructive-Developmental Pedagogy*. Nashville: Vanderbilt University Press.

Beal, P., and L. Noel. 1980. *What Works in Student Retention*. Iowa City: American

College Testing Program and the National Center for Higher Education Management Systems.

Bean, J. 1980. "Dropouts and Turnover: The Synthesis and Test of a Causal Model of Student Attrition." *Research in Higher Education* 12 (2): 155–87.

Beatty, I. 2004. "Transforming Student Learning with Classroom Communication Systems." *Research Bulletin*, 3. Boulder, CO: EDUCAUSE Center for Applied Research.

Becker, D., and M. Devine. 2007. "Automated Assessments and Student Learning." *International Journal of Learning Technology* 3 (1): 5–17.

Becker, D., and S. Haugen. 2001. "Classroom Assessment Techniques and Student Intrinsic Motivation." *Accounting Instructors' Report*, Spring.

Beeson, M., and R. Wessel. 2002. "The Impact of Working on Campus on the Academic Persistence of Freshmen." *Journal of Student Financial Aid* 32 (2): 37–45.

Belcheir, M. 2001. *What Predicts Perceived Gains in Learning and in Satisfaction?* Report, no. BSU-RR-2001–02. Boise, ID: Office of Institutional Advancement. ERIC Document Reproduction Service, no. ED480921.

Belgarde, M., and R. Lore. 2003. "The Retention/Intervention Study of Native American Undergraduates at the University of New Mexico." *Journal of College Student Retention: Research, Theory and Practice* 5 (2): 175–203.

Berger, J. 1997. "Students' Sense of Community in Residence Halls, Social Integration, and First-Year Persistence." *Journal of College Student Retention: Research, Theory and Practice* 38 (5): 441–52.

———. 2001. "Understanding the Organizational Nature of Student Persistence: Recommendations for practice." *Journal of College Student Retention: Research, Theory and Practice* 3 (1): 3–21.

Berger, J., and J. Braxton. 1998. "Revising Tinto's Interactionalist Theory of Student Departure through Theory Elaboration: Examining the Role of Organizational Attributes in the Persistence Process." *Research in Higher Education* 39 (2): 103–19.

Berkner, L., S. He, M. Mason, S. Wheeless, and T. Hunt-White. 2007. *Persistence and Attainment of 2003–2004 Beginning Postsecondary Students: After Three Years.* NCES 2007–169. Washington, DC: National Center for Education Statistics, U.S. Department of Education.

Berger, J., and J. Milem. 2000. "Organizational Behavior in Higher Education and Student Outcomes." In *Higher Education: Handbook of Theory and Research*, vol. 15, edited by John Smart, 268–38. New York: Agathon Press.

Bettinger, E. 2004. "How Financial Aid Affects Persistence." In *College Choices*, edited by C. Hoxby, 207–38. Chicago: University of Chicago Press.

Bettinger, E., and B. Terry Long. 2004a. *Shape Up or Ship Out: The Effects of Remediation on Students at Four-Year Colleges.* Cambridge, MA: National Bureau of Economic Research.

———. 2004b. *Do College Instructors Matter? The Effects of Adjuncts and Graduate Assistants on Students' Interests and Success.* NBER Working Paper, no. 10370. JEL, no. 12, H4. http://www.nber.org/papers/w10370.

———. 2005. "Remediation at the Community College: Student Participation and Outcomes." In *Responding to the Challenges of Developmental Education. New Directions for Community Colleges*, no. 129, edited by C. Kozeracki, 17–26. San Francisco: Jossey-Bass.

Billson, J., and M. Terry. 1987. "A Student Retention Model for Higher Education." *College and University* 62 (Summer): 290–305.

Blanc, R., L. DeBuhr, and D. Martin. 1983. "Breaking the Attrition Cycle: The Effects of Supplemental Instruction on Undergraduate Performance and Attrition." *Journal of Higher Education* 54 (1): 80–90.

Blanc, R., and D. Martin. 1994. "Supplemental Instruction: Increasing Student Performance and Persistence in Difficult Academic Courses." *Academic Medicine* 69 (6): 452–54.

Blanco, C. 2005. *Early Commitment Financial Aid Programs: Promises, Practices, and Policies.* Boulder, CO: Western Interstate Commission on Higher Education.

Bligh, D. 2000. *What's The Use of Lectures?* 2nd ed. San Francisco: Jossey-Bass.

Bloom, D, and C. Sommo. 2005. *Building Learning Communities: Early Results from the Opening Doors Demonstration at Kingsborough Community College.* New York: MDRC.

Blumberg, P. 2000. "Evaluating the Evidence That Problem-Based Learners Are Self-Directed Learners: A Review of the Literature," In *Problem-based Learning: A Research Perspective on Learning Interactions*, edited by D. Evensen and C. Hmelo, 199–226. Mahwah, NJ: Erlbaum.

Blumenfeld, P., E. Soloway, R. Marx, J. Krajcik, M. Guzdial, and A. Palincsar. 1991. "Motivating Project-Based Learning: Sustaining the Doing, Supporting the Learning." *Educational Psychologist* 26 (3): 369–98.

Boggs, G. 1984. "An Evaluation of the Instructional Effectiveness of Part-Time Community College Development Writing Faculty." PhD dissertation, University of Texas at Austin.

Bolge, R. 1995. *Examination of Student Learning as a Function of Instructor Status (Full Time vs. Part Time) at Mercer Community College.* ERIC Document 382 241.

Bonham, S. 2007. "Measuring Student Effort and Engagement in an Introductory Physics Course." Physics Education Research Conference. *American Institute of Physics Conference Proceedings* 951 (1): 57–60.

Bonous-Hammarth, M. 2000. "Value Congruence and Organizational Climates for Undergraduate Persistence." In *Higher Education: Handbook of Theory and Research*, vol. 15, edited by J. Smart, 339–70. New York: Agathon Press.

Bonous-Hammarth, M., and W. Allen. 1994. "A Dream Deferred: The Critical Factor of Timing in College Preparation and Outreach." In *Preparing for College:*

Nine Elements of Effective Outreach, edited by W. Tierney, Z. Corwin, and J. Colyar, 155–72. Albany: State University of New York Press.

Bontrager, B. 2004a. "Enrollment Management: An Introduction to Concepts and Structures." *College and University* 79 (3): 11–16.

———. 2004b. "Strategic Enrollment Management: Core Strategies and Best Practices." *College and University* 79 (4): 9–15.

Bonwell, C., and J. Eison. 1991. *Active Learning: Creating Excitement in the Classroom.* ASHE-ERIC Higher Education Report, no. 1. ERIC Clearinghouse on Higher Education. Washington, DC: George Washington University.

Borglum, K., and T. Kubala. 2000. "Academic and Social Integration of Community College Students: A Case Study." *Community College Journal of Research and Practice* 24 (7): 567–76.

Bothell, T., and T. Henderson. 2004. "Evaluating the Return on Investment of Faculty Development." In *To Improve the Academy: Resources for Faculty, Instructional, and Organizational Development*, vol. 22, edited by C. Wehlburg and S. Chadwick-Blossey. San Francisco: Anker Publication.

Boud, D. 2001. "Introduction: Making the Move to Peer Learning." *Peer Learning in Higher Education: Learning From and With Each Other*, edited by D. Boud, R. Cohen, and J. Sampson, 1–17. Sterling: Stylus Publishing.

Bound, J., M. Lovenheim, and S. Turner. 2007. *Understanding the Increased Time to the Baccalaureate Degree.* Population Studies Center Research Report 07–626, November. Ann Arbor: University of Michigan, Institute for Social Research.

———. 2009. *Why Have College Completion Rates Declined? An Analysis of Changing Student Preparation and Collegiate Resources.* NBER Working Paper, no. 15566. Cambridge, MA: National Bureau of Economic Research.

Bourdieu, P. 1986. "The Forms of Capital." In *Handbook of Theory and Research for the Sociology of Education*, edited by John Richardson. New York, Greenwood, 241–58.

Bowen, W., M. Chingos, and M. McPherson. 2009. *Crossing the Finish Line: Completing College at America's Public Universities.* Princeton: Princeton University Press.

Bowen, W., M. Kurzwell, and E. Tobin. 2005. *Access and Excellence in American Higher Education.* Charlottesville: University of Virginia Press.

Bowles, T., and J. Jones. 2004. "The Effect of Supplemental Instruction on Retention: A Bivariate Probit Model." *Journal of College Student Retention: Research, Theory and Practice* 5 (4): 431–37.

Boyland, H. 2002. *What Works: Research-Based Best Practices in Developmental Education.* Boone: Appalachian State University.

Braxton, J., ed. 2000. *Reworking the Student Departure Puzzle.* Nashville: Vanderbilt University Press.

———, ed. 2001. "Using Theory and Research to Improve College Student

Retention." Special Issue of *College Student Retention: Research, Theory and Practice* 3 (1). Amityville: Baywood Publishing Company.

———, ed. 2008. *The Role of the Classroom in College Student Persistence. New Directions for Teaching and Learning*, no. 115. San Francisco: Jossey-Bass.

Braxton, J., N. Bray, and J. Berger. 2000. "Faculty Teaching Skills and Their Influence on the College Student Departure Process." *Journal of College Student Development* 41 (2): 215–27.

Braxton, J., A. Hirschy, and S. McClendon, 2004. *Understanding and Reducing College Student Departure*. ASHE-ERIC Higher Education Report 30 (3). San Francisco: Jossey-Bass.

Braxton, J., W. Jones, A. Hirschy, and H. Hartley III. 2008. "The Role of Active Learning in College Student Persistence." In *The Role of the Classroom in College Student Persistence. New Directions for Teaching and Learning*, no. 115, edited by J. Braxton, 71–83. San Francisco: Jossey-Bass.

Braxton, J., and S. McClendon. 2001. "The Fostering of Social Integration and Retention through Institutional Practice." *Journal of College Student Retention: Research, Theory, and Practice* 3 (1): 57–71.

Braxton, J., J. Milem, and A. Sullivan. 2000. "The Influence of Active Learning on the College Student Departure Process." *Journal of Higher Education* 71 (5): 569–90.

Braxton, J., and M. Mundy. 2001–2. "Powerful Institutional Levers to Reduce College Student Departure." *Journal of College Student Retention: Research, Theory, and Practice* 3 (1): 91–118.

Braxton, J., N. Vespar, and D. Hossler. 1995. "Expectations for College and Student Persistence." *Research in Higher Education* 36 (5): 595–612.

Bresciani, M. 2005. "Electronic Co-curricular Student Portfolios: Putting Them into Practice." In *New Directions in Student Services*, no. 112, edited by K. Kruger, 69–76. San Francisco: Jossey-Bass.

———. 2006. *Outcomes-Based Academic and Co-Curricular Program Review: A Compilation of Institutional Good Practices*. Sterling: Stylus Publishing.

Bresciani, M., M. Gardner, and J. Hickmott. 2010. *Demonstrating Student Success: A Practical Guide to Outcomes-Based Assessment of Learning and Development*. Sterling: Stylus Publishing.

Bringle, R. 1996. *Service Learning in Higher Education: Concepts and Practices*. San Francisco: Jossey-Bass.

Bringle, R., and J. Hatcher. 1996. "Implementing Service Learning in Higher Education." *Journal of Higher Education* 67 (2): 221–39.

Brookhart, S. 1999. *The Art and Science of Classroom Assessment: The Missing Part of Pedagogy*. Washington, DC: George Washington Press.

Broughton, E., and S. Otto. 1999. "On-Campus Student Employment: Intentional Learning Outcomes." *Journal of College Student Development* 40 (1): 87–89.

Brown, R. 2011. "University of Alaska Researcher Presses More-Inclusive Approach to Measuring Student Achievement." *Chronicle of Higher Education* (on-line), July 17.

Bruff, D. 2009. *Teaching with Classroom Response Systems: Creating Active Learning Environments.* San Francisco: Jossey-Bass.

———. 2010. "Multiple-Choice Questions You Wouldn't Put on a Test: Promoting Deep Learning Using Clickers." *Essays on Teaching Excellence* 21 (3): 1–6.

Bruffee, K. 1995. "Sharing our Toys: Cooperative verses Collaborative Learning." *Change* 27 (1): 12–18.

Buck, C. 1985. "Summer Bridge: A Residential Learning Experience for High-Risk Freshmen at the University of California." Paper presented at the National Conference on the Freshmen Year Experience, San Diego.

Burd, S. 2004. "Graduation Rates Called a Poor Measure of Colleges." *Chronicle of Higher Education*, April 2.

Burgess, L., and C. Samuels. 1999. "Impact of Full-Time versus Part-Time Instructor Status on College Student Retention and Academic Performance in Sequential Course." *Community College Journal of Research and Practice* 23 (5): 487–98.

Cabrera, A., K. Burkum, and S. La Nasa. 2005. "Pathways to a Four-Year Degree: Determinants of Transfer and Degree Completion." In *College Student Retention: A Formula for Student Success,* edited by A. Seidman. 155–214. Westport: ACE/Praeger Series on Higher Education.

Cabrera, A., M. Castaneda, A. Nora, and D. Hengstler. 1992. "The Convergence between Two Theories of College Persistence." *Journal of Higher Education* 63 (2): 143–64.

Cabrera, A., A. Nora, and M. Castañeda. 1992. "The Role of Finances in the Persistence Process: A Structural Model." *Research in Higher Education* 33 (5): 571–93.

Cabrera, A., A. Nora, P. Terenzini, E. Pascarella, and L. Hagedorn. 1999. "Campus Racial Climate and the Adjustment of Students to College: A Comparison between White and African-American Students." *Journal of Higher Education* 70 (2): 134–60.

Calhoun, C. 1992. *Bourdieu: Critical Perspectives.* Chicago: University of Chicago Press.

Campbell, T., and D. Campbell. 1997. "Faculty/Student Mentor Program: Effects on Academic Performance and Retention." *Research in Higher Education* 38 (6): 727–42.

Cambridge, D. 2010. *E-Portfolios for Lifelong Learning and Assessment.* San Francisco: Jossey-Bass.

Campus Computing Project. 2009. *Managing Online Education: The 2009 WCET-Campus Computing Project Survey of Online Education.* Encino: Campus Computing.

Capaldi, E., J. Lombardi, and V. Yellen. 2006. "Improving Graduation Rate: A Simple Method that Works." *Change* 38 (4): 44–50.

Carey, K. 2004. *A Matter of Degree: Improving Graduation Rates in Four-Year Colleges and Universities.* New York: Education Trust.

———. 2005a. *One Step From the Finish Line: Higher Education Graduation Rates are Within our Reach.* New York: Education Trust.

———. 2005b. *Choosing to Improve: Voices from Colleges and Universities with Better Graduation Rates.* New York: Education Trust.

Carey, K., and F. Hess. 2009. *Diplomas and Dropouts: Which Colleges Actually Graduate Their Students (and Which Don't).* Washington DC: Education Sector.

Carini, R., G. Kuh, and S. Klein. 2006. "Student Engagement and Student Learning: Testing the Linkages." *Research in Higher Education* 47 (1): 1–32.

Carnegie Foundation for the Advancement of Teaching. 2008. *Basic Skills for Complex Lives: Designs for Learning in the Community College.* A Report from Strengthening Pre-collegiate Education in Community Colleges. Stanford.

Carnevale, A., and Rose, S. 2003. *Socioeconomic Status, Race/Ethnicity and Selective College Admissions.* New York: Century Foundation.

———. 2011. *The Undereducated American.* Washington DC: Georgetown University, Center on Education and the Workforce.

Carroll, J. 1988. "Freshman Retention and Attrition Factors at a Predominately Black Urban Community College." *Journal of College Student Development* 29 (1): 52–59.

Carter, D. 2006. "Key Issues in the Persistence of Underrepresented Minority Students." *New Directions for Institutional Research* 130 (Summer): 33–46.

Castro-Cedeno, M. 2005. "A Quantitative Assessment of the Benefit of a Learning Community Environment." Presented at the 35th Annual Conference of the ASEE/IEEE Frontiers in Education Conference, Indianapolis.

Catt, S. 1998. "Adjustment Problems of Freshmen Attending Distant, Non-Residential Community College." PhD dissertation, University of Pittsburgh.

CCSSE. *See* Community College Survey of Student Engagement.

Center for Student Success. 2007. *Basic Skills as a Foundation for Student Success in California Community Colleges.* Sacramento: Research and Planning Group for California Community Colleges.

Center for Community College Student Engagement. 2009. *Benchmarking and Benchmarks: Effective Practices with Entering Students.* Austin: University of Texas at Austin, Community College Leadership Program.

Chaney, B., L, Muraskin, M. Cahalen, and R. Rak. 1997. *National Study of Student Support Services: Third-Year Longitudinal Study of Results and Program Implementation Study Update.* Washington, DC: U.S. Department of Education.

Chemers, M., L. Hu, and B. Garcia. 2001. "Academic Self-Efficacy and First-Year College Student Performance and Adjustment." *Journal of Educational Psychology* 93 (1): 55–64.

Chen, X., and D. Carroll. 2005. *First-Generation Students in Postsecondary Education:*

A Look at Their College Transcripts. Washington, DC: National Center for Education Statistics, U.S. Department of Education.

———. 2007. *Part-time Undergraduates in Postsecondary Education: 2003–2004.* Washington, DC: National Center for Education Statistics, U.S. Department of Education.

Chism, N., and T. Banta. 2007. "Enhancing Institutional Assessment Efforts through Qualitative Methods." *New Directions for Institutional Research* 136 (Winter): 15–28.

Chizmar, J., and A. Ostrosky. 1998. "The One Minute Paper: Some Empirical Findings. *Journal of Economic Education* 1 (Winter): 3–10.

Clewell, B., and M. Ficklen. 1986. *Improving Minority Retention in Higher Education: A Search for Effective Institutional Practices.* Princeton: Educational Testing Service.

Coffman, D. 2002. "Social Support, Stress, and Self-Efficacy: Effects on Student Satisfaction." *Journal of College Student Retention: Research, Theory, and Practice* 4 (1): 53–66.

Coghlan, C., J. Fowler and M. Messel. 2010. "The Sophomore Experience: Identifying Factors Related to Second-Year Attrition." Paper presented at the annual meeting of the Consortium for Student Retention Data Exchange, Mobile.

Cohen, J., and P. Kugel, 1994. "The Class Committee and other Recipes for Gourmet Teaching." *College Teaching* 42 (3): 82–90.

College Board, 2009. *How Colleges Organize Themselves to Increase Student Persistence.* New York.

Collins, M. 2008. *It's Not About the Cut Score: Redesigning Placement Assessment Policy to Improve Student Success.* An Achieving the Dream Policy Brief. Indianapolis: Lumina Foundation for Education.

———. 2009. *Setting Up Success in Developmental Education: How State Policy can Help Community Colleges Improve Student Outcomes.* An Achieving the Dream Policy Brief. Indianapolis: Lumina Foundation for Education.

Commander, N., C. Stratton, C. Callahan, and B. Smith. 1996. "A Learning Assistance Model for Expanding Academic Support." *Journal of Developmental Education* 20 (2): 8–16.

Commander, N., M. Valeri-Gold, and K. Darnell. 2004. "The Strategic Thinking and Learning Community: An Innovative Model for Providing Academic Assistance." *Journal of the First Year Experience* 16 (1): 61–76.

Community College Survey of Student Engagement (CCSSE). 2005. *Overview of 2005 National Survey: Community College Faculty Survey of Student Engagement.* Austin: University of Texas at Austin, Community College Leadership Program.

———. 2006. *Tips for Understanding and Using Your CCSSE Results.* Austin: University of Texas at Austin, Community College Leadership Program.

———. 2008. *High Expectations and High Support.* Austin: University of Texas at Austin, Community College Leadership Program.

———. 2009. *Benchmarking and Benchmarks: Effective Practice with Entering Students.* Austin: University of Texas at Austin, Community College Leadership Program.

———. 2010. *The Heart of Student Success: Teaching, Learning, and College Completion.* Austin: University of Texas at Austin, Community College Leadership Program.

Conley, D. 2005. *College Knowledge: What It Really Takes for Students to Succeed and What We Can Do to Get Them Ready.* San Francisco: Jossey-Bass.

———. 2007. *Toward a Comprehensive Conception of College Readiness.* Eugene, OR: Educational Policy Improvement Center.

Conley, D., A. Lombardi, M. Seburn, and C. McGaughy. 2009. "Formative Assessment for College Readiness: Measuring Skill and Growth in Five Key Cognitive Strategies Associated with Postsecondary Success." Paper presented at the annual conference of the American Educational Research Association, San Diego.

Congos, D. 2003. "Is Supplemental Instruction (SI) help helpful?" *Research and Teaching in Developmental Education* 19 (2): 79–90.

Congos, D., D. Langsam, and N. Schoeps. 1997. "Supplemental Instruction: A Successful Approach to Learning How to Learn College Introductory Biology." *Journal of Teaching and Learning* 2 (1): 2–17.

Congos, D., H. Schoeps, and N. Schoeps. 2003. "Inside Supplemental Instruction (SI) Sessions: One Model of What Happens That Improves Grades and Retention Revisited." *Journal of Student Centered Learning* 1 (3): 159–70.

Cooper, J., S. Prescott, L. Cook, L. Smith, R. Meuck, and J. Cuseo. 1990. *Cooperative Learning and College Instruction: Effective Use of Student Learning Teams.* Carson: California State University Foundation.

Cooper, J., and P. Robinson. 1995. *An Annotated Bibliography of Cooperative Learning in Higher Education, Part III: The 1990's.* Stillwater: New Forums Press.

Cooper, J., and P. Robinson. 2000. "Getting Started: Informal Small Groups Strategies in Large Classes." In *Strategies for Energizing Large Classes. New Directions for Teaching and Learning,* no. 81, edited by J. MacGregor et al., 17–24. San Francisco: Jossey-Bass.

Cooper, J., P. Robinson, and M. McKinney. 1994. "Cooperative Learning in the Classroom." In *Changing College Classrooms: New Directions and Learning Strategies for an Increasingly Complex World,* edited by D. Halpern, 74–92. San Francisco: Jossey-Bass.

Corno, L., and E. Mandinach. 1983. "The Role of Cognitive Engagement in Classroom Learning and Motivation." *Educational Psychologist* 18 (2): 88–108.

Cottell, P., and E. Harwood. 1998. "Do Classroom Assessment Techniques (CATs) Improve Student Learning?" In *Classroom Assessment and Research: An Update on Uses, Approaches, and Research Findings. New Directions for Teaching and Learning,* no. 75, edited by T. Angelo, 37–46. San Francisco: Jossey-Bass.

Cox, M. 2001. "Faculty Learning Communities: Change Agents for Transformation of Institutions into Learning Organizations." In *To Improve the Academy*, edited by D. Lieberman and C. Wehlburg, 69–93. Boston: Anker Publishing.
———. 2003. "Proven Faculty Development Tools That Foster the Scholarship of Teaching in Faculty Learning Communities." In *To Improve the Academy*, edited by C. Wehlburg and S. Chadwick-Blossey, 109–42. Boston: Anker Publishing.
Cox, M., and L. Richlin, eds. 2004. *Building Faculty Learning Communities. New Directions for Teaching and Learning*, no .97. San Francisco: Jossey-Bass.
Crisp, G. 2010. "The Impact of Mentoring on the Success of Community College Students." *Review of Higher Education* 34 (4): 39–60.
Crisp, G., and I. Cruz. 2009. "Mentoring College Students: A Critical Review of the Literature between 1990 and 2007." *Research in Higher Education* 50 (6): 525–45.
Critical Issues Bibliography (CRIB): Summer Bridge Programs. 2001. Washington DC: ERIC Clearinghouse on Higher Education. Document no. ED 466 854.
Cross, P. 1998. "Classroom Research: Implementing the Scholarship of Teaching." In *Classroom Assessment and Research: An Update on Uses, Approaches, and Research Findings. New Directions for Teaching and Learning*, no. 75, edited by T. Angelo, 5–12. San Francisco: Jossey-Bass.
Cross, P., and M. Steadman. 1996. *Classroom Research: Implementing the Scholarship of Teaching.* San Francisco: Jossey-Bass.
Cruce, T., G. Wolniak, T. Seifert, and E. Pascarella. 2006. "Impacts of Good Practices on Cognitive Development, Learning Orientations, and Graduate Degree Plans during the First Year of College." *Journal of College Student Development* 47 (4): 365–83.
Davis, B., Jr. 1992. "Freshman Seminar: A Broad Spectrum of Effectiveness." *Journal of the Freshman Year Experience* 4 (1): 79–94.
DeBard, R., and C. Sacks. 2010. "Fraternity/Sorority Membership: Good News about First-Year Impact." *Oracle: The Research Journal of the Association of Fraternity/Sorority Advisors* 5 (1): 12–23.
DeNeef, A. 2002. "The Preparing Future Faculty Program: What Difference Does it Make?" In *Occasional Papers*. Washington, DC: Association of American Colleges and Universities.
DesJardins, S., D. Ahlberg and B. McCall. 2002, "A Temporal Investigation of Factors Related to Timely-Degree Completion." *Journal of Higher Education* 73 (5): 555–81.
———. 2002. "Simulating the Longitudinal Effects of Changes in Financial Aid on Student Departure from College." *Journal of Human Resources* 37 (3): 653–79.
Dey, E., H. Burn, and D. Gerdes. 2009. "Bringing the Classroom to the Web: Effects of Using New Technologies to Capture and Deliver Lectures." *Research in Higher Education* 50 (4): 377–93.
Diaz, D. 2002. "As Distance Education Comes of Age, the Challenge is Keeping the Students." *Chronicle of Higher Education*, February 11.

Diel-Amen, R. 2011. "Socio-Academic Integrative Moments: Rethinking Academic and Social Integration among Two-Year College Students in Career-Related Programs." *Journal of Higher Education* 82 (1): 54–91.

Donaldson, J. 1999. "A Model of College Outcomes for Adults." *Adult Education Quarterly* 50 (1): 24–40.

Donaldson, J., S. Graham, W. Martindill, and S. Bradley. 2000. "Adult Undergraduate Students: How Do They Define their Experiences and Success?" *Journal of Continuing Higher Education* 48 (2): 2–11.

Dougherty, K. 1987. "The Effects of Community Colleges: Aid or Hindrance to Socioeconomic Attainment?" *Sociology of Education* 60 (2): 86–103.

Dougherty, K., and G. Kienzl. 2006. "Its Not Enough to Get through the Open Door: Inequalities by Social Background in Transfer from Community Colleges to Four-Year Colleges." *Teachers College Record* 108 (3): 452–87.

Douglas College. 2002. *Academic Probation Study: Transcript Analysis of Fall 98 Probationary Students.* New Westminster, BC: Douglas College.

Dowd, A., and T. Coury. 2006. "The Effect of Loans on the Persistence and Attainment of Community College Students." *Research in Higher Education* 47 (1): 33–62.

Duch, B. 1995. "Problem-Based Learning in Physics: The Power of Students Teaching Students." *About Teaching* 47 (1): 6–7.

Duch, B., S. Gron, and D. Allen, eds. 2001. *The Power of Problem-Based Learning: A Practical "How To" for Teaching Undergraduates.* Sterling: Stylus Publishing.

Duncan, D. 2005. *Clickers in the Classroom: How to Enhance Science Teaching Using Classroom Response Systems.* New York: Pearson Addison-Wesley.

Dynarski, S. 2002. "The Behavioral and Distributional Implications of Aid for College." *American Economic Review* 92 (2): 279–85.

———. 2003. "Does Aid Matter? Measuring the Effect of Student Aid on College Attendance and Completion." *American Economic Review* 93 (1): 279–88.

Eagan, M., and A. Jaeger. 2009. "Part-time Faculty at Community Colleges: Implications for Student Persistence and Transfer." *Research in Higher Education* 50 (2): 168–88.

———. 2008. "Closing the Gate: Part-Time Faculty Instruction in Gatekeeper Courses and First-Year Persistence." In *The Role of the Classroom in College Student Persistence. New Directions for Teaching and Learning,* no. 115, edited by J. Braxton, 39–53. San Francisco: Jossey-Bass.

Ebert-May, D., C. Brewer, and S. Alfred. 1997. "Innovations in Large Lectures: Teaching for Active Learning." *BioScience* 47 (9): 601–7.

Edgecombe, N. 2011. *Accelerating the Academic Achievement of Students Referred to Developmental Education.* CCRC Working Paper, no. 30. New York: Community College Research Center, Teachers College, Columbia University.

Ehrenberg, R., and L. Zhan. 2005. "Do Tenure and Tenure-Track Faculty Matter?" *Journal of Human Resources* 40 (3): 647–59.

Elkins, S., J. Braxton, and G. James. 2000. "Tinto's Separation Stage and Its Influence on First-Semester College Student Persistence." *Research in Higher Education* 41 (2): 251–68.

Elliott, K., and M. Healy. 2001. "Key Factors Influencing Student Satisfaction Related to Recruitment and Retention." *Journal of Marketing for Higher Education* 10 (4): 1–11.

Endo, J., and R. Harpel. 1982. "The Effect of Student-Faculty Interaction on Students' Educational Outcomes." *Research in Higher Education* 16 (2): 115–35.

Engle, J., A. Bermeo, and C. O'Brien. 2006. *Straight from the Source: What Works for First-Generation College Students.* Washington, DC: Pell Institute for the Study of Opportunity in Higher Education.

Engstrom, C. 2008. "Curricular Learning Communities and Unprepared Students: How Faculty Can Provide a Foundation for Success." In *The Role of the Classroom in College Student Persistence. New Directions for Teaching and Learning*, no. 115, edited by J. Braxton, 5–20. San Francisco: Jossey-Bass.

Engstrom, C., and V. Tinto. 2007. *Pathways to Student Success: The Impact of Learning Communities on the Success of Academically Under-Prepared College Students.* Final Report Prepared for the Lumina Foundation for Education. Syracuse: Syracuse University.

———. 2008. "Access without Support Is Not Opportunity." *Change* 40 (1): 46–51.

Erickson, B., C. Peters, and D. Strommer. 2006. *Teaching First Year Students.* 2nd edition. San Francisco: Jossey-Bass.

Erickson, E. 1968. *Identity: Youth and Crisis.* New York: Faber & Faber.

Evans, R. 1999. "A Comparison of Success Indicators for Program and Non-Program Participants in a Community College Summer Bridge Program for Minority Students." *Visions: The Journal of Applied Research for the Florida Association of Community Colleges* 2 (2): 6–14.

Ewell, P. 1997. "Strengthening Assessment for Academic Quality Improvement." In *Planning and Management for a Changing Environment: A Handbook on Redesigning Postsecondary Institutions*, edited by M. Peterson, D. Dill, and L. Mets, 360–81. San Francisco: Jossey-Bass.

———. 2009. *Community College Data and Performance Measurement Toolkit.* Austin: Community College Bridges to Opportunity Initiative, University of Texas.

Ewell, P., and M. Boeke. 2007. *Critical Connections: Linking States' Unit Record Systems to Track Student Progress.* Indianapolis: Lumina Foundation for Education.

Ewell, P., and P. Kelly. 2009. *State-Level Completion and Transfer Rates: Harnessing a New National Resource.* Draft Report. Boulder: National Center for Higher Education Management Systems.

Eyler, J. 2002. "Reflection: Linking Service and Learning—Linking Students and Communities." *Journal of Social Issues* 58 (3): 517–34.

Eyler, J., D. Giles, Jr., C. Stenson, and C. Gray. 2001. *At a Glance: What We Know about The Effects of Service-Learning on College Students, Faculty, Institutions and Communities, 1993- 2000.* 3rd edition. Nashville: Vanderbilt University.

Farrell, E. 2007. "High-Income Students Get Bulk of Merit Aid." *Chronicle of Higher Education*, February 2.

Fayne, H., and L. Ortquist-Ahrens. 2006. "Learning Communities for First-Year Faculty: Transition, Acculturation, and Transformation." In *To Improve the Academy*, edited by S. Chadwick-Blossey and D. Robertson, 277–90. Boston: Anker Publishing.

Fencl, H., and K. Scheel. 2005. "Engaging Students." *Journal of College Science Teaching* 35 (1): 20–24.

Fenske, R., C. Geranios, J. Keller, and D. Moore. 1997. *Early Intervention Programs: Opening the Door to Higher Education.* ERIC Clearinghouse on Higher Education. Document no. ED 412862.

Filkins, J., and S. Doyle. 2002. "First Generation and Low-Income Students: Using the NSSE Data to Study Effective Educational Practice and Students Self-Reported Gains." Paper presented at the annual forum of the Association for Institutional Research, Toronto.

Fischer, M. 2007. "Settling into Campus life: Differences by Race/Ethnicity in College Involvement and Outcomes." *Journal of Higher Education* 78 (2): 125–61.

Fleming, J. 1984. *Blacks in College.* San Francisco: Jossey-Bass.

Folsom, P. ed. 2007. *The New Advisor Guidebook: Mastering the Art of Academic Advising through the First Year and Beyond.* Monograph no. 16. Manhattan, KS: National Academic Advising Association.

Franklin, M. 1995. "The Effects of Differential College Environments on Academic Learning and Student Perceptions of Cognitive Development." *Research in Higher Education* 36 (2): 127–53.

Freedman, M. 1956. "The Passage Through College." *Journal of Social Issues* 12 (4): 13–28.

Friedlander, J. 1980. "Are College Support Programs and Services Reaching High-Risk Students?" *Journal of College Student Personnel* 21 (1): 23–28.

Friedman, D., and J. Alexander. 2007, "Investigating a First-Year Seminar as an Anchor Course in Learning Communities." *Journal of The First-Year Experience and Students in Transition* 19 (1): 63–74.

Fries-Britt, S., and B. Turner. 2001. "Facing Stereotypes: A Case Study of Black Students on a White Campus." *Journal of College Student Development* 42 (5): 420–29.

Frost, S. 1991. *Academic Advising for Student Success: A System of Shared Responsibility.* San Francisco: Jossey-Bass.

Gaffner, D., and R. Hazler. 2002. "Factors Related to Indecisiveness and Career Indecision in Undecided College Students." *Journal of College Student Development* 43 (3): 317–26.

Gahagan, J., and M. Hunter. 2006. "The Second-Year Experience: Turning Attention to the Academy's Middle Children." *About Campus* 11 (3): 17–22.

Gancarz, C., A. Lowry, C. McIntyre, and R. Moss. 1998. "Increasing Enrollment by Preparing Underachievers for College." *Journal of College Admission* 160 (Summer): 6–13.

Gaide, S. 2004. "Best Practices for Helping Students Complete Online Degree Programs." *Distance Education Report* 8 (20): 8.

Gansermer-Topf, A., and J. Schuh. 2005. "Institutional Grants: Investing in Student Retention and Graduation." *Journal of Student Financial Aid* 35 (3): 5–20.

Garcia, P. 1991. "Summer Bridge: Improving Retention Rates for Underprepared Students." *Journal of the Freshman Year Experience* 3 (2): 91–105.

Gardner, J. 1996. "Helping America's First-Generation College Students." *About Campus* 1 (5): 31–32.

Gardner, P. 2000. "From Drift to Engagement: Finding Purpose and Making Career Connections in the Sophomore Year." In *Visible Solutions for Invisible Students: Helping Sophomores Succeed*, edited by L. Schreiner, and J. Pattengale, 67–77. Columbia, SC: National Resource Center for the First-Year Experience and Students in Transition.

Gardner, J., G. Van der Veer, and Associates. 1997. *The Senior year Experience: Facilitating Integration, Reflection, Closure, and Transition*. San Francisco: Jossey-Bass.

Garis, J., and J. Dalton. eds. 2007. *E-Portfolios: Emerging Opportunities for Student Affairs. New Directions for Student Services*, no.119. San Francisco: Jossey-Bass.

Garth, R. 1999. "Group-Based Learning." In *Teaching and Learning on the Edge of the Millennium. New Directions for Teaching and Learning*, no. 80, edited by M. Svinicki, 55–60. San Francisco: Jossey-Bass.

Gather, G. ed. 2005. *Minority Retention: What Works?* San Francisco: Jossey-Bass.

Giaquinto, R. 2009–10. "Instructional Issues and Retention of First-Year Students." *Journal of College Student Retention: Research, Theory, and Practice* 11 (2): 267–85.

Giddan, N. 1988. *Community and Social Support for Students*. Springfield, IL: Charles C. Thomas.

Gloria, A., and S. Kurpuis. 2001. "Influences of Self-Beliefs, Social Support, and Comfort in the University Environment on the Academic Nonpersistence Decisions of American Indian Undergraduates." *Cultural Diversity and Ethnic Minority Psychology* 7 (1): 88–102.

Gloria, A., S. Kurpius, S., K. Hamilton, K., and M. Wilson. 1999. "African American Students' Persistence at a Predominantly White University: Influences of Social Support, University Comfort, and Self-Beliefs." *Journal of College Student Development* 40 (3): 257–268.

Gohn, Lyle, J. Swartz, and S. Donnelly. 2000. "A Case Study of Second Year Student Persistence." *Journal of College Student Retention: Research, Theory, and Practice* 2 (4): 271–94.

Gold, M. 1992. "The Bridge: A Summer Enrichment Program to Retain African-American Collegians." *Journal of the Freshman Year Experience* 4 (2): 101–17.

Gold, L., and L. Albert. 2006. "Graduation Rates as a Measure of College Accountability." *American Academic* 2 (1): 89–106.

Golde, C., and D. Pribbenow. 2000. "Understanding Faculty Involvement in Residential Learning Communities." *Journal of College Student Development* 41 (1): 27–40.

Gonzales, K. 2002. "Campus Culture and the Experiences of Chicano Students in a Predominantly White Campus." *Urban Education* 37 (2): 193–218.

Goodman, K., and E. Pascarella. 2006. "First-Year Seminars Increase Persistence and Retention: A Summary of the Evidence from How College Affects Students." *Peer Review* 8 (3): 26–28.

Gordon, V. 2005. *Career Advising—An Academic Advisor's Guide.* San Francisco: Jossey Bass.

———. 2007. *The Undecided College Student: An Academic and Career Advising Challenge.* 3rd ed. Springfield, IL: Charles C. Thomas.

———. 2010. "Academic Advising: Helping Sophomores Succeed." In *Helping Sophomore Success: Understanding and Improving the Second-Year Experience,* edited by M. Hunter, B. Tobokowsky, J. Gardner, S. Evenbeck, J. Pattengale, M. Schiller, and L Schreiner. San Francisco: Jossey-Bass.

Gordon, V., and W. Habley. eds. 2000. *Academic Advising: A Comprehensive Handbook.* San Francisco: Jossey-Bass.

Gordon, V., W. Habley, and T. Grites. 2008. *Academic Advising: A Comprehensive Handbook.* 2nd ed. San Francisco: John Wiley and Sons.

Gordon, V., and G. Steele. 1992. "Advising Major Changers: Students in Transition." *NACADA Journal* 12 (1): 22–27.

Grant-Vallone, E. Reid, C. Umali, and E. Pohlert. 2003. "An Analysis of the Effects of Self-Esteem, Social Support, and Participation in Student Support Services on Students' Adjustment and Commitment to College." *Journal of College Student Retention: Research, Theory, and Practice* 5 (3): 255–74.

Graunke, S., and S. Woolsey. 2005. "An Exploration of the Factors That Affect the Academic Success of College Sophomores." *College Student Journal* 39 (2): 367–76.

Greene, J., and G. Foster. 2003. *Public High School Graduation and College Readiness Rates in the United States.* Education Working Paper. New York: Manhattan Institute, Center for Civic Information.

Greene, T. 2005. *Bridging the Divide: Exploring the Relationship between Student Engagement and Educational Outcomes for African American and Hispanic Community College Students in the State of Florida.* Austin: University of Texas, Institute for Community College Research.

Grier-Reed, T., N. Madyun, and C. Buckley. 2008. "Low Black Student Retention on a Predominantly White Campus: Two Faculty Respond with the African

American Student Network." *Journal of College Student Development* 49 (5): 476–85.

Griffin, A., and J. Romm, eds. 2008. *Exploring the Evidence*, vol. 4: *Reporting Research on First-Year Seminars*. Columbia, SC: National Resource Center for the First-Year Experience and Students in Transition. http://www.sc.edu/fye/resources/fyr/index.html. Retrieved October 30, 2010.

Grinnell College. 2008. *Issue Brief: Curricular Breadth*. Grinnell, IA.

Gross, J. Hossler, D., and Ziskin, M. 2007. "Institutional Aid and Student Persistence: An Analysis of the Effects of Campus-Based Financial Aid at Public Four-Year Institutions." *NASFAA Journal of Student Financial Aid* 37 (1): 29–39.

Grubb, N. 1991. "The Decline of Community College Transfer Rates: Evidence from National Longitudinal Surveys." *Journal of Higher Education* 62 (2): 194–217.

Grubb, W., and Associates. 1999. *Honored but Invisible: An Inside Look at Teaching in Community Colleges*. New York: Routledge.

Grubb, W., and R. Cox. 2005. "Pedagogical Alignment and Curricular Consistency: The Challenges for Developmental Education." In *Responding to the Challenges of Developmental Education. New Directions for Community Colleges*, no. 129, edited by C. Kozeracki, 93–103. San Francisco: Jossey-Bass.

Guiffrida, D. 2003. "African American Student Organizations as Agents of Social Integration." *Journal of College Student Development* 44 (3): 304–19.

Guskin, A. 1994. "Reducing Student Costs and Enhancing Student Learning: Restructuring the Role of Faculty." *Change* 26 (5): 16–25.

Hagedorn, L. 2005. "Transcript Analyses as a Tool to Understand Community College Student Academic Behaviors." *Journal of Applied Research in the Community College* 13 (1): 45–57.

Hagedorn, L., W. Maxwell, S. Cypers, H. Moon, and J. Lester. 2007. "Course Shopping in Urban Community Colleges: An Analysis of student Drop and Add Activities." *Journal of Higher Education* 78 (4): 464–85.

Hagerty, B., et al. 1996. "Sense of Belonging and Indicators of Social and Psychological Functioning." *Archives of Psychiatric Nursing* 10 (4): 235–44.

Hall, J., and M. Ponton. 2005. "Mathematics Self-Efficacy of College Freshmen." *Journal of Developmental Education* 28 (3): 26–32.

Hamrick, F., N. Evans, and J. Schuh. 2002. *Foundations of Student Affairs Practice: How Philosophy, Theory, and Research Strengthen Educational Outcomes*. San Francisco: Jossey-Bass.

Hamrick, F., J. Schuh, and M. Shelley. 2004. "Predicting Higher Education Graduation Rates from Institutional Characteristics and Resource Allocation." *Education Policy Analysis Archives* 12 (19): 1–24.

Harper, S. 2007. "Using Qualitative Methods to Assess Student Trajectories and College Impact." *New Directions for Institutional Research* 136 (Winter): 55–68.

Harper, S., and S. Quaye. eds. 2008. *Student Engagement in Higher Education:*

Theoretical Perspectives and Practical Approaches for Diverse Populations. London: Routledge.

Harrington, C., and T. Schibik. 2001. "Caveat Emptor: Is There a Relationship between Part-Time Faculty Utilization and Student Learning Outcomes and Retention?" Paper presented at the annual meeting of the Association for Institutional Research, Long Beach.

Harris, B. 2006. "The Importance of Creating a 'Sense of Community.'" *Journal of College Student Retention: Research, Theory, and Practice* 8 (1): 83–105.

Haugen, S., and D. Becker. 2005. "Classroom Assessment and Accounting Student Performance." *International Journal of Innovation and Learning* 2 (1): 36–45.

Hatcher, J., R. Bringle, and R. Muthiah. 2004. "Designing Effective Reflection: What Matters to Service-Learning?" *Michigan Journal of Community Service Learning* 11 (1): 38–46.

Hausmann, L., F. Ye, J. Schofield, and R. Woods. 2007. "Sense of Belonging as a Predictor of Intentions to Persist among African American and White First-Year Students." *Research in Higher Education* 48 (7): 803–39.

———. 2009. "Sense of Belonging and Persistence among White and African American First-Year Students." *Research in Higher Education* 50 (7): 649–69.

Haycock, K. 2006. *Promised Abandoned: How Policy Choices and Institutional Practices Restrict College Opportunities.* New York: The Education Trust.

Heffernan, K. 2001. *Fundamentals of Service-Learning Course Construction.* Providence: Campus Compact, Brown University.

Heiberger, G., and R. Harper. 2008. "Have You Facebooked Astin Lately? Using Technology to Increase Student Involvement." In *Using Emerging Technologies to Enhance Student Engagement. New Directions for Student Services,* no. 124, edited by R. Junco and D. Timm, 19–35. San Francisco: Jossey-Bass.

Heller, D. 1996. "Rising Public Tuition Prices and Enrollment in Community Colleges and Four-Year Institutions." Presented at the Annual Meeting of the Association for the Study of Higher Education, Memphis.

———. 2003. *Informing Public Policy: Financial Aid and Student Persistence.* Boulder: Western Interstate Commission on Higher Education.

———. 2008. "The Impact of Student Loans on College Access." In *The Effectives of Student Aid Policies: What the Research Tells Us?* edited by S. Baum, M. McPherson, and P. Steele, 39–68. New York: The College Board.

Henscheid, J., ed. 2004. *Integrating the First-Year Experience: The Role of First-Year Seminars in Learning Communities.* Columbia, SC: National Resource Center for the First-Year Experience and Students in Transition; and Olympia, WA: Washington Center for Improving the Quality of Undergraduate Education.

Herzog, S. 2005. "Measuring Determinants of Student Return vs. Dropout/Stopout vs.Transfer: A First-to-Second Year Analysis of New Freshmen." *Research in Higher Education* 46 (8): 883–928.

Hess, F., M. Schneider, K. Carey, A. Kelly. 2009. *Diplomas and Dropouts: Which*

Colleges Actually Graduate Their Students (and Which Don't). Washington, DC: American Enterprise Institute.

Heverly, M. 1999. "Predicting Retention from Students' Experiences with College Processes." *Journal of College Student Retention: Research, Theory, and Practice* 1 (1): 3–11.

Hodges, L. 2010. "Engaging Students, Assessing Learning: Just a Click Away." *Essays on Teaching Excellence* 21 (4). http://www.podnetwork.org/publications/ teachingexcellence/09–10/V21_N4_Hodges.pdf. Retrieved October 21. 2010.

Hodges, R., C. Dochen, and D. Joy. 2001. "Increasing Students' Success: When Supplemental Instruction Becomes Mandatory." *Journal of College Reading and Learning* 31 (2): 143–56.

Hoffman, M., J. Richmond, J. Morrow, and K. Salomone. 2003. "Investigating 'Sense of Belonging' in First-Year College Students." *Journal of College Student Retention: Research, Theory, and Practice* 4 (3): 227–57.

Holmes, S., L. Ebbers, D. Robinson, and A. Mugenda. 2000. "Validating African-American Students at Predominantly White Institutions." *Journal of College Student Retention: Research, Theory, and Practice* 2 (1): 41–58.

Horn, L., R. Berger, and D. Carroll. 2004. *College Persistence on the Rise? Changes in 5-year Degree Completion and Postsecondary Persistence Rates between 1994 and 2000*. NCES 2005–156. Washington DC: National Center for Education Statistics, U.S. Department of Education.

Horn, L., and D. Carroll. 2006. *Placing College Graduation Rates in Context: How 4-Year College Graduation Rates Vary with Selectivity and the Size of Low-Income Enrollment*. NCES 2007–1610. Washington DC: National Center for Education Statistics, U.S. Department of Education.

Horn, L., and S. Lew. 2007a. "California Community College Transfer Rates: Who Is Counted Makes a Difference." In *MPR Research Brief*. Washington, DC: MPR Associates Inc.

———. 2007b. "Unexpected Pathways: Transfer Patterns of California Community College Students." In *MPR Research Brief*. Washington, DC: MPR Associates Inc.

Horn, L., and S. Nevill. 2006. *Profile of Undergraduates in U.S . Postsecondary Education Institutions: 2003–04, With a Special Analysis of Community College Students*. NCES 2006–184. Washington DC: National Center for Education Statistics, U.S. Department of Education.

Horn, L., and A. Nuñez. 2000. *Mapping the Road to College: First-Generation Students' Math Track, Planning Strategies, and Context of Support*. NCES 2000– 153. Washington, DC: National Center for Education Statistics, U.S. Department of Education.

Hossler, D., J. Bena, & Associates, eds. 1990. *The Strategic Management of Enrollments*. San Francisco: Jossey-Bass.

Hossler D., A. Dadashova, M. Ziskin, J. Lucido and S. Schulz. 2010. "National

Survey of Student Retention Practices." Report presented at the 2010 AIR Annual Forum. Chicago.

Hossler, D., J. Gross, and M. Ziskin. 2009. "Lessons Learned: A Final Look" In *Enhancing Institutional and State Initiatives to Increase Student Success: Studies of the Indiana Project on Academic Success*, edited by Hossler, D. J. Gross, and M. Ziskin. Readings in Equal Education, 24. New York: AMS Press.

Hossler, D., M. Ziskin, J. Gross, S. Kim, and O. Cekic. 2009. "Student Aid and Its Role in Encouraging Persistence." In *Higher Education: Handbook of Theory and Research*, edited by J. Smart. New York: Springer.

Hossler, D., M. Ziskin, S. Kim, O. Cekic, and J. Gross. 2008. "Student Aid and Its Role in Encouraging Persistence." In *The Effectives of Student Aid Policies: What the Research Tells Us*, edited by S. Baum, M. McPherson, and P. Steele. New York: The College Board.

Hossler, D., M. Ziskin, and P. Orehovec. 2007. "Developing the Big Picture: How Postsecondary Institutions Support Student Persistence." In *College Board Forum 2007*. New York, NY.

Hotchkiss, J., R. Moore, and M. Pitts, 2005. *Freshman Learning Communities, College Performance, and Retention*. Working Paper, no. 2005–22. Atlanta: Federal Bank of Atlanta.

Howell, J., M. Kurlaender, and E. Grodsky, 2010. "Postsecondary Preparation and Remediation: Examining the Effect of the Early Assessment Program at California State University." *Journal of Policy Analysis and Management* 29 (4): 726–48.

Huba, M, and J. Freed. 2000. *Learner-Centered Assessment on College Campuses: Shifting the Focus from Teaching to Learning*. Boston: Allyn and Bacon.

Huber, M. 2008. "The Promise of Faculty Inquiry for Teaching and Learning Basic Skills." In *Strengthening Pre-collegiate Education in Community Colleges (SPECC)*. Stanford.: Carnegie Foundation for the Advancement of Teaching,

Hunter, M., B. Tobokowsky, J. Gardner, S. Evenbeck, J. Pattengale, M. Schiller, and L. Schreiner, eds. 2010. *Helping Sophomore Success: Understanding and Improving the Second-Year Experience*. San Francisco: Jossey-Bass.

Hunter, M. S. 2006. "Lessons Learned: Achieving Institutional Change in Support of Students in Transition." In *Understanding Students in Transition. New Directions for Student Services* 114, edited by F. Laanan, 7–15. San Francisco: Jossey-Bass.

Hunter, M., and C. Linder. 2005. First-Year Seminars. In *Challenging and Supporting the First-Year Student: A Handbook for Improving the First Year of College*, edited by L. Upcraft, J. Gardner, and B. Barefoot. San Francisco: Jossey-Bass.

Hurd, S., and R. Stein. 2004. *Building and Sustaining Learning Communities: The Syracuse University Experience*. Bolton: Anker.

Hurley, M., G. Jacobs, and M. Gilbert. 2006. "The Basic SI Model." In *Supplemental Instruction. New Directions for Teaching and Learning*, no. 106, edited by M. Stone and G. Jacobs, 11–22. San Francisco: Jossey-Bass.

Hurtado, S. 1994. "The Institutional Climate for Talented Latino Students." *Research in Higher Education* 35 (1): 539–69.

Hurtado, S., and D. Carter. 1996. "Latino Students' Sense of Belonging in the College Community: Rethinking the Concept of Integration on Campus." In. *College Students: The Evolving Nature of Research*, edited by F. Stage, J. Anaya, J. Bean, D. Hossler, and G. Kuh, 123–36. Needhan Heights, MA: Simon and Schuster Custom Publishing.

———. 1997. "Effects of College Transition and Perceptions of the Campus Racial Climate on Latino College Students' Sense of Belonging." *Sociology of Education* 70 (40): 324–45.

Hurtado, S., D. Carter, and A. Spuler. 1996. "Latino Student Transition to College: Understanding Racial and Ethnic Differences." *Journal of Higher Education* 72 (2): 265–86.

Inkelas, K., and J. Weisman. 2003. "Different by Design: An Examination of Student Outcomes among Participants in Three Types of Living-Learning Programs." *Journal of College Student Development* 44 (3): 335–68.

Institute for Higher Education Policy (IHEP). 2011. "The Role of Mentoring in College Access and Success." *Research to Practice Brief.* Washington DC: Institute for Higher Education Policy.

Jackson, T., A. Soderlind, and K. Weiss. 2000. "Personality Traits and Quality of Relationships as Predictors of Future Loneliness among American College Students." *Social Behavior and Personality* 28 (5): 463–47.

Jacobi, M. 1991. "Mentoring and Undergraduate Academic Success: A Literature Review." *Review of Educational Research* 64 (4): 505–32.

Jacoby, D. 2006. "Effects of Part-Time Faculty Employment on Community College Graduation Rates." *Journal of Higher Education* 77 (6): 1081–1103.

Jaeger, A., and M. Eagan. 2009. "Effects of Exposure to Part-Time Faculty on Associate's Degree Completion." *Community College Review* 36 (3): 167–94.

Jaeger, A., and D. Hinz. 2008. "The Effects of Part-Time Faculty on First-Year Freshman Retention: A Predictive Model Using Logistic Regression." *Journal of College Student Retention: Research, Theory and Practice* 10 (3): 265–86.

Jaeger, A., C. Thornton, and K. Eagan. 2007. "Effects of Faculty Type on First Year Student Retention and Performance." Paper presented at the annual meeting of the Association for the Study of Higher Education, Louisville.

Jenkins, D. 2006. *What Community College Management Practices Are Effective in Promoting Student Success? A Study of High- and Low-Impact Institutions.* New York: Community College Research Center, Teachers College, Columbia University.

Jenkins, D., D. McKusick, and P. Adams. 2011. "Preliminary Analysis of Effectiveness of the Accelerated Learning Program (ALP) at the Community College of Baltimore County." Presentation given at the 2011 Achieving the Dream Strategy Institute, Indianapolis.

Jenkins, D., C. Speroni, C. Belfield, S. Jaggers, and N. Edgecombe. 2010. A Model for Accelerating Academic Success of Community College Remedial English Students: Is the Accelerated Learning Program (ALP) Effective and Affordable? *CCRC Working Paper no. 21.* New York: Columbia University, Teachers College, Community College Research Center.

Jenkins, D., M. Zeidenberg, and G. Kienzl. 2009. *Building Bridges to Postsecondary Training for Low-Skill Adults: Outcomes of Washington State's I-BEST Program.* CCRC Brief, no. 42. New York: Community College Research Center Teachers College, Columbia University.

Johnson, J. 2000. "Learning Communities and Special Efforts in the Retention of University Students: What Works, What Doesn't, and Is the Return Worth the Investment?" *Journal of College Student Development* 2 (3): 219–38.

Johnson, D., and R. Johnson. 1994. *Learning Together and Alone: Cooperative and Individualistic Learning.* Boston: Allyn and Bacon.

Johnson, D., R. Johnson, and K. Smith. 1991. "Cooperative Learning: Increasing College Faculty Instructional Productivity." In *Social Psychological Applications to Education,* edited by R. Feldman. Cambridge: Cambridge University Press.

———. 1998a. *Active learning: Cooperation in the College Classroom.* 2nd ed. Edina: Interaction Books.

———. 1998b. "Cooperative Learning Returns to College: What Evidence Is There That It Works?" *Change* 30 (4): 26–35.

Johnson, D., S. Matthew, J. Leonard, P. Alvarez, K. Inkelas, H. Rowan-Keyan, and S. Longerbeam. 2007. "Examining Sense of Belonging among First-Year Undergraduates from Different Racial/Ethnic Groups." *Journal of College Student Development* 48 (5): 525–42.

Johnson, J., J. Richkind, with A. Ott and S. DuPont, 2009. *With Their Whole Lives Ahead of Them.* Seattle: Bill and Melinda Gates Foundation.

Johnston, G. 2006. "The Date of Course Enrollment as a Predictor of Success and Persistence." Paper presented at the annual forum of the Association for Institutional Research, Chicago.

Jones, L., J. Castellanos, and D. Cole. 2002. "Examining The Ethnic Minority Student Experience at Predominantly White Institutions: A Case Study." *Journal of Hispanic Higher Education* 1 (1): 19–39.

Jones, S., and E. Abes. 2004. "Enduring Influences of Service-Learning on College Students' Identity Development." *Journal of College Student Development* 45 (2): 149–66.

Kadar, R. 2001. "A Counseling Liaison Model of Academic Advising." *Journal of College Counseling* 4 (2): 174–78.

Kaleta, R., and T. Joosten. 2007. "Student Response Systems: A University of Wisconsin System Study of Clickers." In *Research Bulletin, Issue 10.* Boulder: EDUCAUSE Center for Applied Research.

Kanoy, K., and J. Bruhn. 1996. "Effects of a First-Year Living and Learning

Residence Hall on Retention and Academic Performance." *Journal of the Freshman Year Experience and Students in Transition* 8 (1): 7–23.

Karp, M., K. Hughes, and L. O'Gara. 2010. "An Exploration of Tinto's Integration Framework for Community College Students." *Journal of College Student Retention: Research, Theory and Practice* 12 (1): 69–86.

Kaya, N. 2004. "Residence Hall Climate: Predicting First-Year Students' Adjustment to College." *Journal of the First-Year Experience* 16 (1): 101–18.

Kegan, R. 1994. *In Over Our Heads: The Mental Demands of Modern Life*. Cambridge, MA: Harvard University Press.

Kennedy, G., and Q. Cutts. 2005. "The Association between Students' Use of an Electronic Voting System and Their Learning Outcomes." *Journal of Computer Assisted Learning* 21 (4): 260–68.

Kenney, P., and J. Kallison Jr. 1994. "Research Studies on the Effectiveness of Supplemental Instruction in Mathematics." In *Supplemental Instruction: Increasing Achievement and Retention. New Directions in Teaching and Learning*, no. 60, edited by D. Martin, and D. Arendale 75–82. San Francisco: Jossey-Bass.

Kezar, A. 2000. *Summer Bridge Programs: Supporting All Students*. Washington DC: ERIC Clearinghouse on Higher Education. Document Number ED 442 421.

Kezar, A., and P. Eckel. 2007. "Ensuring Success for Students of Color." *Change* 39 (4): 18–24.

Khuri, M. 2004. "Working with Emotion in Educational Intergroup Dialogue." *Journal of Intercultural Relations* 28 (6): 595–612.

King, J. 2004. *Missed Opportunities: Students Who Do Not Apply for Financial Aid*. Washington DC: American Council on Education.

King, M. 2003. "Organizational Models and Delivery Systems for Faculty Advising." In *Faculty Advising Examined*, edited by G. Kramer, 125–43. Bolton: Anker.

King, M., and T. Kerr. 2005. "Academic Advising." In *Challenging and Supporting the First-Year Student: A Handbook for Improving the First Year of College*, edited by M. Upcraft, J. Gardner, and B. Barefoot, 320–38. San Francisco: Jossey-Bass.

Kinzie, J. 2005. "Promoting Student Success: What Faculty Members Can Do." In *Occasional Paper*, no. 6. Bloomington: Indiana University Center for Postsecondary Research.

Kinzie, J., R. Gonyea, R. Shoup, and G. Kuh. 2008. "Promoting Persistence and Success of Underrepresented Students: Lessons for Teaching and Learning." In *The Role of the Classroom in College Student Persistence. New Directions for Teaching and Learning*, no. 115, edited by J. Braxton, 21–38. San Francisco: Jossey-Bass.

Kirk, D. 2005. *Taking Back the Classroom: Tips for the College Professor on Becoming a More Effective Teacher*. Des Moines: Tiberius Publications.

Kirst, M., and A. Venezia, eds. 2004. *From High School to College: Improving Opportunities for Success in Postsecondary Education*. San Francisco: Jossey-Bass.

Kisker, C., R. Wagoner, and A. Cohen. 2011. *Implementing Statewide Transfer and*

Articulation Reform. Center for the Study of Community Colleges Report 11–1. Los Angeles: University of California Los Angeles.

Knapp, L., J. Kelly-Reid, and S. Ginder. 2010. *Enrollment in Postsecondary Institutions, Fall 2008; Graduation Rates, 2002 & 2005 Cohorts and Financial Statistics, Fiscal Year 2008.* NCES 2010–152. Washington, DC: National Center for Education Statistics, U.S. Department of Education.

Knight, W. 2003. "Learning Communities and First-Year Programs: Lessons for Planners." *Planning for Higher Education* 31 (4): 5–12.

Koring, H., and S. Campbell, eds. 2005. *Peer Advising: Intentional Connections to Support Student Learning.* Monograph no. M13. Manhattan, KS: National Academic Advising Association.

Korschgen, A., and J. Hageseth. 1997. "Undecided Students: How One College Developed a Collaborative Approach to Help Students Choose Majors and Careers." *Journal of Career Planning and Employment* 57 (3): 49–51.

Kozeracki, C. 2005. "Preparing Faculty to Meet the Needs of Developmental Students." *New Directions for Institutional Research* 125 (Spring): 39–49.

Kramer, G. 2000. "Advising Students at Different Educational Levels." In *Academic Advising: A Comprehensive Handbook,* edited by V. Gordon and W. Habley, 84–104. San Francisco: Jossey-Bass.

Kramer, G., H. Higley, and D. Olsen. 1994. "Changes in Academic Major among Undergraduate Students." *College and University* 69 (2): 88–98.

Kreaden, M. 2001. "Mandatory Faculty Development Works." *To Improve the Academy* 20 (Fall): 107–27.

Krellwitz, A., J. Pole, and W. Potter. 2005. "Collaborating for Student Success: Teaming Support Center Staff with Study Skill Courses." *Learning Assistance Review* 10 (1): 15–23.

Kuh, G. 1994. "Creating Campus Climates That Foster Student Learning." In *Realizing the Educational Potential of Residence Halls,* edited by C. Schroeder and P. Mable, 109–132. San Francisco: Jossey-Bass.

———. 2003. "What We're Learning about Student Engagement from NSSE: Benchmarks for Effective Educational Practices." *Change* 35 (2): 24–32.

Kuh, G., R. Carini, and S. Klein. 2004. "Student Engagement and Student Learning: Insights from a Construct Validation Study." Paper presented at the annual meeting of the American Educational Research Association. San Diego.

Kuh, G, T. Cruce, R. Shoup, J. Kinzie, and R. Gonyea. 2008. "Unmasking the Effects of Student Engagement on First Year College Grades and Persistence." *Journal of Higher Education* 79 (5): 540–63.

Kuh, G., J. Kinzie, T. Cruce, R. Shoup and R. Gonyea. 2007. *Connecting the Dots: Multi-Faceted Analyses of the Relationships between Student Engagement Results from the NSSE, and the Institutional Practices and Conditions That Foster Student Success.* Revised final report prepared for the Lumina Foundation for Education. Indiana University Bloomington: Center for Postsecondary Research.

Kuh, G., J. Kinzie, J. Schuh, E. Whitt, and Associates. 2005. *Student Success in College: Creating Conditions that Matter.* San Francisco: Jossey-Bass.

Kuh, G., J. Schuh, E. Whitt, and Associates. 1991. *Involving Colleges: Successful Approaches to Fostering Student Learning and Development Outside the Classroom.* San Francisco: Jossey-Bass.

Kwan, F. 2010. "Formative Assessment: The One-Minute Paper vs. The Daily Quiz." *Journal of Instructional Pedagogies* 5 (May): 1–8.

Laird, N., T. Buckley, and J. Schwarz. 2005. *Student Engagement and Faculty Development: Faculty Perceptions and Practices.* Bloomington: National Survey of Student Engagement, Indiana University.

Laird, T., D. Chen, and G. Kuh. 2008. "Classroom Practices at Institutions with Higher Than Expected Persistence Rates: What Student Engagement Data Tell Us." In *The Role of the Classroom in College Student Persistence. New Directions for Teaching and Learning*, no. 115, edited by J. Braxton, 85–99. San Francisco: Jossey-Bass.

Larimore, J., and G. McClellan, 2005. "Native American Student Retention in U.S. Postsecondary Education." In *Serving Native American Students. New Directions for Student Services* 109, edited by M. Tippeconnic Fox, S. Lowe, and G. McClellon, 17–32. San Francisco: Jossey-Bass.

Lavin, D., R Alba, and R. Silberstein. 1981. *Right versus Privilege: The Open Admissions Experiment at the City University of New York.* New York: Free Press.

Lee, D., A. Olson. B. Locke, S. Michelson, and E. Odes. 2009. "The Effects of College Counseling Services on Academic Performance and Retention." *Journal of College Student Development* 50 (3): 305–19.

Lee, J., W. Donlan, and E. Brown. 2010–11. "American Indian/Alaskan Native Undergraduate Retention at Predominantly White Institutions: An Elaboration of Tinto's Theory of College Student Departure." *Journal of College Student Retention: Research, Theory and Practice* 12 (3): 257–76.

Leinbach, T., and D. Jenkins. 2008. *Using Longitudinal Data to Increase Community College Student Success: A Guide to Measuring Milestone and Momentum Point Attainment.* New York: Community College Research Center, Teachers College, Columbia University.

Lemons, L., and D. Richmond. 1987. "A Developmental Perspective of Sophomore Slump." *NASPA Journal* 24 (3): 15–19.

Lent, R., S. Brown, and K. Lark. 1984. "Relation of Self-Efficacy Expectations to Academic Achievement and Persistence." *Journal of Counseling Psychology* 31 (3): 356–62.

Levin, M., and J. Levin. 1991. "A Critical Examination of Academic Retention Programs for At-Risk Minority College Students." *Journal of College Student Development* 32 (4): 323–34.

Levine, J., and N. Shapiro. 2000. "Hogwarts: The Learning Community." *About Campus* 5 (4): 8–13.

Levine-Laufgraben, J., and N. Shapiro. 2004. *Sustaining and Improving Learning Communities*. San Francisco: Jossey-Bass.

Lewallen, W. 1993. "The Impact of Being 'Undecided' on College Student Persistence." *Journal of College Student Development* 34 (2): 103–12.

Lichtenstein, M. 2005. "The Importance of Classroom Environments in the Assessment of Learning Community Outcomes." *Journal of College Student Development* 46 (4): 341–56.

Lidy, K., and J. Kahn. 2006. "Personality as a Predictor of First-Semester Adjustment to College: The Mediational Role of Perceived Social Support." *Journal of College Counseling* 9 (2): 123–34.

Light, R. 1990. *The Harvard Assessment Seminars*. Cambridge, MA: Harvard University Press.

Lohfink, M., and M. Paulsen. 2005. "Comparing the Determinants of Persistence for First-Generation and Continuing Generation Students." *Journal of College Student Development* 46 (4): 409–28.

London, H. 1989. "Breaking Away: A Study of First Generation College Students and their Families." *The American Journal of Sociology* 97 (1): 144–70.

Lotkowski, V., S. Robbins, and R. Noeth. 2004. *The Role of Academic and Non-Academic Factors in Improving College Retention*. ACT Policy Report. Washington, DC: American College Testing Program.

Lowe, H., and A. Cook. 2003. "Mind the Gap: Are Students Prepared for Higher Education?" *Journal of Further and Higher Education* 27 (1): 53–76.

Lundberg, C., and L. Schreiner. 2004. "Quality and Frequency of Faculty Student Interaction as Predictors of Learning: An Analysis by Student Race/Ethnicity." *Journal of College Student Development* 45 (5): 549–65.

Luzzo, D. ed. 2000. *Career Counseling of College Students: An Empirical Guide to Strategies that Work*. Washington DC: American Psychological Association.

Mabrito, M. 2004. "Guidelines for Establishing Interactivity in Online Courses." *Innovate* 1:1. http://www.innovateonline.info/index.php?view=article&id=12. Retrieved October 27, 2009.

MacGregor, J. 2000. "Restructuring Large Classes to Create Communities of Learners." In *Strategies for Energizing Large Classes. New Directions for Teaching and Learning*, no. 81, edited by J. MacGregor et al., 47–61. San Francisco: Jossey-Bass.

Major, C., and B. Palmer. 2001. "Assessing the Effectiveness of Problem-Based Learning in Higher Education." *Academic Exchange Quarterly* 5 (1): 4–9.

Malaney, G. D., and M. Shively. 1995. "Academic and Social Expectations and Experiences of First-Year Students of Color." *NASPA Journal* 32 (1): 3–18.

Mallinckrodt, B. 1988. "Student Retention, Social Support and Dropout Intentions: Comparison of Black and White Students." *Journal of College Student Development* 29 (1): 60–64.

Malnarich, G., B. Sloan, van Slyck, P., P. Dusenberry, and J. Swinton. 2003.

The Pedagogy of Possibilities: Developmental Education, College-Level Studies, and Learning Communities. Olympia, WA: Washington Center for Improving the Quality of Undergraduate Education, in cooperation with the American Association for Community Colleges.

Martin, D., and R. Blanc. 2001. "Video-Based Supplemental Instruction (VSI)." *Journal of Developmental Education* 24 (3): 12–19.

Martinez, M. 2003. "High Attrition Rates in e-Learning: Challenges, Predictors, and Solutions." *The e-Learning Developers Journal,* July14: 1–7.

Martyn, M. 2007. "Clickers in the Classroom: An Active Learning Approach" *Educause Quarterly* 30 (2): 71–74.

Maxwell, W. 1998. "Supplemental Instruction, Learning Communities, and Studying Together." *Community College Review* 26 (2): 1–18.

McClenney, K., and E. Waiwaiole. 2005. "Focus on Student Retention: Promising Practices in Community Colleges." *Community College Journal* 75 (6): 36–41.

McClenney, K., B. McClenney, and G. Peterson. 2007. "A Culture of Evidence: What Is It? Do We Have One?" *Planning for Higher Education* 35 (3): 26–33.

McCormick, A. 2003. *Swirling and Double-Dipping: New Patterns of Student Attendance and Their Implications for Higher Education.* New Directions for Higher Education, 121 (Spring): 13–24.

McCracken, H. 2008. "Best Practices in Supporting Persistence of Distance Education Students through Integrated Web-Based Systems." *Journal of College Student Retention: Research, Theory and Practice* 10 (1): 65–91.

McGee Banks, C. 2005. *Improving Multicultural Education: Lessons from the Intergroup Education Movement.* New York: Teachers College.

McGrath, M., and A. Braunstein. 1997. "The Prediction of Freshman Attrition: An Examination of the Importance of Certain Demographic, Academic, Financial, and Social Factors." *College Student Journal* 31 (3): 396–408.

McGuire, S. 2006. "The Impact of Supplemental Instruction on Teaching Students How to Learn." In *Supplemental Instruction. New Directions for Teaching and Learning,* no. 106, edited by M. Stone and G. Jacobs, 3–10. San Francisco: Jossey-Bass.

McKeachie, W. 1986. *Teaching and Learning in the College Classroom: A Review of the Research Literature.* Ann Arbor: University of Michigan.

McLeod, W., and J. Young. 2005. "A Chancellor's Vision: Establishing an Institutional Culture of Student Success." *New Directions for Institutional Research* 125 (Spring): 73–85.

McShannon, J. 2002. "Gaining Retention and Achievement for Students Program (GRASP): A Faculty Development Program to Increase Student Success." Paper presented at the ASEE Gulf-Southwest annual conference, University of Louisiana, March 20–22.

Merisotis, J., and K. McCarthy. 2005. "Retention and Student Success at Minority-Serving Institutions." *New Directions for Institutional Research* 125 (Spring): 45–58.

Merriam, S., T. Thomas, and C. Zeph. 1987. "Mentoring in Higher Education: What We Know Now." *Review of Higher Education* 11 (2): 199–210.

Merton, R. 1936. "The Unanticipated Consequences of Purposive Social Action." *American Sociological Review* 1 (6): 894–904.

Metzner, B. 1989. "Perceived Quality of Academic Advising: The Effect on Freshman Attrition." *American Educational Research Journal* 26 (3): 422–42.

Meyer, K. ed. 2002. *Quality in Distance Education: Focus on On-Line Learning.* ASHE-ERIC Higher Education Report 29 (4). San Francisco: Jossey-Bass.

Michaels, J., and T. Miethe. 1989. "Academic Efforts and College Grades." *Social Forces* 68 (1): 309–19.

Michaelsen, L., and L. Pelton-Sweet. 2008. "The Essential Elements of Team-Based Learning." In *Team-Based Learning. New Directions for Teaching and Learning,* no. 116, edited by L. Michaelson et al., 7–27. San Francisco: Jossey-Bass.

Miller, C., M. Binder, V. Harris, and K. Krause. 2011. *Staying on Track: Early Findings from a Performance-Based Scholarship Program at the University of New Mexico.* New York: MDRC.

Millis, B. 2010. *Cooperative Learning in Higher Education.* Sterling: Stylus Publishing.

Millis, B., and P. Cottell, Jr. 1998. *Cooperative Learning for Higher Education Faculty.* Phoenix: Oryx Press.

Mina, L., J. Cabrales, C. Juarez, and F. Rodriguez-Vasquez. 2004. "Support Programs That Work." In *Addressing the Unique Needs of Latino American Students. New Directions for Student Services,* no. 105, edited by A. Ortiz, 79–88. San Francisco: Jossey-Bass.

Morales, E. 2009. "Legitimizing Hope: An Exploration of Effective Mentoring for Dominican American Male College Students." *Journal of College Student Retention: Research, Theory and Practice* 11 (3): 385–406.

Morest, V., and D. Jenkins. 2007. *Institutional Research and the Culture of Evidence at Community Colleges.* New York: Community College Research Center, Teachers College, Columbia University.

Morris, L., and C. Finnegan. 2008. "Best Practices in Predicting and Encouraging Student Persistence and Achievement Online." *Journal of College Student Retention: Research, Theory, and Practice* 10 (1): 55–64.

Mortenson, T. 2009a. *Access to What? Restricted Educational Opportunities for Students from Low and Lower-Middle Income Families, FY1974 to FY 2009.* Oskaloosa, IA: Postsecondary Education Opportunity.

———. 2009b. *ACT National Persistence Rates, 1983 to 2009.* Oskaloosa, IA: Postsecondary Education Opportunity.

Muhr, C., and D. Martin. 2006. "TeamSI: A Resource for Integrating and Improving Learning." In *Supplemental Instruction. New Directions for Teaching and Learning,* no. 106, edited by M. Stone and G. Jacobs, 85–93. San Francisco: Jossey Bass.

Mulcare, D., and V. Ruget. 2010. "Team-Based Learning: A Faculty Learning Community at Salem State College." Paper presented at the American Political Science Association, 2010 Teaching and Learning Conference. Available at SSRN: http://ssrn.com/abstract=1546479.

Mullendore, R., and L. Banahan. 2005. "Designing Orientation Programs." In *Challenging and Supporting the First-Year Student: A Handbook for Improving the First-Year of College*, edited by L. Upcraft, J. Gardner, and B. Barefoot, 391–409. San Francisco: Jossey-Bass.

Mullendore, R., and C. Hatch. 2000. *Helping Your First-Year College Student Succeed: A Guide for Parents*. Columbia, SC: National Resource Center for the First-Year Experience and Students in Transition.

Multon, K., S. Brown, and R. Lent. 1991. "Relation of Self-Efficacy Beliefs to Academic Outcomes: A Meta-Analytic Investigation." *Journal of Counseling Psychology* 38 (1): 30–38.

Muraskin, L., and J. Lee. 2004. *Raising the Graduation Rates of Low-Income Students*. Washington, DC: Pell Institute for the Study of Opportunity in Higher Education.

Museus, S. 2009. "Understanding Racial Differences in the Effects of Loans on Degree Attainment: A Path Analysis." *Journal of College Student Retention: Research, Theory and Practice* 11 (4): 499–527.

Myers, C., and S. Myers. 2006. "Assessing Assessment: The Effects of Two Exam Formats on Course Achievement and Evaluation." *Innovative Higher Education* 31 (4): 227–36.

Nagda, B., et al. 1995. "Bridging Differences through Intergroup Dialogues." In *Peer Programs on a College Campus: Theory, Training, and "Voice of Peers*, edited by S. Hatcher, 378–414. San Jose: Resources Publications.

National Center for Education Statistics. 2000. *Descriptive Summary of 1995–1996 Beginning Postsecondary Students: Three Years Later*. NCES Statistical Analysis Report 2000–154. Washington DC: U.S. Department of Education, Office of Educational Research and Improvement.

National Center for Education Statistics. 2003. *Descriptive Summary of 1995–96 Beginning Postsecondary Students: Six Years Later*. NCES Statistical Analysis Report 2003–151. Washington, DC: U.S. Department of Education, Office of Educational Research and Improvement.

———. 2004. *Remedial Education at Degree-Granting Postsecondary Institutions in Fall 2000*. NCES Statistical Analysis Report 2004–2010. Washington, DC: U.S. Department of Education, Office of Educational Research and Improvement.

———. 2005. *The Condition of Education 2005*. Washington DC: U.S. Department of Education, Office of Educational Research and Improvement.

National Center for Public Policy and Higher Education. 2006. *Measuring Up: The National Report on Higher Education*. San Jose.

National Survey of Student Engagement. 2006a. *Engaged Learning: Fostering Success for All Students, Annual Report 2006*. Bloomington: National Survey of Student Engagement.

———. 2006b. "Using Student Engagement Data for Institutional Improvement." Presentation at the Annual Conference of the Tennessee Association of Institutional Research, Brentwood, TN.

NCES. See National Center for Education Statistics

Newcomb, T. 1966. "The General Nature of Peer Group Influence." In *College Peer Groups: Problems and Prospects for Research*, edited by T. Wilson and E. Wilson, 2–16. Chicago: Aldine.

Nicholson-Crotty, J., and K. Meier. 2003. "Politics, Structure, and Public Policy." *Educational Policy* 17 (1): 80–97.

Nicpon, M., L. Huser, E. Blanks, S. Sollenberger, C. Befort, and S. Kurpius. 2006. "The Relationship of Loneliness and Social Support with College Freshmen's Academic Performance and Persistence." *Journal of College Student Retention: Research, Theory and Practice* 8 (3): 345–58.

Nora, A. 1987. "Determinants of Retention among Chicano College Students: A Structural Model." *Research in Higher Education* 26 (1): 31–59.

———. 2001. "The Depiction of Significant Others in Tinto's "Rites of Passage": A Reconceptualization of the Influence of Family and Community in the Persistence Process." *College Student Retention: Research, Theory and Practice* 3 (1): 41–40.

Nora, A., and A. Cabrera. 1996. "The Role of Perceptions of Prejudice and Discrimination on the Adjustment of Minority Students to College." *Journal of Higher Education* 67 (2): 119–48.

Norris, D., L. Baer, J. Leonard, L. Pugliese, and R. Lefrere. 2008. "Action Analytics: Measuring and Improving Performance That Matters in Higher Education." *EDUCAUSE Review* 43 (1): 42–67.

Nulden, U. 2000. "Computer Support for Formative Assessment." *Information and Technology*. 1 (4): 329–50.

Nutt, C. 2003. "Academic Advising and Student Retention and Persistence." *NACADA Clearinghouse of Academic Advising Resources*. http://www.nacada.ksu.edu/Clearinghouse/AdvisingIssues. Retrieved June 4, 2010.

Nutt, C., et al. 2003. *Advisor Training: Exemplary Practices in the Development of Advisor Skills*. Monograph no. 9. Manhattan, KS: National Academic Advising Association.

O'Banion, T. 1997. *A Learning College for the 21st Century*. Phoenix: American Council on Education / Oryx Press Series on Higher Education.

Obetz, W. 1998. "Using Cluster Analysis for Transcript Analysis of Course-Taking Patterns of General Studies Graduates at Community College of Philadelphia." PhD dissertation, University of Pennsylvania.

O'Gara, L., M. Karp, and K. Hughes. 2009. "Student Success Courses in the

Community College: An Exploratory Study of Student Perspectives." *Community College Review* 36 (3): 195–218.

Ogden, P., D. Thompson, A. Russell, and C. Simons. 2003. "Supplemental Instruction: Short- and Long-Term Impact." *Journal of Developmental Education* 26 (3): 2–8.

O'Neil Green, D. 2007. "Using Qualitative Methods to Assess Academic Success and Retention Programs for Underrepresented Minority Students." *New Directions for Institutional Research* 136 (Winter): 41–53.

Ory, J., and L. Braskamp. 1988. "Involvement and Growth of Students in Three Academic Programs." *Research in Higher Education* 28 (2): 116–29.

Oseguera, L., and B. Rhee. 2009. "The Influence of Institutional Retention Climates on Student Persistence to Degree Completion: A Multilevel Approach." *Research in Higher Education* 50 (6): 548–69.

Ostrove, J., and S. Long. 2007. "Social Class and Belonging: Implications for College Adjustment." *Review of Higher Education* 30 (4): 363–89.

Ostrow, E., S. Paul, V. Dark, and J. Berhman. 1986. "Adjustment of College Women on Campus: Effects of Stressful Life Events, Social Support, and Personal Competencies." In *Stress, Social Support, and Women*, edited by S. Hobfoll, 29–46. Washington, DC: Hemisphere.

Pace, R. 1980. *Measuring the Quality of Student Effort*. Los Angeles: Laboratory for Research in Higher Education, University of California.

———. 1984. *Measuring the Quality of College Student Experience*. Los Angeles: Higher Education Research Institute, University of California.

Padilla, R. 1999. "College student retention: Focus on Success." *Journal of College Student Retention: Research, Theory and Practice* 1 (2): 131–45.

Pagan, R., and R. Edwards-Wilson. 2002. "A Mentoring Program for Remedial Students." *Journal of College Student Retention: Research, Theory and Practice* 43 (3): 207–26.

Pajares, F. 1996. "Self-Efficacy Beliefs in Academic Settings." *Review of Educational Research* 66 (4): 543–78.

Palloff, R., and K. Pratt. 1999. *Building Learning Communities in Cyberspace*. San Francisco: Jossey-Bass.

Palsolé, S., and C. Awalt. 2008. "Team-Based Learning in Asynchronous Online Settings." In *Team-Based Learning. New Directions for Teaching and Learning*, no. 116, edited by L. Michaelson et al., 87–95. San Francisco: Jossey-Bass.

Pardee, C. 2000. "Organizational Models for Academic Advising." In *Academic Advising: A Comprehensive Handbook*, edited by V. Gordon, W. Habley, and Associates. San Francisco: Jossey-Bass.

Parker, J., and J. Schmidt. 1982. "Effects of College Experience." In *Encyclopedia of Educational Research*, 5th ed., edited by H. Mitzel. New York: Free Press.

Pascarella, E. 1980. "Student-Faculty Informal Contact and College Outcomes." *Review of Educational Research* 50 (4): 545–95.

Pascarella, E., et al. 2004. "First-Generation College Students: Additional Evidence on Experiences and Outcomes." *Journal of Higher Education* 75 (3): 249–84.

Pascarella, E., and D. Chapman. 1983. "A Multi-Institutional, Path Analytic Validation of Tinto's Model of College Withdrawal." *American Educational Research Journal* 20 (1): 87–102.

Pascarella, E., T. Seifert, and E. Whitt. 2008. "Effective Instruction and College Student Persistence: Some New Evidence." In *The Role of the Classroom in College Student Persistence. New Directions for Teaching and Learning*, no. 115, edited by J. Braxton, 55–70. San Francisco: Jossey-Bass.

Pascarella, E., and P. Terenzini. 1980. "Predicting Persistence and Voluntary Dropout Decisions from a Theoretical Model." *Journal of Higher Education* 51 (1): 60–75.

———. 1983. "Predicting Voluntary Freshman Year Persistence/Withdrawal Behavior in a Residential University: A Path Analytic Validation of Tinto's Model." *Journal of Educational Psychology* 75 (2): 215–26.

———. 1991. *How College Affects Students: Findings and Insights from Twenty Years of Research*. San Francisco: Jossey-Bass.

———. 2005. *How College Affects Students: A Third Decade of Research*. Vol. 2. San Francisco: Jossey-Bass.

Patry, M. 2009. "Clickers in Large Classes: From Student Perceptions Towards an Understanding of Best Practices." *International Journal of the Scholarship of Teaching and Learning* 3 (2): 1–11.

Paulsen, M., and E. St. John. 2002. "Social Class and College Costs: Examining the Financial Nexus between College Choice and Persistence." *Journal of Higher Education* 73 (2): 189–236.

Pavel, M. 1991. "Assessing Tinto's Model of Institutional Departure Using American Indian and Alaskan Native Longitudinal Data." Paper presented at the annual conference of the Association for the Study of Higher Education, Boston.

Perin, D. 2011. *Facilitating Student Learning through Contextualization*. CCRC Working Paper, no. 59, Assessment of Evidence Series. Community College Research Center. New York: Teachers College, Columbia University.

Perna, L. 2007. "The Sources of Racial-Ethnic Group Differences in College Enrollment: A Critical Examination." *New Directions for Institutional Research* 136 (Spring): 51–66.

Peterfreund, A., K. Rath, S. Xenos, and F. Bayliss. 2008, "The Impact of Supplemental Instruction on Students in STEM Courses: Results from San Francisco State University." *Journal of College Student Retention: Research, Theory and Practice* 9 (4): 487–503.

Pettit, M., and D. Prince. 2010. "Washington State's Student Achievement Initiative." *Journal of Applied Research in the Community College* 17 (2): 6–12.

Pike, G. 2000. "The Influence of Fraternity or Sorority Membership on Students'

College Experiences and Cognitive Development." *Research in Higher Education* 41 (1): 117–39.

Pike, G., and G. Kuh. 2005. "First and Second-Generation College Students: A Comparison of their Engagement and Intellectual Development." *Journal of Higher Education* 76 (3): 276–300.

Pike, G., G. Kuh, and A. McCormick. 2008. "Learning community participation and educational outcomes: Direct, Indirect, and Contingent Relationships." Paper presented at the annual meeting of the Association for the Study of Higher Education. Jacksonville, FL.

Pike, G. 1999. "The Effects of Residential Learning Communities and Traditional Residential Living Arrangements on Educational Gains during the First Year of College." *Journal of College Student Development* 40 (3): 269–84.

Pike, G., C. Schroeder, and T. Berry. 1997. "Enhancing the Educational Impact of Residence Halls: The Relationship between Residential Learning Communities and First-Year College Experiences and Persistence." *Journal of College Student Development* 38 (6): 609–21.

Poirier, C., and R. Feldman. 2007. "Promoting Active Learning Using Individual Response Technology in Large Introductory Psychology Classes." *Teaching of Psychology* 34 (3): 194–96.

Polewchak, J. 2002. *The Effects of Social Support and Interpersonal Dependency upon Emotional Adjustment to College and Physical Health.* Virginia Beach: Virginia Consortium for Professional Psychology.

Polinsky, T. 2003. "Understanding Student Retention through a Look at Student Goals, Intentions, and Behavior." *Journal of College Student Retention: Research, Theory and Practice* 4 (4): 361–76.

Porter, S. 2003. "Understanding Retention Outcomes: Using Multiple Data Sources to Distinguish between Dropouts, Stopouts, and Transfer-Outs," *Journal of College Student Retention: Research, Theory and Practice* 5 (1): 53–70.

Portes, A. 1998. "Social Capital: Its Origins and Applications in Modern Society." *Annual Review of Sociology* 24:1–24.

Prince, D., L. Seppanen, L., D. Stephens, and C. Stewart. 2010. "Turning State Data and Research into Information: An Example from Washington State's Student Achievement Initiative." *New Directions for Institutional Research* 147 (Fall): 47–64.

Quirk, K. 2005. "A Comprehensive Approach to Developmental Education." *New Directions for Community Colleges* 129 (Spring): 83–92.

Radford, A., L. Berkner, S. Wheeless, and B. Shepherd. 2010. *Persistence and Attainment of 2003–2004 Beginning Postsecondary Students: After 6 Years.* NCES 2011–151. U.S. Department of Education, Office of Educational Research and Improvement.

Raftery, S. 2005. "Developmental Learning Communities at Metropolitan Community College." *New Directions for Community Colleges* 129 (Spring): 63–72.

Ramirez, G. 1997. "Supplemental Instruction: The Long-Term Impact." *Journal of Developmental Education* 21 (1): 2–10.

Rau, W., and A. Durand. 2000. "The Academic Ethic and College Grades: Does Hard Work Help Students to 'Make the Grade?'" *Sociology of Education* 73 (1): 19–38.

Ravitz, J. 2009. "Introduction: Summarizing Findings and Looking Ahead to a New Generation of PBL Research." *Interdisciplinary Journal of Problem-Based Learning* 3 (1): 4–11. Available at: http://docs.lib.purdue.edu/ijpbl/v013/iss1/2/.

Rayle, A., and K. Chung. 2007. "Revisiting First-Year College Students' Mattering: Social Support, Academic Stress, and the Mattering Experience." *Journal of College Student Retention: Research, Theory and Practice* 9 (1): 21–37.

Reason, R, P. Terenzini, and R. Domingo. 2006. "First Things First: Developing Competence in the First Year of College." *Research in Higher Education* 47 (2): 149–76.

Reason, R., P. Terenzini, and R. Domingo. 2007. "Developing Social and Personal Competence in the First Year of College." *Review of Higher Education* 30 (3): 271–99.

Redden, E. 2007. "Automatic Access or Raised Retention?" *Inside Higher Education*, January 10, 2007.

Reichard, C. 2001. "Will They Ever Graduate? An Analysis of Long-Term Students." Paper presented at the 2001 annual meeting of the Southern Association of Institutional Research, Panama City.

Rendon, L. 1994. "Validating Culturally Diverse Students: Toward New Model of Learning and Student Development." *Innovative Higher Education* 19 (1): 33–51.

Rendon, L., R. Jalomo, and A. Nora. 2000. "Theoretical Considerations in the Study of Minority Retention in Higher Education." In *Reworking the Student Departure Puzzle*, edited by J. Braxton, 127–56. Nashville: Vanderbilt University Press.

Reumann-Moore, R., A. El-Haj, and E. Gold. 1997. *Friends for School Purposes: Learning Communities and Their Role in Building Community at a Large Urban University*. Philadelphia: Temple University.

Rice, N., and O. Lightsey. 2001. "Freshman Living Learning Community: Relationship to Academic Success and Affective Development." *Journal of College and University Housing* 30 (1): 11–17.

Richburg-Hayes, L., et al. 2009. *Rewarding Persistence: Effects of a Performance-Based Scholarship Program for Low-Income Parents*. New York: Manpower Demonstration Research Corporation.

Richmond, D., and L. Lemons. 1985. "Sophomore Slump: An Individual Approach to Recognition and Response." *Journal of College Student Personnel* 26 (2): 176–77.

Rocconi, L. 2010. "The Impact of Learning Communities on First Year Students' Growth and Development in College." *Research in Higher Education* 27 (2): 1–16.

Roksa, J., D. Jenkins, S. Jaggars, M. Zeidenberg, and S. Cho. 2009. *Strategies for Promoting Gatekeeper Course Success among Students Needing Remediation:*

Research Report for the Virginia Community College System. New York: Community College Research Center, Teachers College, Columbia University.

Roschelle, J., W. Penuel, and L. Abrahamson. 2004. *Classroom Response and Communication Systems: Research Review and Theory*. Paper presented at the annual meeting of the American Educational Research Association, San Diego.

Rotenberg, K., and J. Morrison. 1993. "Loneliness and College Achievement: Do Loneliness Scale Scores Predict College Dropout?" *Psychological Reports* 73 (3): 1283–88.

Rucker, M., and S. Thomson. 2003. "Assessing Student Learning Outcomes: An Investigation of the Relationship among Feedback Measures." *College Student Journal* 37 (3): 400–404.

Rutschow, E. et al. 2011. *Turning the Tide: Five Years of Achieving the Dream in Community Colleges*. New York: MDRC.

Ryan, J. 2004. "The Relationship between Institutional Expenditures and Degree Attainment at Baccalaureate Colleges." *Research in Higher Education* 45 (2): 97–116.

Ryan, M., and P. Glenn. 2003. "Increasing One-Year Retention Rates by Focusing on Academic Competence: An Empirical Odyssey." *Journal of College Student Retention: Research, Theory and Practice* 4 (3): 297–324.

Saenz, V., S. Hurtado, D. Barrera, D. Wolf, and F. Yeung. 2007. "First in My Family: A Profile of First-Generation College Students at Four-Year Institutions Since 1971." Los Angeles: Cooperative Institutional Research Program, Higher Education Research Institute, University of California, Los Angeles.

Salinitri, G. 2005. "The Effects of Formal Mentoring on the Retention Rates for First-Year, Low-Achieving Students." *Canadian Journal of Education* 28 (4): 853–73.

Sand, J., S. Robinson Kurpuis, and A. Dixon Rayle. 2004. "Academic Stress and Social Support Factors in Latino and Euro-American Male and Female College Students." Paper presented at the annual meeting of the American Psychological Association. Honolulu.

Sanford, N. 1966. *Self and Society: Social Change and Individual Development*. New York: Atherton.

Santos, S., and E. Riegadas. 2004. "Understanding the Student-Faculty Mentoring Process: Its Effects on At-Risk University Students." *Journal of College Student Retention: Research, Theory and Practice* 6 (3): 337–57.

Schaller, M. 2005. "Wandering and Wondering: Traversing the Uneven Terrain of the Second College Year." *About Campus* 10 (3): 17–24.

Schilling, K. M., and K. L. Schilling. 1999. "Increasing Expectations for Student Effort." *About Campus* 4 (2): 4–10.

Schlossberg, Nancy. 1989. "Marginality and Mattering: Key Issues in Building Community." In *Designing Campus Activities to Foster a Sense of Community. New Directions for Student Services*, no. 48, edited by D. Roberts. 5–15. San Francisco: Jossey-Bass.

Schreiner, L., and J. Pattengale, eds. 2000. *Visible Solutions for Invisible Students:*

Helping Sophomores Succeed. Columbia, SC: National Resource Center for the
First-Year Experience and Students in Transition.

Schroeder, C., F. Minor, and T. Tarkow. 1999. "Freshman Interest Groups:
Partnership for Promoting Student Success." In *Creating Successful Partnerships
Between Academic and Student Affairs. New Directions for Student Services*, no. 87,
edited by J. Schuh and E. Whitt. 37–49. San Francisco: Jossey-Bass.

Scrivener, S. 2007. "The Opening Doors Demonstration and Evaluation." In
*Community College Fellowship Seminar, The Hechinger Institute on Education and
the Media.* New York: Community College Research Center, Teachers College,
Columbia University.

Scrivener, S., et al. 2008. *A Good Start: Two-Year Effects of a Freshman Learning
Community Program at Kingsborough Community College.* New York: Manpower
Demonstration Research Corporation.

Scrivener, S., C. Sommo, and H. Collado. 2009. *Getting Back on Track: Effects of
a Community College Program for Probationary Students.* New York: Manpower
Demonstration Research Corporation.

Seidman, A. 1991. "The Evaluation of a Pre/Post Admission/Counseling Process
at a Suburban Community College: Impact on Student Satisfaction with the
Faculty and the Institution, Retention, and Academic Performance." *College and
University* 66 (4): 223–32.

———, ed. 2005. *College Student Retention: Formula for Student Success.* Westport,
CT: ACE/Praeger.

———, ed. 2007. *Minority Student Retention: The Best of the Journal of College
Student Retention: Research, Theory and Practice.* Amityville, NY: Baywood
Publishing Company.

Shapiro, N., and J. Levine. 1999. *Creating Learning Communities: A Practical Guide
to Winning Support, Organizing for Change, and Implementing Programs.* San
Francisco: Jossey-Bass.

Sharkin, B. 2004. "College Counseling and Student Retention: Research Findings
and Implications for Counseling Centers." *Journal of College Counseling* 7 (2):
99–108.

Shaw, K. 1997. "Remedial Education as Ideological Battleground: Emerging
Remedial Education Policies and Their Implications for Community College
Student Mobility." *Educational Evaluation and Policy Analysis* 19 (3): 284–96.

Shotton, H., S. Oosahwe, and R. Cintron. 2007. "Stories of Success: Experiences of
American Indian Students in a Peer-Mentoring Retention Program." *Review of
Higher Education* 31 (1): 81–107.

Shulman, G., M. Cox, and L. Richlin. 2004. "Institutional Considerations in
Developing a Faculty Learning Community Program." In *Building Faculty
Learning Communities. New Directions for Teaching and Learning*, no. 97, edited by
M. Cox and L. Richlin, 41–49. San Francisco: Jossey-Bass.

Shultz, M., and S. Zedeck. 2008. "Final Report: Identification, Development, and Validation of Predictors for Successful Lawyering." University of California, Berkeley, September. Available at http://www.law.berkeley.edu/files/LSAC REPORTfinal-12.pdf.

Simons, L., and B. Cleary. 2006. "The Influence of Service Learning on Students' Personal and Social Development." *College Teaching* 54 (4): 307–19.

Simpson, O. 1999. *Student Retention in Online, Open, and Distance Learning*. London: Kogan Page.

Singell, L. Jr. 2004. "Come and Stay a While: Does Financial Aid Affect Retention Conditioned on Enrollment at a Large Public University?" *Economics of Education Review* 23 (5): 459–71.

Skahill, M. 2002. "The Role of Social Support Network in College Persistence among Freshman Students." *Journal of College Student Retention: Research, Theory and Practice* 4 (1): 39–52.

Smith, A., M. Street, and A. Olivarez. 2002. "Early, Regular, and Late Registration and Community College Success." *Community College Journal of Research and Practice* 26 (3): 261–73.

Smith, B., J. MacGregor, R. Matthews, and F. Gabelnick. 2004. *Learning Communities: Reforming Undergraduate Education*. San Francisco: Jossey-Bass.

Smith, K. 2000. "Going Deeper: Formal Small-Group Learning in Large Classes." In *Strategies for Energizing Large Classes. New Directions for Teaching and Learning*, no. 81, edited by J. MacGregor et al., 25–46. San Francisco: Jossey-Bass.

Snyder, T., and S. Dillow. 2010. *Digest of Education Statistics 2009*. NCES 2010–013. Washington, DC: National Center for Education Statistics, U.S. Department of Education.

Solberg, V., and P. Villarreal. 1997. "Examination of Self-Efficacy, Social Support, and Stress as Predictors of Psychological Stress among Hispanic College Students." *Journal of the Behavioral Sciences* 19 (2): 182–201.

Solorzano, D., M. Ceja, and T. Yosso. 2000. "Critical Race Theory, Racial Microaggressions, and Campus Racial Climate: The Experiences of African American College Students." *Journal of Negro Education* 69 (1–2): 60–73.

Somera, L., and B. Ellis. 1996. "Communication Networks and Perceptions of Social Support as Antecedents to College Adjustments: A Comparison between Student Commuters and Campus Residents." *Journal of the Association for Communication Administration* 2 (2): 97–110.

Song, B. 2006. "Content-Based ESL Instruction: Long-Term Effects and Outcomes." *English for Specific Purposes* 25 (4): 420–37.

Sorcinelli, M. 1991. "Research Findings on the Seven Principles." In *Applying the Seven Principles for Good Practice in Undergraduate Education. New Directions for Teaching and Learning*, no. 47, edited by A. Chickering and Z.Gamson, 13–25. San Francisco: Jossey-Bass.

Sorrentino, D. 2007. "The SEEK Mentoring Program: An Application of the Goal Setting Theory." *Journal of College Student Retention: Research, Theory and Practice* 8 (2): 241–50.

Sporn, B. 1996. "Managing University Culture: An Analysis of the Relationship between Institutional Culture and Management Approaches." *Higher Education* 32 (1): 41–61.

Springer, L., M. Stanne, and S. Donovan. 1999. "Effects of Small-Group Learning on Undergraduates in Science, Mathematics, Engineering, and Technology: A Meta-Analysis." *Review of Educational Research* 69 (1): 50–80.

Stark, K. 2002. "Advising Undecided Students: What Works Best?" *Mentor: An Academic Advising Journal* 4 (3): 1–5. http://www.psu.edu/dus/mentor. Retrieved October 12, 2008.

Steadman, M. 1998. "CAT's: Using Classroom Assessment to Change Both Teaching and Learning." In *Classroom Assessment and Research: Uses, Approaches, and Research Findings. New Directions for Teaching and Learning*, no. 75, edited by T. Angelo, 23–35. San Francisco, Jossey-Bass.

Steadman, M., and M. Svinicki. 1998. "A Student's Gateway to Better Learning." In *Classroom Assessment and Research: Uses, Approaches, and Research Findings. New Directions for Teaching and Learning*, no. 75, edited by T. Angelo, 13–20. San Francisco, Jossey-Bass.

Steele, C. 1999. "Thin Ice: Stereotype Threat and Black College Students." *Atlantic Monthly* 284 (2): 44–54.

Steele, C., and J. Aronson. 1998. "Stereotype Threat and the Test Performance of Academically Successful African Americans." In *The Black-White Test Score Gap*, edited by C. Jencks and M. Phillips, 401–30.Washington, DC: Brookings Institution Press.

Steele, G. 2003. "A Research-Based Approach to Working with Undecided Students: A Case Study." *NACADA Journal* 23 (1–2): 10–20.

Steinke, P., and S. Buresh. 2002. "Cognitive Outcomes of Service-Learning: Reviewing the Past and Glimpsing the Future." *Michigan Journal of Community Service Learning* 8 (2): 5–14.

Stetson, N. 1993. "Professional Development for Two-Way Teaching and Learning." *Leadership Abstracts* 6: (7). ERIC Digest: ED367430.

Stevenson, C., R. Duran, K. Barrett, and G. Colarulli. 2005. "Fostering Faculty Collaboration in Learning Communities: A Developmental Approach." *Innovative Higher Education* 30 (1): 23–36.

St. John, E. 1990. "Price Response in Enrollment Decisions: An Analysis of the High School and Beyond Sophomore Cohort." *Research in Higher Education* 31 (2): 161–76.

———. 1991. "The Impact of Student Financial Aid: A Review of Recent Research." *Journal of Student Financial Aid* 21 (1): 18–32.

———. 2001. "The Impact of Aid Packages on Educational Choices: High Tuition /

High Loan and Educational Opportunity." *Journal of Student Financial Aid* 31 (2): 35–54.

———. 2004. "The Nexus between Finances and Student Involvement in Persistence." Paper presented at the annual meeting of the American Education Research Association, San Diego.

———. 2005. *Affordability of Postsecondary Education: Equity and Adequacy across the 50 States.* Report prepared for: Renewing Our Schools, Securing our Future. A National Task Force on Public Education. The Center for American Progress.

———. 2006. "Lessons Learned: Institutional Research as Support for Academic Improvement." *New Directions for Institutional Research* 130: 95–107.

St. John, E., S. Hu, and T. Tuttle. 2000. "Persistence in an Urban Public University: A Case Study of the Effects of Student Aid." *Journal of Student Financial Aid* 30 (2): 23–37.

St. John, E., S. Hu, and J. Weber. 2001. "State Policy and the Affordability of Public Higher Education: The Influence of State Grants on Persistence in Indiana." *Research in Higher Education* 42 (4): 401–28.

Stone, E., and G. Jacobs, eds. 2006. "Supplemental Instruction: New Visions for Empowering Student Learning." In *Supplemental Instruction. New Directions for Teaching and Learning*, no. 106, edited by M. Stone and G. Jacobs. San Francisco: Jossey Bass.

Strobel, J., and A. van Barneveld. 2008. "When is PBL More Effective? A Meta-Synthesis of Meta-Analyses Comparing PBL to Conventional Classrooms." *Interdisciplinary Journal of Problem-Based Learning* 3 (1): 44–58. Available at: http://docs.lib.purdue.edu/ijpbl/v013/iss1/4.

Suen, H. 1983. "Alienation and Attrition of Black College Students on a Predominantly White Campus." *Journal of College Student Personnel* 24 (2): 117–21.

Supiano, B. 2011. "College Enrollments Continue to Climb, While Graduation Rates Hold Steady." *Chronicle of Higher Education*, February 2.

Svanum, S., and S. Bigatti. 2006. "The Influence of Course Effort and Outside Activities on Grades in a College Course." *Journal of College Student Development* 47 (5): 564–76.

Swail, S, K. Redd, and L. Perna. 2003. *Retaining Minority Students in Higher Education: A Framework for Success.* ASHE-ERIC Higher Education Report 30 (20). San Francisco: Jossey-Bass.

Sweet, M., and L. Pelton-Sweet. 2008. "The Social Foundation of Team-Based Learning: Students Accountable to Students." In *Team-Based Learning. New Directions for Teaching and Learning*, no. 116, edited by L. Michaelson et al., 29–40. San Francisco: Jossey-Bass.

Swenson, L., A. Nordstrom, and M. Hiester. 2008. "The Role of Peer Relationships in Adjustment to College." *Journal of College Student Development* 49 (6): 551–67.

Swing, R. 2003. "What Matters in First-Year Seminars: Results from a National Survey." Paper presented at First Year Experience West Conference, Costa Mesa.

———. 2004. "The Improved Learning Outcomes of Linked versus Stand-Alone First-Year Seminars" In *Integrating the First-Year Experience: The Role of First-Year Seminars in Learning Communities*, 9–17. Columbia, SC: National Resource Center for the First-Year Experience and Students in Transition; and Olympia, WA: Washington Center for Improving the Quality of Undergraduate Education.

Tagg, J. 2003. *The Learning Paradigm College*. Boston: Anker.

Tatum, B. 2003. "Talking about Race, Learning about Racism: The Application of Racial Identity Development Theory in the Classroom." In *Race and Higher Education: Rethinking Pedagogy in a Diverse College Classroom*, edited by A. Howell and F. Tuitt,139–62. Cambridge, MA: Harvard Education Press.

Taylor, K., with W. Moore, J. MacGregor, and J. Lindblad. 2003. *Learning Community Research and Assessment: What We Know Now*. National Learning Communities Monograph Series. Olympia, WA: Washington Center for Improving the Quality of Undergraduate Education.

Terenzini, P., et al. 1994. "The Transition to College: Diverse Students, Diverse Stories." *Research in Higher Education* 35 (1): 57–73.

Terenzini, P, W. Lorang, and E. Pascarella. 1981. "Predicting Freshman Persistence and Voluntary Dropout Decisions: A Replication." *Research in Higher Education* 15 (2): 109–27.

Terenzini, P., and E. Pascarella. 1980. "Student/faculty Relationships and Freshman Year Educational Outcomes: A Further Investigation." *Journal of College Student Development* 21 (6): 521–28.

Thayer, P. 2000. "Retaining First-Generation and Low-Income Students." *Opportunity Outlook* (May): 2–8.

Thomas, S. 2000. "Ties That Bind: A Social Network Approach to Understanding Student Integration and Persistence." *Journal of Higher Education* 75 (5): 591–615.

Tierney, T. 2006. "How Is American Higher Education Measuring Up? An Outsider's Perspective." In *American Higher Education: How Does it Measure Up for the 21st Century?* edited J. Hunt Jr., and T. Tierney. San Jose: National Center for Public Policy and Higher Education.

Tierney, W. 1992. "An Anthropological Analysis of Student Participation in College." *Journal of Higher Education* 63 (3): 603–18.

———. 2000. "Power, Identity, and the Dilemma of College Student Departure." In *Reworking the Student Departure Puzzle*, edited by J. Braxton, 213–34. Nashville: Vanderbilt University Press.

Tinto, V. 1975. "Dropouts from Higher Education: A Theoretical Synthesis of Recent Research." *Review of Educational Research* 45 (1): 89–125.

———. 1993. *Leaving College: Rethinking the Causes and Cures of Student Attrition*. 2nd. ed. Chicago: University of Chicago Press.

———. 1997. "Colleges as Communities: Exploring the Educational Character of Student Persistence." *Journal of Higher Education* 68 (6): 599–623.

———. 1999. "Adapting Learning Communities to the Needs of Development Education Students." Paper presented at the National Center for Postsecondary Improvement, Stanford University. Stanford.

———. 2005. "Epilogue: Moving from Theory to Action." In *College Student Retention: Formula for Student Success*, edited by A. Seidman, 317–34. Westport, CT: ACE/Praeger.

———. 2008. "Access without Support Is Not Opportunity." Keynote speech given at the annual Institute for Chief Academic Officers, Council of Independent Colleges, Seattle, Washington.

———. 2010. "From theory to Action: Exploring the Institutional Conditions for Student Retention." In *Higher Education: Handbook of Theory and Research*, vol. 25, edited by J. Smart, 51–90. New York: Springer.

Tinto, V., and A. Goodsell. 1994. "Freshman Interest Groups and the First Year Experience: Constructing Student Communities in a Large University." *Journal of the Freshman Year Experience* 6 (1): 7–28.

Tinto, V., A. Goodsell, and P. Russo. 1993. "Building Community among New College Students." *Liberal Education* 79 (1): 16–21.

Tinto, V., and P. Russo. 1994. "Coordinated Studies Programs: Their Effect on Student Involvement at a Community College." *Community College Review* 22 (2): 16–25.

Titley, W., and B. Titley. 1980. "The Major Changers: Are Only the 'Undecided' Undecided?" *Journal of College Student Development* 21 (4): 293–98.

Tobolowsky, B., and B. Cox, eds. 2007. *Shedding Light on Sophomores: An Exploration of the Second Year of College*. Columbia, SC: National Resource Center for the First-Year Experience and Students in Transition.

Tobolowsky, B., B. Cox, and M. Wagner, eds. 2005. *Exploring the Evidence*, vol. 3: *Reporting Research on First-Year Seminars*. Columbia, SC: National Resource Center for the First Year Experience and Students in Transition.

Tokuno, K. 1993. "Long Term and Recent Student Outcomes of Freshman Interest Group Program." *Journal of the Freshman Year Experience* 5 (2): 7–28.

Torres, V. 2003a. "Influences on Ethnic Identify Development of Latino Students in the First Two Years of College." *Journal of College Student Development* 44 (4): 532–47.

———. 2003b. "Mi Casa is Not Exactly Like Your House." *About Campus* 8 (2): 2–8.

———. 2004. "Familial Influences on the Identity Development of Latino First Year Students." *Journal of College Student Development* 45 (4): 457–69.

———. 2006. "A Mixed Method Study Testing Data-Model Fit of a Retention Model for Latino/a Students at Urban Universities." *Journal of College Student Development* 47 (3): 299–318.

Torres, J., and S. Solberg. 2001. "Role of Self-Efficacy, Stress, Social Integration, and

Family Support in Latino College Student Persistence and Health." *Journal of Vocational Behavior* 59 (1): 53–63.

Tucker, J. 1999. "Tinto's Model and Successful College Transitions." *Journal of College Student Retention: Research, Theory and Practice* 1 (2): 163–75.

Turner, A., and T. Berry. 2000. "Counseling Center Contributions to Student Retention and Graduation: A Longitudinal Assessment." *Journal of College Student Development* 41 (6): 627–36.

Twigg, C. 2005. *Increasing Success for Underserved Students: Redesigning Introductory Courses.* Saratoga Springs: National Center for Academic Transformation.

Twomey, J. 1991. *Academic Performance and Retention in a Peer Mentor Program of a Two-Year Campus of a Four-Year Institution.* Alamogordo: New Mexico State University Press.

Umbach, P., and S. Porter. 2002. "How Do Academic Departments Impact Student Satisfaction?" *Research in Higher Education* 43 (2): 209–34.

Umbach, P., and M. Wawrzynski. 2005. "Faculty Do matter: The Role of College Faculty in Student Learning and Engagement." *Research in Higher Education* 46 (2): 153–84.

Upcraft, M., J. Gardner, and Associates. 1989. *The Freshman Year Experience.* San Francisco: Jossey-Bass.

Upcraft, M., J. Gardner, and B. Barefoot, eds. 2005. *Challenging and Supporting: A Handbook for Improving the First Year of College.* San Francisco: Jossey-Bass.

Upcraft, M., and J. Schuh. 1996. *Assessment in Student Affairs: A Guide for Practitioners.* San Francisco: Jossey-Bass.

Valeri-Gold, M., M. Deming, and K. Stone. 1992. "The Bridge: A Summer Enrichment Program to Retain African-American Collegians." *Journal of the Freshman Year Experience* 4 (2): 101–17.

Valley, P. 2004a. "Entertaining Strangers: Providing for the Development Needs of Part-Time Faculty." In *To Improve the Academy*, vol. 23, edited by S. Chadwick-Blossey and D. Robertson. Boston: Anker Publishing.

———. 2004b. "Faculty Development in Community Colleges: A Model for Part-Time Faculty" In *To Improve the Academy*, vol. 23, edited by Chadwick-Blossey, S., and D. Robertson. Boston: Anker Publishing.

Visher, M., E. Schneider, H. Wathington, and H. Collado. 2010. *Scaling Up Learning Communities: The Experience of Six Community Colleges.* New York: Manpower Demonstration Research Corporation.

Vogelgesang, L., and A. Astin. 2000. "Comparing the Effects of Community Service and Service Learning." *Michigan Journal of Community Service Learning* 7 (Fall): 25–34.

Voorhees, R. 1997. "Student Learning and Cognitive Development in College." In *Higher Education Handbook of Theory and Research*, vol. 12, edited by J. Smart and W. Tierney, 313–70. New York: Agathon Press.

Vuong, M., S. Brown-Welty, and S. Tracz. 2010. "The Effects of Self-Efficacy on

Academic Success of First-Generation College Sophomore Students." *Journal of College Student Development* 51 (1): 50–64.

Wagner College. 2010. *Liberal Education and Reflective Practice: Faculty Guide to the First-Year Learning Community*. Staten Island, NY: Wagner College.

Walpole, M., H. Simmerman, C. Mack, J. Mills, M. Scales, and D. Albano. 2008. "Bridge to Success: Insight into Summer Bridge Program Students' College Transition." *Journal of the First-Year Experience and Students in Transition* 20 (1): 11–30.

Walters, E. 2003. "Editors Choice: Becoming Student Centered via the One-Stop Shop Initiative: A Case Study of Onondaga Community College." *Community College Review* 31 (3): 40–54.

Wang, D. 2005. "Students' Learning and Locus of Control in Web-Supplemental Instruction." *Innovative Higher Education* 30 (1): 67–82.

Warburton, E.C., R. Bugarin, R., and A. Nuñez. 2001. *Bridging the Gap: Academic Preparation and Postsecondary Success of First-Generation Students*. NCES 2001–153. Washington, DC: National Center for Education Statistics, U.S. Department of Education.

Ward, K., L. Trautvetter, and L Braskamp. 2005. "Putting Students First: Creating a Climate of Support and Challenge." *Journal of College and Character* 6 (8): 1–5.

Ward-Roof, J. 2010. *Designing Successful Transitions: A Guide to Orienting Students to College*. 3rd ed. Columbia, SC: National Resource Center for the First Year Experience and Students in Transition.

Ward-Roof, J., and C. Hatch. 2003. *Designing Successful Transitions: A Guide to Orienting Students to College*. 2nd ed. Columbia, SC: National Resource Center for the First Year Experience and Students in Transition.

Washington Center News. 1990. *Freshman Interest Groups at the University of Washington: Building Community for Freshmen at a Large University*. Olympia, WA: Washington Center for Improving the Quality of Undergraduate Education.

Wathington, H., J. Pretlow III, and C. Mitchell. 2010–11. "The Difference a Cohort Makes: Understanding Developmental Learning Communities in Community Colleges." *Journal of College Student Retention: Research, Theory and Practice* 12 (2): 225–42.

Wergin, J., and J. Swinger, eds. 2000. *Departmental Assessment: How Some Campuses Are Effectively Evaluating the Collective Work of Faculty*. A Publication of the AAHE Forum on Faculty Roles and Rewards, American Association of Higher Education, Sterling: Stylus Publishing.

White, C. 2005. "Student Portfolios: An Alternative Way of Encouraging and Evaluating Student Learning." In *Alternate Strategies for Evaluating Student Learning. New Directions for Teaching and Learning*, no. 100, edited by M. Achacoso and M. Svinicki, 37–42. San Francisco: Jossey-Bass.

Wholey, J., H. Hatry, and K. Newcomer, eds. 1994. *Handbook of Practical Program Evaluation*. San Francisco: Jossey-Bass.

Wilcox, P., S. Winn, and M. Fyvie-Gauld. 2005. "'It was nothing to do with the university, it was just the people': The Role of Social Support in The First-Year Experience of Higher Education." *Studies in Higher Education* 30 (6): 707–22.

Wilkerson, L., and W. Gijselaers, eds. 1996. *Bringing Problem-Based Learning to Higher Education: Theory and Practice. New Directions for Teaching and Learning,* no. 68. San Francisco: Jossey-Bass.

Wilkie, C., and M. Jones. 1994. "Academic Benefits of On-Campus Employment to First Year Developmental Education Students." *Journal of the Freshman Year Experience* 6 (2): 37–56.

Wilson, R., L. Wood, and J. Gaff. 1974. "Social-Psychological Accessibility and Faculty Student Interaction Beyond the Classroom." *Sociology of Education* 47 (1): 74–92.

Wilson, S., T. Mason, and M. Ewing. 1997. "Evaluating the Impact of Receiving University-Based Counseling Services on Student Retention." *Journal of Counseling Psychology* 44 (3): 316–20.

Windham, P. 2006. *Taking Student Life Skills Course Increases Academic Success.* Data Trend, no. 31. Tallahassee: Florida Department of Education.

Wolfe, R. 1988. "A Model Retention Program for the Community College." *Maryland Association for Higher Education Journal* 11 (10): 18–20.

Wolf-Wendel, L., K. Tuttle, and C. Keller-Wolff. 1999. "Assessment of a Freshman Summer Transition Program in an Open-Admissions Institution." *Journal of the First-Year Experience and Students in Transition* 11 (2): 7–32.

Wolverton, M. 1998. "Treading the Tenure-Track Tightrope: Finding a Balance between Research Excellence and Quality Teaching." *Innovative Higher Education* 23 (1): 61–79.

Wolverton, M., and W. Gmelch. 2002. *College Deans: Leading from Within.* Westport: American Council on Education / Oryx Press.

Wright, G., R. Wright, and C. Lamb. 2002. "Developmental Mathematics Education and Supplemental Instruction: Pondering the Potential." *Journal of Developmental Education* 26 (1): 30–35.

Yao, Y., and M. Grady. 2005. "How Do Faculty Make Formative Use of Student Evaluation Feedback? A Multiple Case Study." *Journal of Personnel Evaluation in Education* 18 (2): 107–26.

Young, R., R. Backer, and G. Rogers. 1989. "The Impact of Early Advising and Scheduling on Freshman Success." *Journal of College Student Development* 30 (3): 309–12.

Zachry, E., with E. Schneider. 2008: *Promising Instructional Reforms in Developmental Education: A Case Study of Three Achieving the Dream Colleges.* New York. MDRC.

Zajacova, A., S. Lynch, and T. Espenshade. 2005. "Self-Efficacy, Stress, and Academic Success in College." *Research in Higher Education* 46 (6): 677–708.

Zaritsky, J., and A. Toce. 2006. "Supplemental Instruction at a Community College:

The Four Pillars." In *Supplemental Instruction. New Directions for Teaching and Learning*, no. 106, edited by M. Stone and G. Jacobs, 23–31. San Francisco: Jossey-Bass.

Zeidenberg, M., D. Jenkins, and J. Calcagno. 2007. *Do Student Success Courses Actually Help Community College Students Succeed?* CCRC Brief, no. 36. New York: Community College Research Center, Teachers College, Columbia University.

Zhai, M., S. Ronco, X. Feng, and A. Feiner. 2001. "Assessing Student Course-Taking Patterns and Their Impact on College Persistence." Paper presented at the 41st annual forum of the Association of Institutional Research, Long Beach.

Zhao, C., and G. Kuh. 2004. "Adding Value: Learning Communities and Student Engagement." *Research in Higher Education* 45 (2): 115–38.

Ziskin, M., J. Gross, and D. Hossler. 2006. "Institutional Practices and Student Persistence: Extending the Empirical Record." Paper presented at the 31st annual meeting of the Association for the Study of Higher Education, Anaheim.

Zubizarreta, J. 2009. *The Learning Portfolio: Reflective Practice for Improving Student Learning*. 2nd ed. San Francisco: Jossey-Bass.

Zúñiga, X., A. Nagda, M. Chester, and A. Cytron-Walker. 2007. *Intergroup Dialogue in Higher Education: Meaningful Learning about Social Justice*. ASHE Higher Education Report, 32 (4). San Francisco: Jossey-Bass.

Zúñiga, X., and T. Sevig. 1997. "Bridging the Us/Them Divide through Intergroup Dialogues and Peer Leadership." *Diversity Factor* 6 (2): 23–28.

INDEX

expectations (*continued*)
and peer group, 14, 156n1; and race,
14; shaping, 15–17; and social class, 14;
for student effort, 12–14

faculty and staff: behavior of, 12, 23,
115; and collaboration, 86, 112–13,
122, 163n6; faculty advising, 20–21,
22, 123; faculty development, 77–81,
87–88, 91, 98, 108, 115, 116, 124;
and learning communities, 86; and
program development, 85–86; and
program implementation, 91, 92–93;
rewards and incentives for, 115; and
social support, 29; and student
involvement, 64, 65, 68. *See also*
classroom
feedback. *See* assessment and feedback
Fencl, H., 69
Ferris State University, 96
Filkins, J., 24
financial aid: awareness of, 53; for low-
income students, 29, 30–31, 51–52,
53; merit-based, 30; need-based,
30; Pell grants, 3, 30, 53, 155n5; and
retention, 29–31, 156n11, 157n4; and
student engagement, 30; work-study
programs, 30, 51, 158n26
first-generation students: advising for,
11–12, 123; and expectations, 11–12,
16; graduation rates of, 3, 131–33,
140–41; and mentoring, 28–29;
and orientation, 11–12, 16; and self-
efficacy, 27; support for, 24, 49–50;
and transcript analysis, 84
first-year seminars, 16–17, 33–36, 38, 72,
94, 98, 103, 107
first-year students: advising for,
17–22, 123; alignment for, 106–10;
experience courses, 16–17; first-year
seminars, 16–17, 33–36, 38, 72, 94,
98, 103, 107; learning communities,

16–17, 29, 103, 107–10, 111–12, 123;
retention of, 3, 97–99; support for, 7,
24, 25–26, 38, 122
Fischer, M., 64
Fleming, J., 28
Florida Department of Education, 26
Florida Gulf Coast University, 61
Florida Southern College, 58
Foothill College, 22
Foothill Community College, 79
Foundations of Excellence Program, 98,
162n1
Fox Valley Technical College, 18, 21
fraternities, 65–66
Friedman, D., 38
Frostburg State University, 49

Gardner, J., 97, 98
gender: and expectations, 14; and
graduation rates, 2, 136, 155n8
George Mason University, 48
Georgetown University, 16
Glen Oaks Community College, 15
Governance Institute for Student
Success, 113
graduation: and administrative
action, 82; assessment of, 146–47;
changes in, 2, 4, 86–87, 110,
142–44; definition of, 127–28; and
effectiveness, 149; of first-generation
students, 3, 131–33, 140–41; and
gender, 2, 136, 155n8; long-term,
134–35; of low-income students, 3, 4,
131–33, 136, 140–41, 166n2, 167n5; of
minority students, 2–3, 136, 139–41,
161n4; of part-time students, 168n19,
169n1; predicated-versus-actual, 150;
requirements for, 10; and selectivity,
135–36, 163n7, 168n10; timing of,
133–34; of transfer students, 136–38,
149, 153–54; variability of, 135–36. *See
also* completion

Mountain View College, 79
Mount St. Mary's College, 58

National Academic Advising Association
   (NACADA), 165n24
National Association of Independent
   Colleges and Universities (NAICU),
   151
National Association of State
   Universities and Land-Grant Colleges
   (NASULGC), 151
National Association of System Heads,
   153
National Center for Academic
   Transformation, 61, 98
National Center for Higher Education
   Management Systems (NCHEMS),
   138, 142, 143, 144
National Educational Longitudinal Study
   (NELS), 26, 147
National Longitudinal Survey of
   Freshman, 64
National Science Foundation, 80
National Student Clearinghouse (NSC),
   138, 142
National Survey of Student Engagement
   (NSSE), 13, 22–23, 62, 66, 83
Native American students, 52–53
Navarro College, 58
NCHEMS. See National Center for
   Higher Education Management
   Systems (NCHEMS)
New York State's Higher Education
   Opportunity Program (HEOP), 50
North Carolina State University, 18, 50
North Carolina State University at
   Raleigh, 106
Northeastern State University, 102
Northern Essex Community Col-
   lege, 70
Northern Virginia Community Col-
   lege, 58

North Lake College, 79
Northwestern State University, 58

Oakland University, 17
Ohio State University, 19, 57
one-minute papers, 54, 57
Oregon State University, 18
orientation programs, 11–12, 15–16, 98,
   157n4
Oseguera, L., 14

Palm Beach Community College, 58
Palmer, Parker, 115
part-time students, 5–6, 29–30, 115,
   168n19, 169n1
Pasadena Community College, 46
pathways, 6, 47, 115, 122, 125, 166n8
Patrick Henry Community College, 44
Paul Smith College, 60
peer group: advising, 21; and
   expectations, 14, 156n1; mentoring,
   12, 48–49, 96; and social support, 29;
   tutors, 46–47
Peer-Led Team Learning (PLTL)
   program, 46–47
Pell grants, 3, 30, 53, 155n5
Pennsylvania State University, 18–
   19, 58
persistence: changes in, 145–46; data
   on, 128–33, 136–38; definition of,
   127–28; long-term, 138; variation in,
   139–41. See also retention
Pew Charitable Trusts, 80
Policy Center on the First Year of
   College, 107
Pomona College, 50
portfolios, 58, 109, 160n13
Portland Community College, 76
Portland State University, 61, 76
Preparing Future Faculty program,
   80–81
prerequisites, 165n28

Southern Arkansas University, 100
Southern Illinois University at
 Edwardsville, 57
South Texas College, 79
SSS. *See* Student Support Services (SSS)
staff. *See* faculty and staff
Stanford University, 51, 100, 102
State University of New York Cort-
 land, 53
State University of New York's
 Educational Opportunity Program
 (EOP), 50
Statistics Pathway (Statway), 47–48
Steadman, M., 54
Stetson, N., 54
St. Lawrence University, 73
St. Louis University, 16
St. Mary's University, 48, 87
Stonehill College, 79
Stony Brook University, 100, 101
stopouts, 127–28, 167n1
Strategic Literacy Initiative, 45
Strengthening Pre-Collegiate Education
 in Community Colleges (SPECC), 44
student effort, 12–14, 120
student experience, 62–63, 83, 121, 125
students of color. *See* minority students
student success, 4, 114–25; and
 the classroom, 114–15, 116, 125;
 conditions for, 6–9; and self-
 efficacy, 26–27; taking it seriously,
 115–16. *See also* assessment and
 feedback; expectations; graduation;
 involvement; momentum points;
 retention; support
Student Support Services (SSS), 11–12,
 49–50
summer bridge programs, 31–33, 96,
 98, 164n13
supplemental instruction, 36–38,
 46–47, 89, 94, 112
support, 7, 8, 24–53, 114; balance with
 expectations, 24–25; basic-skills

courses, 25–26, 43–48; embedded
 academic support, 42–43, 45, 46,
 122; financial, 29–31, 51–53; for
 first-generation students, 24; for
 first-year students, 7, 24, 25–26,
 33–36, 38, 122; investing in, 83;
 learning communities, 38–42; for
 low-income students, 24, 118; social,
 27–29, 35, 48–51; summer bridge
 programs, 31–33; supplemental
 instruction, 36–38, 46–47; for
 underprepared students, 118. *See also*
 mentoring
Survey of Entering Student Engagement
 (SENSE), 14
surveys, 83. *See also* Community College
 Survey of Student Engagement
 (CCSSE); National Survey of Student
 Engagement (NSSE)
swirling, 149, 153
syllabi, 12
Syracuse University, 20, 31, 51, 52–53,
 58, 80, 87, 98, 100, 101

Tacoma Community College, 42, 85
Tallahassee Community College, 59,
 61, 79
Temple University, 38
Terenzini, P., 12, 24
Texas A&M University, 36
Texas Christian University, 100
Tinto, V., 39
Tomas Rivera Center for Student
 Success, 111
Torres, V., 27
transcript analysis, 83–85, 111
transfer students, 103, 136–38, 149,
 153–54, 169n8
Troy University, 87
Turner, A., 48
Twenty-First Century Scholars
 Program, 52
Twigg, Carol, 61, 98